ACT!® 2000 For Windows®
FOR DUMMIES®

by Jeffrey J. Mayer

Hungry Minds™

HUNGRY MINDS, INC.

New York, NY ◆ Cleveland, OH ◆ Indianapolis, IN

ACT!® 2000 For Windows® For Dummies®

Published by
Hungry Minds, Inc.
909 Third Avenue
New York, NY 10022
www.hungryminds.com
www.dummies.com (Dummies Press Web site)

Library of Congress Catalog Card No.: 99-66086

ISBN: 0-7645-0561-0

Printed in the United States of America

10 9 8 7 6 5

1B/SS/QR/QS/IN

Distributed in the United States by Hungry Minds, Inc.

Distributed by CDG Books Canada Inc. for Canada; by Transworld Publishers Limited in the United Kingdom; by IDG Norge Books for Norway; by IDG Sweden Books for Sweden; by IDG Books Australia Publishing Corporation Pty. Ltd. for Australia and New Zealand; by TransQuest Publishers Pte Ltd. for Singapore, Malaysia, Thailand, Indonesia, and Hong Kong; by Gotop Information Inc. for Taiwan; by ICG Muse, Inc. for Japan; by Intersoft for South Africa; by Eyrolles for France; by International Thomson Publishing for Germany, Austria and Switzerland; by Distribuidora Cuspide for Argentina; by LR International for Brazil; by Galileo Libros for Chile; by Ediciones ZETA S.C.R. Ltda. for Peru; by WS Computer Publishing Corporation, Inc., for the Philippines; by Contemporanea de Ediciones for Venezuela; by Express Computer Distributors for the Caribbean and West Indies; by Micronesia Media Distributor, Inc. for Micronesia; by Chips Computadoras S.A. de C.V. for Mexico; by Editorial Norma de Panama S.A. for Panama; by American Bookshops for Finland.

For general information on Hungry Minds' products and services please contact our Customer Care Department within the U.S. at 800-762-2974, outside the U.S. at 317-572-3993 or fax 317-572-4002.

For sales inquiries and reseller information, including discounts, premium and bulk quantity sales, and foreign-language translations, please contact our Customer Care Department at 800-434-3422, fax 317-572-4002, or write to Hungry Minds, Inc., Attn: Customer Care Department, 10475 Crosspoint Boulevard, Indianapolis, IN 46256.

For information on licensing foreign or domestic rights, please contact our Sub-Rights Customer Care Department at 212-884-5000.

For information on using Hungry Minds' products and services in the classroom or for ordering examination copies, please contact our Educational Sales Department at 800-434-2086 or fax 317-572-4005.

For press review copies, author interviews, or other publicity information, please contact our Public Relations Department at 317-572-3168 or fax 317-572-4168.

For authorization to photocopy items for corporate, personal, or educational use, please contact Copyright Clearance Center, 222 Rosewood Drive, Danvers, MA 01923, or fax 978-750-4470.

Hungry Minds™ is a trademark of Hungry Minds, Inc.

About the Author

Jeffrey J. Mayer — America's #1 ACT! and Time Management expert — is an outstanding speaker, best-selling author, and personal advisor and counselor to thousands of people.

Jeff works with entrepreneurs who want to grow their business, with executives who want to expand their careers, and with anyone who wants to enhance their lives and live their dreams.

Jeff works with people individually in their office or by telephone. He conducts presentations and workshops for business owners, corporate executives, and sales professionals on a variety of issues related to growing a business, getting ahead in life, and living your dreams.

In his dynamic program, Growing Your Business With ACT!, Jeff shares his tips, techniques, and strategies for using ACT! to get organized; set your priorities; manage your time; stay in touch with your important customers, clients, and prospects; and build relationships with the important people in your business and personal life. And most importantly, Jeff shares with you his secret to success: Managing your time!

Feature stories about Jeffrey Mayer have appeared in many newspapers and magazine, including *The Wall Street Journal, The New York Times, USA Today; People, Newsweek, Fortune, Esquire, Entrepreneur,* and *The Ladies Home Journal.* He has also been interviewed on radio and television in every major city in the United States.

Jeffrey Mayer has also done national media tours as a corporate spokesperson for Sharp Electronics, Kentucky Fried Chicken, Pacific Bell, and Kellogg's Smart Start cereal.

Jeff's three previous *ACT! For Dummies* books have sold more than 100,000 copies. His best-selling *Time Management For Dummies,* (now in its 2nd edition) has sold more than 400,000 copies and has been translated into 12 languages. His first best-selling book, *If You Haven't Got The Time To Do It Right, When Will You Find The Time To Do It Over?* has sold more than 500,000 copies and been translated into 8 languages. *Success is a Journey* is Jeff's newest non-computer book.

Jeff is also the publisher of *ACT! in ACTion ,* the #1 ACT! newsletter. For a free sample issue, complete the coupon at the back of this book, or you can fill out the form on Web site at www.ACTnews.com.

To have Jeffrey J. Mayer speak at your next conference or business meeting, or to learn about his individual and telephone programs, contact him at 312-944-4184, or jeff@ACTnews.com. You can write to him at Succeeding In Business, Inc., 50 East Bellevue Place, Suite 305, Chicago IL 60611.

Other Books by Jeffrey J. Mayer

If You Haven't Got the Time to Do It Right, When Will You Find the Time to Do It Over?

Find the Job You've Always Wanted in Half the Time with Half the Effort

Winning the Fight Between You and Your Desk

Time Management For Dummies

Time Management For Dummies Briefcase Edition

ACT! For Windows For Dummies

Act! 3 For Windows For Dummies

Act! 4 For Windows For Dummies

Success is a Journey

Time Management For Dummies, 2nd edition

Dedication

To my daughter DeLaine, whom I love very much. She has just discovered the computer and will soon be using ACT! to keep track of all of her play dates.

Author's Acknowledgments

There are many people I would like to thank and acknowledge for their help and contributions for the creation of this book.

I want to congratulate Erin Hintz, Director, Product Management; John Mitzel, ACT! Product Manager; Dale Elliot, Sr. Development Manager; and Sanjiv Bhargava Sr. Director, Development for a job well done. Erin, John, Dale, and Sanjiv all deserves a hearty round of applause for a job well done. On behalf of all ACT! users, thank you.

John — who has become a good friend over the past few months that we have been working together — was my ACT! 2000 contact person. It would have been impossible for me to complete this book without his help and assistance. Thank You.

Dale and I have been working together for years. He was my technical liaison for my *ACT! 3 For Windows For Dummies* book, and I couldn't have written that book without his help and assistance. And he was development manager for ACT! 4.0. Whenever I've had a question, or two, or three, about how some feature was supposed to work, I gave Dale a call. (And before we knew it, he had given me an hour of his time.) If he didn't know the answer, he always got back to me very quickly. Dale is a very dear friend.

Sanjiv has been ACT!'s Director of Development for ACT! 3.0, ACT! 4.0, and ACT! 2000. He has done just a great job over the past few years.

I want to thank Linda Keating for all of her help, support, and encouragement. Linda was the technical consultant for my last ACT! book, *ACT! 4 For Windows For Dummies,* and for this book. All of her thoughts, comments, and ideas have been greatly appreciated.

When it comes to database marketing, Linda is brilliant. She's been a frequent contributor to my *ACT! in ACTion* newsletter. You can reach Linda at JL Technical (phone 650-323-9141; e-mail linda@jltechnical.com; Web www.jltechnical.com).

A BIG thank you goes to Martine Edwards, my acquisitions editor for this book. She was great to work with and helped me to create a wonderful book. We worked very closely in laying out the book, and she offered great insights for ways in which we could *improve* upon the *ACT! 4 For Windows For Dummies* book.

I want to also thank Gwenette Gaddis. Gwenette was my copy editor, and she did a masterful job of making my words come out just right.

I want to thank my editor and good friend, Tim Gallan, for all of his help, assistance, encouragement, and patience during the five years we've been working together. Tim, you made everything much easier for me and helped me write six great books. It's been a pleasure working with you. (I'm looking forward to working with you on *ACT! 3000 For Dummies*.) Thank you.

And finally, I would like to thank the two women in my life, my wife Mitzi and my daughter DeLaine, for their love, support, and encouragement during the four months it took me to complete this book. They left me alone on the weekends so that I could write, and they didn't ask too many questions about why I was sitting at the computer at 5:00 a.m.

Publisher's Acknowledgments

We're proud of this book; please send us your comments through our Online Registration Form located at www.dummies.com.

Some of the people who helped bring this book to market include the following:

Acquisitions, Editorial, and Media Development

Senior Project Editor: Tim Gallan

Acquisitions Editor: Martine Edwards

Copy Editor: Gwenette Gaddis

Technical Editor: Linda Keating

Editorial Manager: Seta K. Franz

Editorial Assistant: Alison Walthall

Production

Project Coordinator: Regina Snyder

Layout and Graphics: Amy M. Adrian, Brian Drumm, Angela F. Hunckler, Barry Offringa, Tracy Oliver, Jill Piscitelli, Douglas L. Rollison, Brent Savage, Janet Seib, Michael A. Sullivan, Brian Torwelle, Mary Jo Weis

Proofreaders: Nancy Reinhardt, Marianne Santy, Rebecca Senninger, Toni Settle

Indexer: Ann Norcross

Hungry Minds Technology Publishing Group: Richard Swadley, Senior Vice President and Publisher; Mary Bednarek, Vice President and Publisher, Networking; Joseph Wikert, Vice President and Publisher, Web Development Group; Mary C. Corder, Editorial Director, Dummies Technology; Andy Cummings, Publishing Director, Dummies Technology; Barry Pruett, Publishing Director, Visual/Graphic Design

Hungry Minds Manufacturing: Ivor Parker, Vice President, Manufacturing

Hungry Minds Marketing: John Helmus, Assistant Vice President, Director of Marketing

Hungry Minds Production for Branded Press: Debbie Stailey, Production Director

Hungry Minds Sales: Michael Violano, Vice President, International Sales and Sub Rights

Contents at a Glance

Cartoons at a Glance

By Rich Tennant

page 221

"NIFTY CHART, FRANK, BUT NOT ENTIRELY NECESSARY."

page 97

page 7

"IT'S ANOTHER DEEP SPACE PROBE FROM EARTH, SEEKING CONTACT FROM EXTRATERRESTRIALS. I WISH THEY'D JUST INCLUDE AN E-MAIL ADDRESS."

page 143

Maintenance is chagrined to find out the squeak in Clark's disk drive is really a whistle in Clark's nose.

page 67

"Can someone please tell me how long 'Larry's Lunch Truck' has had his own page on the intranet?"

page 295

"I'm just not sure it's appropriate to send a digital resume to a paper stock company looking for a sales rep."

page 197

"MY GIRLFRIEND RAN A SPREADSHEET OF MY LIFE, AND GENERATED THIS CHART. MY BEST HOPE IS THAT SHE'LL CHANGE HER MAJOR FROM 'COMPUTER SCIENCES' TO 'REHABILITATIVE SERVICES.'"

page 339

Cartoon Information:
Fax: 978-546-7747
E-Mail: richtennant@the5thwave.com
World Wide Web: www.the5thwave.com

Table of Contents

Introduction

• •

*A*CT! 2000 for Windows is a brand-new product. Well, it's not really a new product; it's just ACT!'s newest version.

I've been using ACT! since version 1.1b for Windows and have written three ACT! books, *ACT! 4 For Windows For Dummies*, *ACT! 3 For Windows For Dummies* and *ACT! For Windows For Dummies* (covering version 2). I've also been publishing ACT! in ACTion, the #1 newsletter for ACT! users who want to grow their business, since 1995. So I can honestly say that I know a lot about ACT!.

ACT! 2000 For Windows For Dummies is written for experienced ACT! users — some go back to the days of ACT! for DOS — and for the people who have just purchased ACT! and installed it on their computers.

This book is filled with information that will help you to use ACT! 2000's many timesaving and productivity-improving features so that you can grow your business, expand your career, save time, and make more money.

In addition, I've included many of the ACT! tips, techniques and strategies that I've learned from using ACT! every day since the early '90s, since that's what I do for a living: I work with people who want to use ACT! to grow their businesses and expand their careers.

Why I Love ACT!

When I began my business career almost 25 years ago, I was told that if you want to succeed in business you *must* keep track of all your calls, meetings, and to-dos, so I started using a daily-planning book. In addition, I began to keep detailed notes of all my meetings, phone conversations, and observations in manila folders. Over the years, I found this process helped me grow my business and expand my career immeasurably. It enabled me to focus my time and energy on the *right* people. The people who *wanted* to do business with me.

Then I discovered ACT!. Once I started using it, I became hooked. With ACT!, I could do everything that I had been trained to do with a pencil and a piece of paper. Today, I have information on thousands of people in my databases, and with just a few keystrokes, all of this information is at my fingertips. Since I began using ACT!, my business success has skyrocketed.

With ACT! I'm able to set my daily, weekly, and long-term priorities; focus on my most important tasks and capitalize on my business opportunities. And so can you.

In addition to writing books, I've a thriving business as a speaker and advisor. I work with people who want to grow their businesses and with individuals who want to get ahead in life. During the past few years, I discovered that many of my clients had ACT! loaded on their computers, but they didn't really know how to use it. So I started teaching them how they could use ACT! to keep track of all the important things that are going on their lives, and keep in touch with all the important people in their lives.

In just a couple of hours, I can teach people how to make ACT! work for them so they can grow their businesses and expand their careers — even if they've never used a computer before. And that's what I've done for you in *ACT! 2000 For Windows For Dummies*. I'm giving you the information that you need to make ACT! work for you.

How to Use This Book

Like all *...For Dummies* books, this book is a reference, which means that you don't have to read it from cover to cover. Each chapter focuses on a single topic and is meant to stand on its own; however, I've tried to organize the parts of this book in a logical manner, just in case some of you want to read it from start to finish.

To get started, look up a topic in the table of contents or index. When you see something that interests you, flip to that section of the book. If I've done my job, you'll find out how to use ACT! in a new and interesting way, and you'll want to read more chapters. Fortunately, I've sprinkled cross-references throughout the book to help you find information on topics related to whatever you happen to be reading.

How This Book Is Organized

This book contains eight parts. Each part contains a few chapters covering related topics. Here's a brief summary of the aforementioned parts:

Part I: Getting to Know ACT!

In Part I, you get an overview of how to use ACT!. I explain how to get contacts into your ACT! database; how to set up your general preference settings; how to get the most out of the Contact window; how to work with the Contact window's different tabs; and how to define the fields of your ACT! database.

Part II: Using Your Database

In Part II, I guide you through the process of entering information into ACT!. I show you how to move from one field to another and how to customize your individual fields. I also show you how to view your contact information as a list. And most importantly, I help you get contacts into ACT!. After all, ACT! is almost useless unless you fill it with the information about the important people in your life.

Part III: Working with ACT! Contacts

In Part III, I show you how to find people. You've got Instant lookups, standard lookups, and advanced queries. And you can even look up people over the Internet and add them to your ACT! database. Once you've created a lookup, then I show you how to save your lookup by creating ACT! groups.

Part IV: Scheduling: A Play in Four Acts

In Part IV, I help you use ACT! to take control of your day. I present the nitty-gritty details of scheduling activities. ACT! provides several different ways for you schedule activities, and I show how to do them all. That way, you can select the method that's best for you.

Part V: Using ACT! as a Sales Tool

ACT! 2000 has some new features that will help you automate your sales processes. You can create sales opportunities, keep track of those opportunities, and schedule a series of activities that remind you to do specific things on specific dates for your contacts.

Part VI: Communicating with the Outside World

ACT! makes it easy for you to keep in touch with your contacts. In Part VI, I describe how to use these communications features, everything from phone and e-mail management to custom reports and letter templates.

Part VII: More ACT! Features

ACT! is a very powerful program, and this part of the book will walk you through some of its coolest features, which include customizing commands, managing your database, and designing your own contact layouts.

Part VIII: The Part of Tens

Every ...*For Dummies* book is supposed to end with top-ten lists, and this book is no exception. In my Part of Tens, I offer some tips on keeping your database in shape. I also provide lists of resources that can provide more information.

Conventions Used in This Book

ACT! provides several different ways to activate the same function or feature. You can use your mouse to pull down a menu and select a command from that menu. When I want you to choose a command from a menu, I present the menu first, then an arrow, and then the command, as in, for example, File, Save. I'm basically saying, "Select the Save command from the File menu."

You can also access commands using Ctrl key keyboard shortcuts, which I provide to you like this: Ctrl+S. This means press and hold down the Ctrl key and then press the S key. ACT! stores many commands in buttons on its Toolbar.

ACT! allows you to access many commands from a menu that appears when you click the right button on your mouse (also called right-clicking). Different commands appear on this menu depending on where your pointer is when you click the right mouse button.

Icons Used in This Book

This icon indicates that I'm telling a story of some kind. These stories usually have a point, but I won't make any promises. I tend to ramble sometimes, which reminds me of something that happened to me on the way to. . . .

I use this icon to point out important conceptual information that you shouldn't forget.

As you might expect, this icon flags tips, tricks, hints, and secrets that can help you get your work done quickly and efficiently.

This icon has two purposes: It lets the technologically inclined know that I'm about to cover something complex and exciting, and it lets technophobes know that they ought to skip over that section because the information flagged by the Technical Stuff icon will only confuse and/or frighten them.

This icon lets you know of some potential danger, like if you click the wrong button in the ACT! Self Destruct dialog box, your computer might explode. Just kidding. I do try to warn you of situations that may cause awful things to happen, like data loss, hair loss, weight gain, and insomnia. By the way, some parts of this book are a great cure for insomnia. Ask my editor.

Where to Go from Here

If you have never used ACT! before, head to Chapter 1. If you're upgrading from a previous version of ACT!, I suggest that you skim through the entire book to get an overview of all of ACT! 2000's features.

Then look for the ACT! features that you use most frequently and read those sections because ACT!'s developers have added a lot of new features and enhancements.

And finally, go through the index or table of contents and look for ACT! Features that you've never used before.

One Last Thing

If you're using ACT! to grow your business and expand your career, you'll certainly want to become a subscriber to my monthly ACT! newsletter, *ACT! in ACTion*. It is filled with ACT! information that will help you to use ACT! to get more done each day.

You can obtain a free, three-month trial subscription to my *ACT! in ACTion* newsletter by filling out the form at the back of this book. (You can fax or mail it in.) You can also fill out a Web form by visiting my Web site at www.ACTnews.com. My ACT! in ACTion Online Web site has articles from previous issues and lots of other ACT! information.

I also send out a free ACT! Tip of the Week via e-mail. If you would like to be added to the list, place your e-mail address in the message body and send it to subscribe@actnews.com.

And finally, my newest book *Success is a Journey,* has two chapters that describe how to use ACT!. One chapter explains how to use ACT! to set your priorities and get your most important work done each day; the other walks you through the process of how to use ACT! to stay in touch with the important people in your life.

Part I

Getting to Know ACT!

The 5th Wave — By Rich Tennant

In this part . . .

ACT! is a very powerful tool, on par with a top-of-the-line database or spreadsheet program, and if you take the time to fine-tune its features to match your specific needs, you'll soon find yourself using this tool to its fullest potential. Driving a Porsche is probably a great experience, but it'd be an even better experience if you took the time to adjust the seat and mirrors before hitting the road. (Lame analogy, I know, but I'm just getting warmed up.)

This part helps you set up ACT! so that it meets your needs. I show you how to insert contact information into ACT! and get your preferences in order. I also explain how all of the windows and tabs work.

One last thing: Don't skip Chapter 1. It's the most important chapter in this book.

Chapter 1

ACT! 2000: An Overview

● ●

In This Chapter

▶ Knowing very important ACT! information

▶ Using ACT! windows

▶ Getting help when you need it

● ●

Read this chapter before you look at any other part of this book! While you may be itching to jump ahead and find out about scheduling activities and creating custom reports or whatever, I strongly urge you to give this chapter a good once-over. You may think you know it all, or maybe you think that this section, because it comes early in the book, won't contain any real information. Well, it does, darn it, so humor me and continue reading!

End of tirade. I promise not to yell at you anymore.

Some Very Important ACT! Information

The stuff I talk about here will save you hours of frustration and maybe even save your life — maybe. You'll discover the importance of keeping all your contact information in one place. I'll share secrets about protecting your ACT! data. And you'll find out some of the fun and important things that ACT! can do for you.

ACT! is people-oriented, not task-oriented

The whole concept of ACT! is that it's people-oriented, not task-oriented. For most of us, this is a different way of approaching the subject of how to set our priorities, to stay on top of all of our unfinished work, tasks, and projects, and to maintain relationships with the important people in our lives. When you become comfortable with this concept, ACT! is a very easy program to use.

For years, we've all been keeping track of our activities by using some version of a things-to-do list. Some people write down all of their tasks on pads of paper and update the list every few days, others use daily planning books, and still others write everything on sticky notes and paste them to the desktop, wall, and computer monitor.

With ACT!, you don't make lists. You schedule a specific task and include the task's date, time, and regarding information, and then you assign the task to a specific person. Then you use ACT! to help you to keep track of all your unfinished tasks.

So instead of having an item on your things-to-do list that says, "Call Jeffrey Mayer," you use ACT! to go to Jeffrey Mayer's contact record and schedule the item "Follow-up on last week's presentation" as a call.

In ACT!'s Task List you can view information on your calls, meetings, and to-dos, for any date you choose — past, present, or future — as a list. Click the Daily, Weekly, or Monthly calendar icons, and you can view your schedule on a calendar. And by clicking the Activities tab within the Contact window, you can view all the activities that are scheduled for a specific contact. For more information on the Task List, see Chapter 16. Chapter 15 covers ACT!'s calendars, and Chapter 5 covers the Activities tab.

Remember to record history items

Keeping a history of your activities and other things is a very important part of ACT!. Your history notations are automatically recorded and can be viewed by clicking a contact's Notes/History tab. History records serve several important purposes:

- ✔ They provide an automatic record of the date, time, and purpose for all the activities that you have cleared for each contact. (If you don't clear an activity, it's not recorded as a history item.)

- ✔ ACT!'s history feature automatically records the date and regarding information of any correspondence — letters, memos, faxes, and e-mail — that you have sent to the contact. Use the attachment feature, and you automatically attach the document to the contact record. Double-click on the attachment icon, and ACT! opens the document.

- ✔ Make an ACT! field a History field, and whenever you make an entry in that field, ACT! automatically creates a history notation that appears within the Notes/History Tab. The Last Results field, for example, is a History field.

- ✔ Use ACT!'s Record History dialog box (press Ctrl+H), which offers a quick and easy way to record the results of a meeting, a telephone call, or a completed to-do.

The recording of history notations is extremely important because it gives you the capability to automatically record all the events and communications that have taken place between you and the important people in your life. After you've created this information, you can then include it in a report for your boss or supervisor. With ACT!'s Record History feature, ACT!'s reporting capabilities become huge productivity-improving and timesaving tools that will help you to grow your business and expand your career.

For the lowdown on the Notes/History tab, turn to Chapter 5.

Put everybody you know into ACT!

Because ACT! is contact-oriented, you really need to get people into the program. (See Chapter 7 on how to import information from another database, word processing merge file, or contact management program into ACT!.)

If you're a new ACT! user, you should plan on using it a little bit at a time while you continue using your present system (such as your daily-planning book). You do more and more things with ACT! as you become familiar with its features and add more people to the database. Then one day you realize that you're using ACT! all of the time.

If you're an ACT! 3 or ACT! 4 user, ACT! 2000 automatically installs over it. If you're converting from ACT! 2 or an earlier version of ACT!, you may want to spend a bit of time learning its ins and outs before you convert your data and go live.

If you're sharing ACT! data with other users, everybody *must* be using ACT! 2000. An ACT! 2000 database can be saved in either the ACT! 3 or the ACT! 4 format, but is not compatible with the ACT! 3 or the ACT! 4 format.

Turn ACT! into your electronic Rolodex file

Feel free to include the names, addresses, and phone numbers of your family, your friends, your doctor, your dentist, your lawyer, your auto mechanic, and the butcher, the baker, and the candlestick maker, as well as all your business contacts. The more people you have in your ACT! database, the easier it will be for you to use the program.

Initially, your goal should be to get as many people as you can, as quickly as you can, into the program. The basic information includes each person's name, company name, and phone number. You can fill in additional pieces of information — such as address, city, zip code, and so on — as time permits.

When talking on the phone to a person you want to add to your ACT! database, make sure that you get all of the person's important information — company name, address, phone number, and so on. You can save time by typing the information directly into ACT!. However, you *must* take a moment to read this information back to the person, especially to check the spelling of his or her name, mailing address, phone number, e-mail address, and Web site to ensure that you recorded it properly.

The best way to learn how to use ACT! is to play with it. Click the different icons and watch what happens. Select the different commands listed on the menus and see what each of them does.

Back up your ACT!

The more you use ACT!, the more important it becomes that you back up your database on a regular basis. Losing data or other files can be disastrous.

ACT! 2000 includes a backup feature whereby you can backup your database, as well as your attached e-mail messages, documents, envelopes, labels, layouts, reports, SideACT! Data, and form letter templates. Backing up and restoring your ACT! database is covered in Chapter 28.

Practical Sales Tools has an ACT! utility, called Backup Your ACT!, that has some neat features. For more information, give them a call toll-free at 888-433-2891 or visit their Web site at www.pstools.com.

One of the easiest ways to backup your hard drives and your ACT! databases is to use an automatic backup system with a tape backup or ZIP drive.

ACT! is such an important part of my life that I back it up twice a day. Scheduled, automatic backups of my ACT! files occur every day at 12:30 p.m. and at 6:30 p.m. I back up all files that have changed on my hard drive. (I do a complete backup of my hard drive about once every week.) For years, I've been using Seagate's tape backup systems, and they work just great!

If you're not backing up your computer and your ACT! database on a regular basis, you're taking an unnecessary risk because sooner or later, something bad is going to happen, and you're going to lose some or all of your data. It's happened to me more than once, and my tape backup system has been both a lifesaver and a huge time-saver.

Protect access to your ACT! database with a password

You should take great care to prevent unauthorized access to your ACT! database by using a password.

If you're using ACT! on your laptop and taking it with you when you leave the office, you should definitely password-protect your ACT! database. If you're using ACT! on a stand-alone computer in a small office environment, password protecting your database may not be necessary.

To assign a password to a database, take the following steps:

1. **Select File⇨Administration and then Set Password from the menu bar.**
2. **If you already have a password and want to change it, enter the current password in the Old Password field.**

   If you don't have a password, leave the Old Password field blank.
3. **Enter your new password in the New Password field.**
4. **Retype your new password in the Retype New Password field to confirm the new password, and then click OK.**

Saving your user password

If you're using ACT! on a network or sharing a database with other users, you must enter your name and password each time you want to use ACT!; otherwise, ACT! doesn't know which user you are. When there are multiple users of an ACT! database, each user has his or her own My Record contact record, and all of that person's activities are associated with that My Record file.

By entering your name and password, you're instructing ACT! to bring up your My Record contact record.

The Remember Password option on the General tab of ACT!'s preference settings (select Edit⇨Preferences) gives you the capability to have ACT! automatically enter your name, or your name and password, in the Login To "name of database" dialog box whenever you turn ACT! on.

Warning: The Remember Password option creates the opportunity for a breach of security. If you select this option, someone else can sit down at your computer, turn on ACT!, and have complete access to your ACT! database.

If you're using ACT! on a laptop or notebook computer, you should *not* use the Remember Password option.

Opening a password-protected database

When you open a password-protected database, the Login To "name of database" dialog box appears. Enter your user name and password and click OK.

If you want ACT! to remember your password for use the next time you log on to this database, choose the Remember Password option. The Remember Password option can also be set by selecting it on the General tab of the Preferences dialog box, which you open by selecting Edit⇨Preferences from the menu bar.

If you forget your password, call ACT! Technical Support at 541-465-8645 and ask about the Password Removal Service.

Using ACT!'s Windows

In ACT! 2000, you can view the Contact Layout; Contact List; Daily, Weekly, and Monthly calendars; Task List; Groups; and E-mail in separate windows. You can open all of these windows at the same time, and you can choose to have them cascaded or tiled (vertically or horizontally). You can move from one open window to another by clicking the window that you want, clicking the appropriate icon at the bottom of the Contact window, or pressing Ctrl+Tab.

Here's an example of working with multiple windows: To schedule an activity, click any portion of a contact's contact record, drag it onto an open calendar, and drop it on the day and time you want. ACT! opens the Schedule Activity dialog box in which you enter the activity's particulars.

You open ACT! windows by clicking the appropriate icon on the View Bar. Figure 1-1 shows the icons.

Right-click on the View Bar, and you can change its position from the left side of the window (Large View Bar), to the bottom-right edge of the window (Mini View Bar). You can also choose large or small icons.

You can also open windows by selecting the View command from the menu bar, or by using these function keys:

- ✔ F3 opens the Weekly calendar.
- ✔ F5 opens the Monthly calendar.
- ✔ F7 opens the Task List window.
- ✔ F8 opens the Contact List window.

✔ F10 opens the Groups window.

✔ F11 brings you to the Contact window.

✔ Shift+F5 opens the Daily calendar.

Figure 1-1:
ACT!
window
icons.

To close any window other than the Contact window, press Ctrl+F4. Pressing Ctrl+F4 in the Contact window closes the database. Pressing Alt+F4 closes ACT!.

Getting Help When You Need It

The reason you bought this book is because you wanted to find out how to use ACT! 2000. A number of resources are available to you if you need information that is beyond the scope of this *...For Dummies* book.

Online ACT! help

The online help feature in ACT! is very good. It's a quick and convenient way to look up information about how to use a particular feature or command. If you have a specific question about an ACT! feature or command, select Help Topics from the Help menu, and you may be able to find the answer to your question all by yourself.

Help for a specific ACT! dialog box

Within any ACT! dialog box, there is usually a Help button at the bottom right-hand corner. Click on it, and the help information for the dialog box's features opens.

You can also use the right mouse button to click an option about which you'd like more information. Click in a blank area of a dialog box and you'll get general help information about that dialog box.

View ACT!'s online manuals

The ACT! 2000 CD-ROM also has online manuals. You access the online manuals by selecting Help⇨Online Manuals.

Symantec Online Support

Technical support for ACT! is available online through Symantec's Web site. Select Help⇨Symantec Online Support, and you've access to:

- **Online Support:** Technical support options available online.
- **Telephone Support:** Look here for your product's telephone support numbers.
- **Online Assistant:** Find what you're looking for on our technical support Web site.

The Internet address for the ACT! Support Center is `service.symantec.com/act`. At the Support Center, you have quick access to the following services: Service File Download Area, Frequently Asked Questions (FAQs), Interactive Technical Support System, Knowledge Bases, and Online Discussion Groups.

You log on to Symantec's Web site by selecting Internet Links⇨Symantec. Then choose from the list of sites that includes ACT! Small Business Resource Center, Mobile Resources, Technical Support, Try It Before You Buy It, and Symantec Corporation. Using ACT!'s Internet Tools is covered in Chapter 25.

Chapter 2

Getting Contacts into ACT!

● ●

In This Chapter

▶ Creating a new ACT! database

▶ Converting a previous ACT! database to ACT! 2000

▶ Importing contacts into ACT!

▶ Opening, closing, and deleting an ACT! database

● ●

A fter you've installed ACT! and have it up and running, you need to create a database of contacts so that you can keep track of them. Just by coincidence, I cover that very topic in this chapter.

Creating a New ACT! Database

You create a new ACT! database by taking the following steps:

1. **Select the File⇨New command from the menu bar.**

   The New dialog box appears.

2. **Select ACT! Database in the File Type box, and click OK.**

   The New Database dialog box appears.

3. **Give the new database a name, and click Save.**

   The Enter "My Record" Information dialog box opens.

4. **Enter information about yourself in the Enter "My Record" Information dialog box, and click OK.**

   ACT! creates the new database.

Do not use the File⇨New command to convert a previous ACT! database to the ACT! 2000 format. If you do, you will overwrite the database and lose all your contact information!

If, by chance, Chris Huffman's contact information — or someone else's — appears in the My Record contact record instead of your contact information, just enter your name, address, phone number, and so on, in the appropriate fields. This little problem sometimes occurs if you were using ACT!'s Demo database at the time you created a new database. You can find the My Record contact record by selecting Lookup⇨My Record.

Converting a Previous ACT! Database to ACT! 2000

You can convert a database from a previous version of ACT! into an ACT! 2000 database, but remember that an ACT! 2000 database cannot be read by a previous version of ACT!.

Before you convert your ACT! database to ACT! 2000, I suggest that you backup your ACT! database. If you don't have a tape backup system or a ZIP drive, open the database directory and copy the files that make up the database to another directory.

And if you're an ACT! 2 user, I suggest that you copy your ACT! 2 database from your ACT! 2 database directory to the ACT! 2000 database directory before you make the conversion.

This is how you convert an ACT! 2, ACT! 3, or ACT! 4 database to the ACT! 2000 format:

1. **Select the File⇨Open command from the menu bar.**

   The Open dialog box appears.

2. **Locate the directory containing the database, which is probably your ACT! database directory.**

3. **Select ACT! Database (*.dbf) from the Files of Type drop-down menu, if it isn't already selected.**

4. **Click Open.**

   The Convert Database dialog box, shown in Figure 2-1, appears with this message: This file was created with a previous version of ACT! and will be converted to ACT! 2000. Would you like to create a backup copy of the existing file?

5. **Select the Create Backup option and the Move Converted Database to Default Folder option.**

   I recommend that you select the Create Backup option as protection in case a failure occurs during the conversion process. The backup copy of your database is stored in ACT! 2000's database\backup directory.

6. **Click OK.**

   ACT! displays the name of the database and asks whether you want to replace it.

7. **Click Yes.**

   ACT! creates the new database and copies the old database to the database\backup directory.

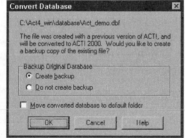

Figure 2-1:
The Convert
Database
dialog box.

For ACT! 2 users only: If you were using the Library field in ACT! 2, be aware that ACT! 2000 doesn't contain a Library field. Any Library files that were part of a contact's record appear as an attachment in the contact's Notes/History tab in ACT! 2000. To avoid losing data stored in the Library field, map the Library field to another ACT! 2000 field. I talk about the map feature later in this chapter.

For ACT! 2 users only: ACT! 2000 does not use description files. If you have more than one description file that you use with your ACT! 2 database, make sure that your primary description file is the one that is applied at the time you convert your ACT! 2 database to the ACT! 2000 format.

Importing Contacts into ACT! from Another Database

If you already have a list of names, addresses, and phone numbers in a database, a contact manager, or a personal information manager (or, for that matter, names and addresses in a word processing merge file), you can import that information directly into ACT! and spare yourself the time and effort of re-entering each individual's information, piece by piece, into your ACT! database.

Follow these steps to import a text-delimited (.TXT) file of names and addresses into ACT!:

1. **Open the ACT! database into which you want to import the records.**

2. **Select File⇨Data Exchange⇨Import from the menu bar.**

   The Import Wizard appears.

3. **Select the type of file that you want to import from the File Type drop-down list.**

   You can select from ACT! 3.x, 4.x or ACT! 2000 (*.DBF) files, dBASE III – V files, Outlook Data, Q&A 4.0 to 5.0 Data files, and Text-Delimited files.

   If you don't see the file type that you want, you may need to convert your existing file to a text-delimited file.

4. **Use the Browse button to open the Open dialog box; then select the directory where the file is located.**

5. **Highlight the file, and click the Open button.**

   The file's path is displayed in the Filename and Location field in the Import Wizard.

6. **Click the Next button.**

   The Wizard asks you what kind of records you want to import.

7. **Pick either Contact Records Only or Group Records Only, and click the Options button.**

   The Import Options dialog box opens. ACT! asks you to make the following choices:

   • Select the type of field separator. It can be either a comma or a tab.

   • Choose the character set. In the character set field, you tell ACT! what kind of character information you're importing. ACT! wants to know whether your imported file is formatted for Windows, DOS, or Macintosh.

   • Do you wish to import the first record? Sometimes, the first record displayed in a text file is the list of field names, such as Company, Contact, Phone, City, State, and so on. You probably don't want to import that record into ACT!. If the first record of the database that you're importing is indeed a list of field names, leave the Yes, Import the First Record check box empty. If the first record is a contact, you should check this box.

8. **Make your selections, and click OK.**

   The options dialog box closes, and you return to the import Wizard.

9. **Click the Next button.**

   ACT! asks you if you want to use a predefined map file. A map file is a template that matches the database fields from other applications (ECCO, FedEx, GoldMine, Janna Contact, Maximizer Organizer, Schedule+, Sharkware, Sidekick, and Tracker) to fields in an ACT! database.

10. **Select the map you wish to use when you import your data.**

    If you wish to use a map, click the Next button and you can view your map in the Contact Map, a feature discussed in the next section. The Contact Map appears, as shown in Figure 2-2.

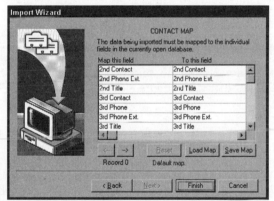

Figure 2-2:
The Contact
Map.

11. **If you do not want to use a predefined map, click the Next button and you can manually map your fields in the Contact Map.**

12. **When the fields you are importing are mapped to the correct ACT! fields, click the Finish button.**

    ACT! imports your contacts into the database.

Mapping your database fields

When you import a file into ACT!, you want to make sure that everything ends up in the right place. For example, you want the company's name to appear in the Company field, the contact's name to appear in the Contact field, and so on. After all, it doesn't do you much good if the contact's phone number is in the City field, does it? So ACT! includes a feature that allows you to map your fields.

Mapping is the process of matching fields from a file that you want to import into ACT! with the appropriate fields on an ACT! database. You can map each field from an import file to any ACT! field that you choose. You can also exclude any field you want from the importing process.

The Contact Map dialog box (refer to Figure 2-2) displays the contents of each field of the import file, beginning with the first record, and it enables you to map, or match, each of those fields to the appropriate ACT! field.

To match the import fields with the appropriate ACT! fields, choose a field in the Map This Field column and then select the ACT! field that you want to map it to from the drop-down list in the To This Field column.

You then work your way through the list of fields you're importing into ACT!, one field at a time and determine to which ACT! field you want to map the import field.

After mapping all the information in your import file to the appropriate ACT! fields and saving your map settings (if desired), it's time to begin the actual import. When you're ready, click Finish, and ACT! imports the contact information into your ACT! database. If you change your mind and don't want to import this information, click Cancel.

Here are some additional ACT! mapping tips:

✔ **Importing first and last names:** If the file you're importing lists the contact's first and last names in separate fields, select the First Name and Last Name fields (rather than the Contact field) from the To This Field column. When you import the file into ACT!, the First Name and Last Name fields automatically combine in the Contact field.

✔ **Excluding a field:** If you don't want to import a particular field into ACT!, you can exclude that field by selecting the Do Not Map selection from the drop-down menu, which leaves the field blank.

✔ **Dealing with dBASE memo and character fields longer than 256 characters:** dBASE memo fields cannot be imported directly into ACT! contact notes. To import this information from the contact records of your previous database, contact manager, or personal information manager, you must use the cut-and-paste features of Windows to move each contact's notes into the ACT! notepad, one record at a time.

✔ **Viewing the contacts information:** After mapping the fields of your first contact, click the View Next Record button to view the contact information of the next contact in the import file. Viewing the records of several contacts helps you determine how the imported fields should be mapped to their corresponding ACT! fields. (To view the previous contact's information, click the View Previous Record button.)

Continue the mapping process until all the fields from the import file have been mapped to the correct ACT! fields or have been excluded from the importing process. These additional tips will help you get the most benefit from the mapping feature:

- **ACT! truncates data:** If the data in an import file field is larger, or longer, than the ACT! field that you are mapping it to, ACT! truncates the data.

- **Saving your map settings:** After mapping your data, you can save your map settings by clicking the Contact Map's Save Map button (refer to Figure 2-2) so that the settings may be used again if you need to import information from the same source into one of your ACT! databases.

- **Using your map settings:** To apply one of your previously saved map settings, click the Contact Map's Load Map button (refer to Figure 2-2) and select the map that you want to use from the list that's displayed in the Open dialog box.

Importing contact information from business cards and lists

We've all got names, addresses, and phone numbers on pieces of paper. They're hard to keep track of, and as you may have guessed, ACT! can't work with them. This section covers two ways to get contact information in paper form into ACT!.

- **Business-card scanners:** Do you have a huge stack of business cards in the bottom of your desk drawer? Put them into ACT!. I know; it's a big pain to type all that information. But with a business-card scanner, you can eliminate the biggest hurdle to getting this important information into your computer. Seiko Instruments' Smart Business Card Reader is a very good business-card scanner. It's available through Seiko Instruments, 1130 Ringwood Court, San Jose, CA 95131-1726; phone 800-688-0817. Seiko's Web site is www.seikos-mart.com.

- **Typing services:** If you've got mailing lists, business cards, or Rolodex files that you want typed into your computer, get in touch with Contact Data Entry, P.O. Box 3998,

Bartlesville, OK 74006; phone 918-335-0252, Web site: www.contactentry.com. You send them your lists, they type the names into their computer, and then send them back to you. Follow the importing steps that have just been described, and within minutes, you have your list of names inside ACT!.

- **Contact information from your Web site and e-mail messages:** AddressGrabber magically copies name and address information from your e-mail messages into ACT!. Just highlight the information, click AddressGrabber's ACT! button, and AddressGrabber inserts the information into the correct ACT! field. It also copies ACT! information into other programs, such as QuickBooks, FedEx Ship, Eudora Pro, Outlook, and Outlook Express. For more information, contact ProdEx Technologies, 14471 Big Basin Way, Suite E, Saratoga, CA 95070, phone 408-872-3102. Their Web site is www.prodexusa.com /addressgrabber.

Chapter 3

ACT!'s General Preferences

I know you're in a hurry to start using ACT!, but I feel that you should first set up the program so that you can use it in the most efficient and effective way. To do this, you need to access ACT!'s Preferences settings. Simply choose Edit⇨Preferences.

The Preferences dialog box contains several tabs for a number of different ACT! settings. In this chapter, I discuss only the settings that pertain to getting started: General and Startup. I cover the other tabs with their specific ACT! features in other parts of the book. (For example, I think that it makes more sense to discuss how to work with the calendar preferences in the chapter on how to use the ACT! calendars.)

The Preferences dialog box has the following tabs:

- **General:** Discussed in this chapter

- **Startup:** Discussed in this chapter

- **Names:** Discussed in Chapter 7

- **Scheduling:** Discussed in Chapter 13

- **Calendar:** Discussed in Chapter 15

- **Dialer:** Discussed in Chapter 20

- **Spelling:** Discussed in Chapter 21

- **WinFax Options:** Discussed in Chapter 22. If WinFax PRO is not installed on your computer, this tab will not be displayed. Since the release of ACT! 4, complete integration exists between ACT! and WinFax PRO 8.03 or higher. If you're using a previous version of WinFax PRO, I suggest that you upgrade to the newest version of WinFax PRO.

✔ **E-mail:** Discussed in Chapter 23

✔ **Colors and Fonts:** Discussed in Chapter 27

✔ **Synchronization:** Discussed in Chapter 28

Preferences Dialog Box Basics

When you select the Preferences command, you can customize the various functions and settings for your ACT! database to your individual tastes. After you make your Preferences setting selections, click the OK button at the bottom of the Preferences dialog box. ACT! saves your settings and returns you to the Contact window.

If you don't want to save your changes to the Preferences settings, click Cancel or press the Esc key. ACT! returns you to the Contact window with your prior Preferences settings still active. Here are some additional things you can do:

✔ To apply a setting without closing the Preferences dialog box, click the Apply button at the bottom-left corner of the box.

✔ To move from one field to another within the Preferences dialog box, you can use the Tab key, click with your mouse, or press the Alt key plus the underlined letter.

✔ To move backward through the dialog box, use the Shift+Tab key combination.

✔ To change tabs, click the tab with your mouse. When a tab is highlighted (with a dotted box around it), use the arrow keys to move between tabs. You can also use the Ctrl+PageUp and Ctrl+PageDown keys to move from one tab to another.

The General tab

In the General tab, you select default applications, file locations, phone formats, and other default settings.

✔ **Select your word processor:** In the Default Applications section of the General tab, you choose your word processor. You have two choices: You can use the ACT! word processor or Microsoft Word. Using word processors is discussed in Chapter 21.

✔ **Select your faxing software:** You choose the fax software that you want from those in the drop-down list in the Default applications section of the General tab.

ACT! QuickStart Wizard makes it easy to select your word processor and faxing software and to set up your e-mail systems. It also gives you the option of converting previous ACT! databases to the ACT! 2000 format. The Wizard walks you through the process. To find the QuickStart Wizard, select Help➪QuickStart Wizard.

✔ **Set your ACT! file location:** The Default Locations settings enable you to define the default directory for your ACT! database, as well as the default directory for your reports, documents, form letter templates, macros, queries, and so on.

If you use databases on both your own computer and on a network drive, you need to know how to change the default location of your database so that ACT! can find it. Read on.

When you select a File Type from the Default Locations drop-down menu, Database for example, its path automatically displays in the Location field. If you want to change the location of a directory, click the Browse button to the right of the Location field, and the Browse For Folder dialog box appears. Use this dialog box to choose a new directory path.

✔ **Decide on the Tab key or the Enter key:** In the Moving Between Fields Using [Tab or Enter Key] section of the General tab, you can choose either the Tab key or the Enter key as the one that moves the cursor from one field to the next.

✔ **Display country codes in phone field:** If you like the field for the country code (1 for the United States, 33 for France, 81 for Japan, and so on) to appear in each Phone field throughout ACT!, select this option.

✔ **Have ACT! prompt you before exiting:** Would you like ACT! to ask you whether you really want to quit each time you exit ACT!? If so, select the Prompt Before Exiting option. (I suggest that you check this box so that you can't close ACT! by accident.)

The Ctrl+F4 key combination automatically closes an ACT! window or database. Alt+F4 automatically closes ACT!.

✔ **Have ACT! remember your password:** If you want ACT! to remember your password each time you open an ACT! database, select the Remember Password option.

✔ **Move between records using ACT! 2.0 shortcut keys:** If you use ACT! 2, you know that Ctrl+Home moves you to the first record in a lookup and Ctrl+End moves you to the last record in a lookup. You also know that the PageUp key moves you to the previous record and the PageDown key moves you to the next record.

If you like to use the ACT! 2 shortcut keys, select this option on the General tab.

In ACT! 2000, the key combinations are different. Alt+Home moves you to the first record in a lookup. Alt+End moves you to the last record in a lookup. Ctrl+PageUp moves you to the previous record. Ctrl+PageDown moves you to the next record.

The Startup tab

The Startup tab enables you to select a default contact and a group layout, which database to open each time you start ACT!, a macro to run when you start ACT!, and more.

- ✔ **Select a default contact layout:** The Default Contact Layout field lets you choose the contact layout ACT! uses when you start the program. Click the Browse button to the right of the Default Contact Layout field, and select from the list of available layouts.

- ✔ **Make all new contacts public or private:** If you want all the new contacts you add to the database to be private (meaning that their contact information is not shared with ACT! users with whom you are sharing your ACT! database), check the Make New Contacts Private check box. Everyone who uses the database can view public activities.

- ✔ **Select default group layout:** The group layout is what ACT! uses when you start the program, and you get to choose the layout you want to use from the list of available layouts in the Default Group Layout field. Click the Browse button to the right of the Default Group Layout field to display the list.

- ✔ **Make all new groups public or private:** If you would like to make all the new groups you add to the database private, check the Make New Groups Private check box. The contact information of private groups is not shared with any ACT! users with whom you are sharing your ACT! database.

- ✔ **Last opened database:** Choose this option if you want ACT! to open the database you were working with when you last exited ACT!.

- ✔ **Named database:** If you want a specific database to open every time you start ACT!, choose this option. To select a specific database, click the Browse button to the right of the Named Database field and select the database you want from the list of available databases.

- ✔ **Macro options:** If you want ACT! to run a macro when you start the program, select that macro and insert its path in the Run Macro On Startup field. To select a macro, click the Browse button and select from the list of available macros.

Chapter 4

The Contact Window

● ●

In This Chapter

▶ Using the fields of an ACT! Contact layout

▶ Executing ACT! commands

● ●

*1*n the ACT! Contact window, shown in Figure 4-1, you view contact information displayed on a contact layout. You switch from one contact layout to another by clicking the Contact Layout button at the bottom of the Contact window. ACT! comes with several contact layouts, including Contact 2000, Contact 4.0, Contact 3.0, Contact Layout, Classic Contact 1, Classic Contact 2, Alternate, Rotary Index, and Large Font.

For ACT! 2 users, the Classic Contact 1 and Classic Contact 2 layouts are the same as the Contact 1 and Contact 2 layouts in ACT! 2000.

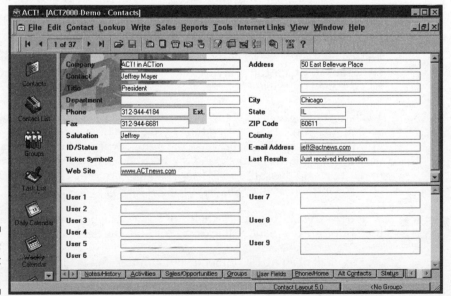

Figure 4-1:
The Contact
window.

The Fields of an ACT! Contact Layout

ACT! layouts have many fields in which to store information about your contacts. ACT! provides so many fields because the more information that you're able to store and record about the important people in your business and personal life, the easier it is to develop and maintain long-term relationships.

A field is where you enter information about a person — such as "Mayer Enterprises." The field name for Mayer Enterprises would be the word "Company." Every field needs to have a field name; otherwise, you wouldn't know what information to enter where.

ACT! enables you to create additional fields with the Edit⇨Define Fields command. This feature is discussed in Chapter 6. After you create a new ACT! field, you have to do two more things:

1. **Put the new field on the contact layout, so that you can enter contact information into it.**

   You do this task by using the Layout Designer. To open the Layout Designer, select Tools⇨Design Layout from the menu bar. The Layout Designer is discussed in Chapter 26.

2. **Add the new field to your reports.**

   Use ACT!'s Report editor to add new fields. To edit a report, select Reports⇨Edit Report Template from the menu bar, and then select the ACT! report that you want to modify from the displayed list. Editing ACT! reports is discussed in Chapter 24.

The ACT! Contact window (refer to Figure 4-1) consists of two parts. The top section contains general contact information, and the bottom section has eight tabs in which you can view different information. The bar between the two is called the *splitter bar*.

To change the size of a split window, position the cursor on the splitter bar so that it changes to the sizing tool, hold down the mouse button, move it upward or downward, and release the mouse when the window sizes are where you want them. To expand the bottom portion of the split window so that it takes up the entire window, place the cursor on the splitter bar until it changes into the sizing tool, and then double-click.

To move forward through the fields of an ACT! layout, press the Tab key. Use the Shift+Tab key to move backward through the fields.

The top half of an ACT! Contact layout contains fields for entering general contact information, such as the company, contact name, phone and fax numbers, title, mailing address, and so on.

The bottom half of an ACT! layout contains eight very useful tabs. These four tabs contain contact information:

- **The User Fields tab:** On the User Fields tab, you find User fields 1 through 9. (User fields 10 through 15 are on the Status tab.) You use these fields to customize ACT! so that it best suits your needs and requirements. (For additional information about customizing your User fields, see Chapter 6.)

- **The Phone/Home tab:** The Phone/Home tab contains fields for the contact's home address and phone number, as well as fields for additional telephone numbers.

- **The Alt Contacts tab:** The Alternate Contacts tab contains fields in which you can store information about the contact's assistant and additional contacts who work closely with the contact.

I suggest that you create a separate contact record for every person with whom you want to maintain a relationship. Use the Assistant, 2nd Contact, and 3rd Contact fields to enter basic information about people who work closely with your contact. Having these additional names and telephone numbers available is very helpful when you're unable to reach your contact.

- **The Status tab:** The Status tab contains reference information about your phone calls, meetings, correspondence, and contact management information. It also contains User fields 10 through 15. Only the Public/Private and Record Manager fields can be modified. The other fields are system fields and cannot be modified. Here's a brief description of the fields in the Status tab:

  - **Last Reach:** The Last Reach field records the date on which you last reached the contact by phone. This field updates automatically when you record a completed telephone call from the Record History dialog box. It is a system field and cannot be modified.

  - **Last Meeting:** The Last Meeting field records the date on which you last met with the contact. This field is updated automatically when you clear a scheduled meeting. It is a system field and cannot be modified.

  - **Last Attempt:** The Last Attempt field records the date on which you last attempted to phone the contact. This field is updated automatically when you record an attempted telephone call from the Record History dialog box. It is a system field and cannot be modified.

  - **Letter Date:** The Letter Date field records the date of the last letter that you sent to the contact. It is a system field and cannot be modified.

- **Create Date:** The Create Date field records the date the contact record was created. It is a system field and cannot be modified.

- **Edit Date:** The Edit Date field records the date on which the contact's record was last edited. This field is updated automatically whenever a change is made to the contact's record. It is a system field and cannot be modified.

You can use the dates displayed in the Edit Date, Last Reach, Last Attempt, Last Meeting, and Letter Date fields to do custom database queries. For example, with ACT!'s Advanced Query feature (select Lookup⇨By Example), you can search for all the contacts with whom you haven't had a meeting since April 1 or all the people you haven't reached on the phone since September 15. For more information on database queries, see Chapter 11.

The edit date does not change when an activity is scheduled or a note is entered. The edit date changes only when the contact record itself is edited, or when the Last Reach, Last Meeting, Last Attempt, or Letter Date fields change. I think this is a serious design flaw because it limits your ability to search your database.

- **Merge Date:** The Merge Date field records the date on which the contact record was merged into this ACT! database. It is a system field and cannot be modified.

- **Record Creator:** The Record Creator field records the name of the person who created the record. It is a system field and cannot be modified.

- **Record Manager:** The Record Manager field records the name of the manager of the contact record. If the record was created in your database, the manager information is automatically inserted from the My Record contact record. If the contact record was imported from another database (yours or someone else's), the Manager field contains the information from that user's database. The information in this field can be edited manually.

- **Public/Private:** If you're using ACT! in a multi-user environment, other users who log on to your ACT! database will be able to see the contacts marked as public. But you may want to add some of your personal contacts to your ACT! database. If you do not want other users to see these records, mark them as private.

In addition to the Contact Layout tabs that contain contact information, four tabs contain information about all the things that are happening, or have happened, between you and your contacts. (The features of these tabs are covered in Chapter 5.)

✔ **Notes/History tab:** The Notes/History tab contains the notepad, the contact history, and the names of any files attached to the contact record.

✔ **Activities tab:** The Activities tab contains a listing of all the activities that you have scheduled for a contact.

✔ **Sales/Opportunities tab:** The Sales/Opportunities tab shows a list, and the status, of each sales opportunity that you have with a specific person.

✔ **Groups tab:** The Groups tab enables you to view the groups of which an individual is a member.

Executing ACT! Commands

Now that you understand how ACT! information appears within an ACT! layout, I'm going to explain how you execute ACT! commands. You can execute ACT! commands in many different ways. You can use the menu bar, shortcut menus, shortcut keys, the toolbar, and the status bar.

The top of the ACT! Contact window (refer to Figure 4-1) contains a menu bar with lots of choices: File, Edit, Contact, Lookup, Write, Sales, Reports, Tools, Internet Links, View, Window, and Help. It is from this menu that you access all ACT! commands.

For example, clicking Contact on the menu bar brings you a list of the various ACT! commands for managing your contacts. From the Contact menu, you can insert a new contact record; duplicate an existing contact record; delete a contact; schedule a call, meeting, or to-do; and so on.

You activate these commands by clicking the specific command with your mouse. You can also use the arrow keys to highlight the specific command, and then press Enter. To the right of each command is the appropriate function key combination, if you like to use shortcut keys.

Here are some menu bar tips:

✔ When you highlight a command either with your mouse or from the keyboard, the status bar at the bottom-left corner of the Contact window displays a description of the command.

✔ To change the position of the menu bar, click on a blank portion — don't click a command — and drag the menu bar to another position on the window. If you want the menu bar to float as a palette, just leave it positioned anywhere you want in the Contact window.

To make changes to the commands that are displayed on the menu bar — add commands, remove commands, or change their positions — select Tools⇨Customize Contacts Window. Customizing ACT! is covered in Chapter 27.

Shortcut menus

Right-click on almost any portion of an ACT! window or tab, and a shortcut menu appears. This makes it easy for you to select an ACT! command. This brief summary tells you about the commands that are available from within the Contact window:

- ✓ **The Contact window:** Right-click on a blank portion of the Contact window, and you can add, duplicate, or delete a contact; schedule an activity; write a letter, memo, fax, or e-mail message; and lots more. The same commands are also available on the Phone/Home, Alt Contacts, and Status tabs.

- ✓ **An ACT! field:** Right-click on highlighted text in an ACT! field, and you can cut, copy, paste or delete the text.

- ✓ **The Notes/History tab:** Right-click on a blank portion of the Notes/History tab, and you can insert a note, record a history, attach a file, and lots more.

- ✓ **The Activities tab:** Right-click on a blank portion of the Activities tab, and you can schedule, reschedule, or clear an activity; phone a contact; and more.

- ✓ **Sales/Opportunities tab:** Right-click on a blank portion of the Sales/Opportunities tab, and you can add a new sales opportunity; edit, delete or list a sale as being completed; and more.

- ✓ **Groups tab:** Right-click on a blank portion of the Groups tab, and you can add or remove people from a group, and more.

Shortcut Keys

Many ACT! commands can be activated by pressing shortcut keys. Tables 4-1 through 4-6 list ACT!'s shortcuts:

Table 4-1	File Menu Commands
Use This:	*To Do This:*
Ctrl+N	Open the New dialog box where you can create a new database, word processing document or template, report, envelope, or letter
Ctrl+O	Open a database or other ACT! file
Ctrl+F4	Close a window and close an ACT! database
Ctrl+W	Close a window
Ctrl+P	Open the Print dialog box
Alt+F4	Exit ACT!

Table 4-2	Edit Menu Commands
Use This:	*To Do This:*
Ctrl+C	Copy
Ctrl+V	Paste
Ctrl+X	Cut
Ctrl+Z	Undo

Table 4-3	Contact Menu Commands
Use This:	*To Do This:*
Insert	Insert new contact
Ctrl+Del	Delete a contact or lookup
Ctrl+L	Schedule a call
Ctrl+M	Schedule a meeting
Ctrl+T	Schedule a to-do
F9	Insert a note
Ctrl+H	Record an action's history
Ctrl+I	Attach a file

Table 4-4	Tools Menu Commands
Use This:	*To Do This:*
Alt+F7	Check spelling
Shift+F4	Set timer
Alt+F5	Record macro
Ctrl+Q	Launches SideACT!

Table 4-5	View Menu Commands
Use This:	*To Do This:*
F4	View the Mini-Calendar
F7	View the Task List
F8	View the Contact List
F10	View Groups
F11	View the Contact window
Alt+F9	View the Activities tab
Shift+F9	View the Notes/History tab
Ctrl+F9	View the Groups tab
Shift+F5	View the Daily Calendar
F3	View the Weekly Calendar
F5	View the Monthly Calendar

Table 4-6	Other Commands
Use This:	*To Do This:*
Ctrl+Tab	Toggle between open windows within ACT!
Alt+Tab	Toggle between open programs

You can also create your own custom commands and assign them to shortcut keys. I cover writing macros and assigning them to shortcut keys in Chapter 27.

The Toolbar

ACT! displays and uses 18 standard buttons — ACT! calls them tools — in the Contact window. If you're using WinFax PRO, ACT! adds a 19th button to the toolbar, called the Quick Fax button. The following buttons are pre-installed on the Contact window toolbar.

✔ **The First Record button** moves you to the first record of the lookup. (To find out more about the powerful Lookup feature, see Chapter 10.)

✔ **The Last Record button** moves you to the last record of the lookup.

To move to the first contact record in your lookup, press either Alt+Home or Ctrl+Home. To move to the last contact record in your lookup, press either Alt+End or Ctrl+End. To move between contact records, select the Move Between Records Using ACT! 2 Shortcut Keys option in the General tab of ACT!'s Preferences. This option is discussed in Chapter 3.

✔ **The Previous Contact button** moves you to the previous contact record.

✔ **The Next Contact button** moves you to the next contact record.

✔ The numbers on **the Contact Number button** tell you the position of the current contact record within the current lookup. It also tells you the number of contacts in the current lookup. (For example, 1 of 37 means that the current contact is the first record in a lookup that contains 37 records.)

✔ **The Open File button** brings up the Open File dialog box so that you can open a new file.

✔ **The Save File button** saves changes that you make to the current contact record.

✔ **The New Contact button** adds a new contact to your ACT! database.

✔ **The Insert Note button** lets you write a note to yourself about a contact.

✔ **The Schedule Call button** schedules a new call. (Scheduling activities — calls, meetings, and to-dos — is discussed in Chapter 13.)

✔ **The Schedule Meeting button** schedules a new meeting.

✔ **The Schedule To-do button** schedules a new to-do.

✔ **The Letter button** opens the letter template (`letter.tpl`). (Writing letters in ACT! is covered in Chapter 21.)

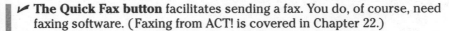

 ✔ **The Quick Fax button** facilitates sending a fax. You do, of course, need faxing software. (Faxing from ACT! is covered in Chapter 22.)

 ✔ **The E-mail Message button** creates an e-mail message for the current contact. Using ACT! to send and receive e-mail is covered in Chapter 23.

 ✔ **The Dial Phone button** displays the Dialer dialog box, which contains all of a current contact's phone numbers. Using ACT! to dial the phone is covered in Chapter 20.

 ✔ **The SideACT! button** launches an ACT! utility that enables you to schedule activities even if ACT! isn't running. SideACT! is discussed in Chapter 21.

 ✔ **LiveUpdate** keeps your ACT! software up to date with the latest fixes and enhancements.

 ✔ **The Help Topics button** opens the Help Topics dialog box, which gives you access to information on the commands and features of ACT!.

The look and feel of the ACT! toolbar can be customized and modified. Here are some of the things you can do:

✔ **Change the toolbar position:** To change the position of the toolbar, click a blank portion of the toolbar — don't click a button — and drag the toolbar to another position on the window. If you want the toolbar to float as a palette, just leave it positioned anywhere you want in the Contact window.

✔ **Change the size of the buttons:** To change the size of a button (large or small), right-click a blank portion of the toolbar, and make your selection from the menu that appears.

✔ **Add Tool Tips:** If you need help remembering what a button does, just place your mouse above the button, and a brief description of the button's function appears. This information is called a Tool Tip. To enable the Tool Tip option, right-click the toolbar, select Customize Window from the menu, and select the Show Tooltips option on the Toolbars tab of the Customize ACT! Contact Window dialog box.

✔ **Customize the toolbar:** Right-click the toolbar, select Customize Window from the subsequent menu, and the Customize ACT! Contact Window dialog box opens. You can also access this dialog box by selecting Tools➪Customize Contacts Window from the menu bar. In this dialog box, you can add or remove buttons from the toolbar, and do lots more. For more information on how to customize the toolbar, menus, and keyboard, check out Chapter 27.

✔ **Add a new toolbar:** You can also create your own toolbars. You do this by selecting the New Toolbar button in the Customize ACT! Contact Window dialog box. Adding new ACT! toolbars is also covered in Chapter 27.

What is a lookup?

Throughout this book, you'll see references to ACT!'s Lookup feature. This feature makes ACT! so powerful because you use it to find people in your ACT! database.

When you do a lookup, you're searching your ACT! database for contact records with similar or identical information, such as everybody who has a last name of Smith or everybody who lives in Chicago. When ACT! finds these records, it groups them together.

For example, let's say that you are planning a business trip and you want to create a list of all the people you know in the city you're visiting so that you can schedule additional meetings or appointments while you are in town. Here's what you do:

1. **Select Lookup⇨City.**

2. **Type in the name of the city.**

3. **Click OK.**

ACT! creates your list in a fraction of a second.

You can also use the Lookup feature to find single contacts in your database. (I use this feature all day long. ACT! has become my personal Rolodex file.) To find someone in ACT!, just select Lookup⇨First Name, Lookup⇨Last Name, or Lookup⇨Company. Then type in the first two or three letters of the name, click OK, and ACT! creates a complete list of all the people who fit that lookup criteria.

If your lookup finds more than one contact record, you can use the PageUp or PageDown keys to move through the list. (You can also use the Ctrl+PageUp and Ctrl+PageDown keys.) Or you can view the results of your lookup as a list by opening the Contact List window (select View⇨Contact List from the menu bar, press F8, or click the Contact List button). I've devoted a whole chapter to the subject of lookups, so see Chapter 10 for more information.

The View Bar

The bar at the left side of the Contact window is called the View bar. It has eight buttons that enable you to open different ACT! windows. The Large View bar is shown in Figure 4-2. Clicking an icon opens a different ACT! window.

You can change the position of the View bar from the Contact window's left edge to the bottom-right corner of the Status bar (which is discussed next), by right-clicking on the View bar and selecting Mini View bar. Here is a brief explanation of how each icon works:

Figure 4-2:
The eight
Large View
bar icons.

✔ **Contacts:** This button displays the contact layout. It is in this window that you enter contact information.

✔ **Contact List:** Clicking this button opens the Contact List window. You use this window to view the list of contacts in the current lookup. The Contact List is discussed in Chapter 15.

✔ **Groups:** This button displays the Groups window, in which you create new groups, modify existing groups, and delete unused groups. Chapter 12 addresses Groups.

✔ **Task List:** This button opens the Task List window, in which you view a list of all your unfinished tasks — your calls, meetings, and to-dos — for past, present, or future dates. The Task List is discussed in Chapter 16.

✔ **Daily Calendar:** Clicking the Daily Calendar button shows you all the activities scheduled for a specific day. ACT!'s calendar features are covered in Chapter 15.

✔ **Weekly Calendar:** Clicking the Weekly Calendar button brings up the ACT! Weekly calendar, where you view all the activities scheduled for a specific week.

✔ **Monthly Calendar:** Click the Monthly Calendar button to bring up the Monthly calendar, which displays all the activities that you have scheduled for a specific month.

✔ **E-mail:** Clicking here opens the e-mail window. In this window, you can view the e-mail messages that are in your inbox, outbox, or briefcase. You also create e-mail messages from this window. See Chapter 23 for a discussion of ACT!'s e-mail features.

The Status Bar

The bar at the bottom of the Contact window is called the status bar. At the left, it displays information about what ACT! is doing. It also contains the Groups and Layout buttons. What follows are descriptions of some of the status bar's functions.

✔ **Viewing your lookup and command descriptions:** Whenever you perform a lookup, the status bar at the bottom-left corner of the Contact window displays the type of lookup. When you highlight a command from the menu bar using either the mouse or the keyboard, a description of the command appears on the status bar.

✔ **Changing layouts with the Layout button:** Click the Layout button on the status bar, and a list of available ACT! layouts is displayed from the drop-down menu. Highlight the layout that you want, and ACT! applies that layout. The name of the layout that is currently selected appears on the Layout button.

✔ **Changing and customizing ACT! layouts:** Use the Layout Designer to customize layouts. You open the Layout Designer by selecting Tools⇨Design Layouts. The features of the Layout Designer are discussed in Chapter 26.

✔ **Changing groups with the Groups button:** Click the Groups button on the status bar, and the drop-down menu displays a list of available groups. Highlight the group you want, and ACT! brings up the members of that group. The name of the group currently selected is displayed on the Groups button. (Using groups is discussed in Chapter 12.)

Chapter 5

Using Some Tabs

At the bottom of the Contact window are eight tabs containing contact information. Four of those tabs — User Fields, Phone/Home, Alt Contacts, and Status — contain contact information that is part of the person's contact record. I cover these tabs in Chapter 4.

The other four tabs — Notes/History, Activities, Sales/Opportunity, and Groups — contain information about recorded notes, history items, and attachments; scheduled activities, sales opportunities, and the groups that the person is a member of. I cover these four tabs in this chapter.

The ACT! Contact window consists of two parts. The top section contains general contact information, and the bottom section has eight tabs in which you can view different information. The bar between the two is called the splitter bar. Resize the bottom part of the Contact window using the splitter bar. See Chapter 4 for more information on the splitter bar.

To scroll through the contact list while the Notes/History tab, Activities tab, or Groups tab is selected, use the Ctrl+PageUp or Ctrl+PageDown keys.

The Notes/History Tab

One of the reasons ACT! is such a powerful tool is that it enables you to keep a record of all of the things that have gone on between you and the important people in both your business life and your personal life. With more information at your fingertips, you can develop closer relationships with your customers, clients, and prospects, which ultimately means more money in your pocket.

You store this information in one of three ways, and access it through the Notes/History tab.

- ✓ **The Insert Note command** lets you write notes to yourself about your meetings, telephone conversations, and other things that may come to mind.

- ✓ **The Record History command** helps you maintain a record of all your meetings, calls, to-dos, and any other information that you want stored as a history entry.

- ✓ **The Attachments command** enables you to attach files to contact records. With a click of your mouse, you can open the attached file in the program that created it.

The Notes/History tab is shown in Figure 5-1.

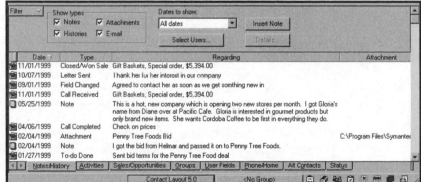

Figure 5-1:
The Notes/
History tab.

The more information you collect about your contacts, the easier it is for you to develop and maintain long-term relationships.

Entering notes of thoughts, meetings, and conversations

ACT! gives you lots of ways to enter notes. You can select Contact⇨Insert Note from the menu bar or press the F9 key from any ACT! window. You can also click the Insert Note button on the Notes/History tab. You can even select the Insert Note command by right-clicking within the Contact window, the Notes/History tab, the User Fields tab, the Phone/Home tab, the Alt Contacts tab, the Status tab, or any other tab that you may add to the contact layout.

Every time you have a conversation with someone, write a note to yourself about the particulars of that call. The more you write down, the less you need to remember.

When you select the Insert Note command, ACT! automatically creates a new note and places the cursor in the Note Regarding field, where you type your note. When you're finished, just press Esc, execute another ACT! command, or click something else with your cursor, and your note is saved.

In addition, ACT! automatically inserts the date in the Date column, inserts the time in the Time column, and inserts "Note" in the Type column. Now isn't that easy?

Recording the results of your activities

The ACT! History feature serves several important purposes. First, it provides an automatic record of the date, time, and purpose for all the activities that you have cleared for each contact. (If you don't clear an activity, a history record is not created, so you won't know what you did or didn't do with that person.)

Second, the History feature automatically stores information about any correspondence — letters, memos, faxes, and e-mail — that you have sent to the contact. (You can also attach the document to the contact record. This is discussed later in this chapter.)

How ACT! notes can improve business relationships

One day, I got a call from a client's assistant who informed me that my appointment with her boss had to be rescheduled. I asked why, and she explained that her son had the leading role in a school play, and she wasn't going to be in the office that day.

I recorded this information as a note in ACT!. When I met with my client a week or two later, I checked my notes in ACT! and asked about her son's performance in the school play.

"He was just great and got a standing ovation," she said. She was very appreciative of the fact that I inquired about her son's performance. I also made the sale.

Third, the History feature can hold any specific information that you entered into an ACT! user field that had been selected as a History field with the Define Fields setting. The Last Results field, for example, is a History field. Whenever information is entered in the Last Results field, it is automatically recorded as a history item.

TIP

To make a field a History field, open the Define Fields dialog box by choosing Edit⇨Define Fields from the menu bar, select the desired field, and choose the Generate History option.

With all this recorded information, you can easily answer your boss's questions: Whom did you meet? When did you meet with him? What happened?

Using the Record History dialog box

You enter history notations into ACT! from the Record History dialog box, shown in Figure 5-2.

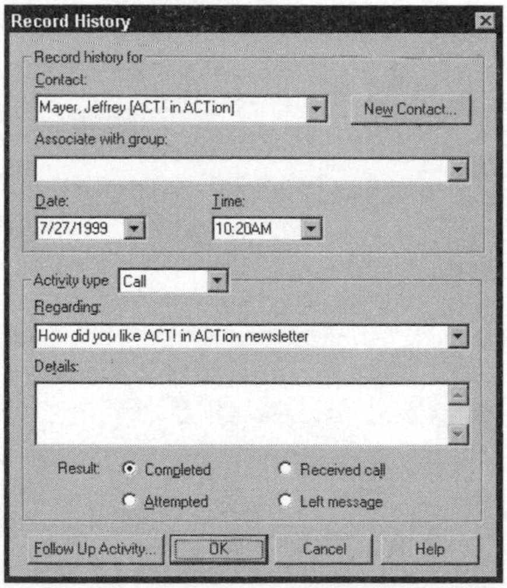

Figure 5-2:
The Record
History
dialog box.

You can open the Record History dialog box in one of three ways:

- ✔ Select Contact⇨Record History from the menu bar.
- ✔ Press Ctrl+H.
- ✔ Select Record History from the shortcut menu that appears when you right-click anywhere within the Contact window, the Notes/History tab, the User Fields tab, the Phone/Home tab, the Alt Contacts tab, the Status tab, or any other tab that you may add to the contact layout.

In the Record History dialog box, choose from the following history choices:

- **Contact:** Select the contact for whom you want to record the history item. Click the down-arrow, and you can assign this activity to any contact within your ACT! database. The list can be sorted alphabetically by the contact's last name or the company name.

- **Associate with Group:** If you wish to associate the history item with a specific group, select the desired group from the Associate with Group drop-down list.

- **Date:** Select the history item's date.

- **Time:** Select the history item's time.

- **Activity Type:** Select Call, Meeting, or To-do as the activity type, and enter information about that activity in the Regarding field, or enter information from the drop-down menu.

The information on the drop-down menu changes to reflect entries in the Call, Meeting, or To-do Regarding field when Call, Meeting, or To-do is selected.

You can select from a pop-up list by pressing F2 when your cursor is in the Regarding field.

- **Activity Results:** You have several choices for the result of an activity.

  - **Call:** When a Call is selected, you have the following Call Results to choose from: Call Attempted, Call Completed, Call Left Message, and Call Received Call.

  - **Meeting:** When a Meeting is selected, you have the following Meeting Results to choose from: Meeting Held and Meeting Not Held.

  - **To-do:** When a To-do is selected, you have the following To-do Results to choose from: To-do Done and To-do Not Done.

- **Details:** If you want to enter a longer description of this call, meeting, or to-do than space allows in the Regarding field, write it in the Details field. You've space for 30,000 characters.

- **New Contact:** Click the New Contact button, and the Add Contact dialog box opens. Here, you can add a new contact to your database. In Chapter 9, I give a complete dissertation on how to add contacts to ACT!.

- **Schedule a Follow-up Activity:** Click the Follow Up Activity button, and the Schedule Activity dialog box opens. Here, you can schedule an activity for this contact or any contact in your ACT! database. I have a whole chapter on how to schedule activities. It's Chapter 13.

Use the Record History dialog box to record the results of impromptu meetings and to-dos that were completed before they were ever scheduled. And every time you speak with someone on the telephone, press Ctrl+H to bring up the Record History box, and write yourself a brief note of the conversation.

From time to time, you may want to record a single history notation for more than one contact. This is how you do it:

1. **Create a lookup of all the contacts to which you want to record this history notation.**

2. **Open the Contact List window (F9), and highlight or tag the specific contacts.**

3. **Press Ctrl+H to open the Record History dialog box, enter your history notation, and click OK.**

Attaching files to contact records

You can attach any kind of file to a contact record. Here are examples of the types of files you can attach:

✓ You may have created a spreadsheet to track sales to a specific contact. When you attach the spreadsheet file to the contact's record, that file will always be part of the contact's record.

✓ You may have created a custom presentation in your word processor or presentation program. Just attach the file to that contact's record.

✓ You may have created a project list in SideACT!, which is covered in Chapter 14. Just attach the SideACT! database to your contact record.

✓ When you print a letter or word processing document, ACT! enables you to automatically attach the document to the contact's record. Chapter 16 covers printing and attaching documents.

When you want to open the document or file, just double-click the attachment icon, and ACT! opens the file in the application that created it. Now isn't that easy?

Attach a file to a contact record by following these steps:

1. **Select the contact record.**

2. **Select Contact⇨Attach File from the menu bar, press Ctrl+I, or choose the Attach File command from the menu that appears after you click the right mouse button.**

   The Attach File dialog box appears.

3. **Select the file you want to attach, and click OK.**

   The file is attached to the contact record.

Here are some tips for attaching file:

- As an alternative to using the Attachment command, you can attach any file to a contact record by dragging it from the desktop or the Windows Explorer and dropping it onto the Notes/History tab.

- When you want to attach the same file to several contacts, perform a lookup to find the contacts, open the Contact List window (press F9), and tag or highlight the contacts. Then press Ctrl+I to bring up the Attach File dialog box, locate the file on your hard drive, and click Open. ACT! then attaches the file to each of the selected contacts.

- To launch a program from an attached file, locate the program's executable file (programfile.exe), and make that file the attachment. To launch the program, just double-click on the attachment icon.

Create your own reference library

You can create your own reference libraries using the ACT! attachment feature and attaching specific documents to contact records.

Here are some of the things you can do with a reference library file:

- You can store information about a person's family members — such as their birth dates, anniversaries, Social Security numbers, and credit card numbers.

- You can create a list of points that you always want to discuss when you're speaking with someone on the phone — for example, a telemarketing script.

- You can store reference information, such as area codes or zip codes, for easy access.

- If you have different price lists for your customers, why not record your price lists in a file and attach the appropriate price list to each of your customers? For example, Client X gets a 20-percent discount, Client Y gets a 10-percent discount, and the rest are 100-percenters. When you're talking with a customer on the phone and you need to quote a price, just open the document, and that person's price list appears. And when your price list changes, all you have to do is make the changes to the attached file.

- If different product descriptions, company guidelines, parameters, statistics, or other types of information are meaningful to a group of your contacts, store that information in a file and attach it to each contact's record.

With ACT!'s attachment feature, any document, spreadsheet, or graphics file can become part of your reference library.

Additional note, history, and attachment features

Here are some more note, history, and attachment features.

✔ **To view the details of a note, history entry, or attachment,** highlight the specific item by clicking its icon and click the Details button. The Details dialog box appears. The Details dialog box shows the following information: Type, Date, Time, Created by, Attachment, and Group Assignment.

✔ **To delete a note, history, or attachment,** highlight the item(s) by clicking the desired icon. Press the Delete key, or select the Delete Selected command after you right-click. A message box appears asking, "Are you sure you want to delete the selected item(s)?" To delete the selected entry, click Yes.

To highlight two or more entries next to each other, hold down the Shift key while you click on the first and last entries. To highlight entries not next to each other, hold down the Ctrl key while you select each entry individually.

A highlighted item can be deleted by pressing the Ctrl+X key.

✔ **Cutting, copying, and pasting notes, histories, and attachments:** From time to time, you may want to move or copy a note, history, or attachment from one contact to another. You do this using the Cut (Ctrl+X), Copy (Ctrl+C), and Paste (Ctrl+V) commands. Just highlight the item that you want to cut or copy, and select either the Cut or Copy command. Switch to another contact record, and paste the note, history, or attachment into the contact's Notes/History tab.

✔ **Modifying the particulars of a note, history item, or attachment:** In the Notes/History tab, you can display up to seven columns. (Adding and removing columns is discussed later in this chapter.) The seven columns are Date, Time, Type, Regarding, Record Manager, Group, and Attachment.

With the exception of the information that ACT! enters in the Type field when it creates a note, records a history item, or creates an attachment, all the information that's in the other ACT! columns can be modified or edited.

• **To modify the Date, Time, or Group,** click on the desired field and select a new date, time, or group from the drop-down menu calendar, Mini calendar, or Group drop-down menu.

• **To associate a note, history item, or attachment with a specific group,** select the group from the drop-down menu in the Groups column.

- **To edit the information in a Regarding field,** simply place your cursor in the field and begin typing.

- **To change an attachment,** click the Attachment field, and the Browse button appears. Click the Browse button, and the Open dialog box appears. Select a new attachment.

When you're finished making your changes, execute another command and your modified note, history item, or attachment is saved. Pressing Esc also saves your changes.

If you would like to prevent history editing, just disable the Allow History Editing feature. To access the Allow History Editing feature, select the Advanced tab in the Define Fields dialog box, which you open by selecting the Edit⇨Define Fields command from the menu bar.

Sorting your notes, history, and attachments

To change the sort order of the notes, history, and attachments, just click any of the column headings — Date, Time, Type, and so on — and ACT! re-sorts the items in the Notes/History Tab. An up arrow or down arrow shows the sorting selection.

Filtering your notes, history, and attachments

With the Filtering command, you choose which information — notes, history, or attachments — you want to view for a given range of dates.

The Filter button is at the top of the Notes/History tab. (Refer to Figure 5-1.) Click the button, and you can make the same selections in the Filter Notes/History dialog box as you can in the Notes/History dialog box.

To open the Filter Notes/History dialog box, select View⇨Filter Activities from the menu bar, or select the Filter Activities command from the menu that appears when you right-click in the Notes/History tab.

In the Filter Notes/History dialog box, you have the following options:

- **Users:** In the Users section, you apply the filter options to selected users or to all users of the database.

- **Show:** Choose which information to view by selecting or not selecting the Notes, Histories, Attachments, or e-mail check boxes.

✔ **Select Dates:** Your options for viewing dates include All dates, Today, Past dates, Future dates, or a range of dates in the Select Dates section.

Working with columns

The Notes/History tab can display up to seven columns: Date, Type, Time, Regarding, Group, Record Manager, and Attachment. ACT! enables you to change the look and feel of your columns. You can do the following:

✔ **Add columns:** Select the Add Columns command from the menu that appears when you right-click within the Notes/History tab, and the Add Columns dialog box appears. Select the column that you want to add, and click OK.

✔ **Change the position of columns:** Click the column heading (the cursor turns into a hand), and drag it to its new position.

✔ **Remove a column:** Click the column heading, and drag it up (the cursor turns into a garbage can) and off the Notes/History tab.

✔ **Show/Hide Column Headings:** Select the Show/Hide Column Headings command from the menu that appears when you right-click. This is a toggle command.

✔ **Change the width of a column heading:** Place the cursor on the line between two column headings. When it turns into a sizing tool, move the column left or right to make the column smaller or wider.

✔ **Lock columns:** To lock your columns in place, click the small bar located at the left edge of the column heading, and drag it to the right of the column(s) you want to lock. The columns to the left of the column lock remain in place when you scroll left or right.

✔ **Show Grid Lines:** Select the Show Grid Lines option in the Notes/History tab settings in the Colors and Fonts tab of the Preferences dialog box. (Did you get all that?) To open preferences, select Edit➪Preferences from the menu bar. The Colors and Fonts tab of the ACT! Preference dialog box is explained in Chapter 27.

✔ **Changing the tab's appearance:** To change the appearance — font, font size, font style, font color, and background color of the Notes/History tab — open the Preferences dialog box and select the Colors and Fonts tab. (Open the Preferences dialog box by selecting Edit➪Preferences from the menu bar.) You use this ACT! feature in the same way for every ACT! window and tab — all 12 of them — so I'm only going to explain it once — in Chapter 27.

✔ **Printing your notes, histories, and/or attachments:** Click the Notes/History tab, select File⇨Print Notes/Histories from the menu bar, and ACT! prints a custom report. You can also access the Print Notes/Histories command from the menu that appears when you right-click from inside the Notes/History tab.

The Activities Tab

The Activities tab, shown in Figure 5-3, displays the activities — calls, meetings, and to-dos — scheduled with the current contact. Click the Activities tab to display all the activities you've scheduled with a specific person.

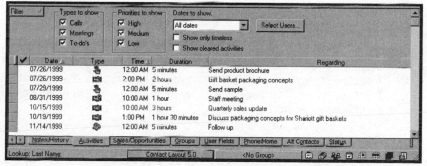

Figure 5-3:
The
Activities
tab.

You can do these things from the Activities tab:

✔ Schedule a new activity

✔ Reschedule an activity

✔ Clear an activity

✔ Unclear a cleared activity

✔ Clear multiple activities

✔ Modify a previously scheduled activity

You can also show Outlook activities. The Show Outlook Activities option enables you to display Outlook appointments and tasks. To display Outlook appointments, you must also select the Meetings option. To display Outlook tasks, you must also select the To-do option. (You do, of course, need to have Microsoft Outlook 98 or Outlook 2000 installed on your computer. I cover ACT!'s integration with Microsoft Outlook 98/2000 in Chapter 13.)

In addition, you can filter your activities by User, Activity, Priority, and Date.

You can change and customize the appearance of your Activities tab. You can add or remove the column headings; change the position of the column headings, as well as their width; change the font, font size, and font color displayed in the Activities tab; and even change the background color.

The features of the Activities tab are identical to those of the Task List, with only one difference: The Task List shows a list of all your scheduled activities, and the Activities tab shows your activities for a single contact.

For this reason, I decided to explain how to use the features of the Activities tab and the Task List in the chapter on how to use the Task List, which is Chapter 16.

To schedule an activity using the Windows drag-and-drop feature, click on a blank portion of the contact layout (the cursor turns into a circle with a line through it), drag the cursor onto the Task List or any of the ACT! calendars, and the Schedule Activity dialog box appears. Scheduling activities is covered in Chapter 13.

To print your Activities, click the Activities tab, select File⇨Print Activities from the menu bar, and ACT! prints a custom report. You can also access the Print Activities command from the menu that appears when you right-click from inside the Activities tab.

The Sales/Opportunity Tab

In the Sales/Opportunity tab, you can create a sales forecast to track all your sales opportunities. You can track specific products, the types of products within the product line, the number of units, unit price, and total amount of the sale.

You can create your own customized list of the different stages that a prospect will go through within your sales cycle. You can then choose a projected closing date and assign a probability percentage for successfully closing the sale.

With all this recorded information, you can easily answer your boss's questions: What are your customers or prospects going to buy? How much are they going to buy? And when will you close the sale?

ACT!'s Sales/Opportunity features are so powerful that I've devoted an entire part of *ACT! 2000 For Windows For Dummies* to this topic. So if you want to read about it right now, turn to Part V.

The Groups Tab

In the Groups tab, you can view a list of all the groups of which the contact is a member. The Groups tab is shown in Figure 5-4. Creating ACT! groups is discussed in Chapter 12. This section contains information on the things you can do from within the Groups tab.

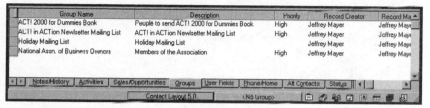

Figure 5-4:
The Groups
tab.

Changing group membership

To change the contact's group membership — you can add a person to a group or remove a person from a group — select Contact⇨Group Membership from the menu bar. You can also select the Group Membership command from the menu that appears when you right-click within the Groups tab. The Group Membership dialog box appears either way.

Changing the Groups tabs

You customize the appearance of the Groups tab by changing the column headings: Any field in a group layout can become a column in the Groups tab. You can also change the position and width of the column headings, as well as the font, font size, font color, and background color. The method for customizing the Groups tab is identical to the method for customizing the Notes/History tab, described earlier in this chapter.

Printing group information

To print your groups, click the Groups tab, select File⇨Print Groups from the menu bar, and ACT! prints a custom report. You can also access the Print Groups command from the menu that appears when you right-click from inside the Groups tab.

Assigning Shortcut Keys to Your Tabs

You can open each tab with shortcut keys while in the Contact window. If you're a keyboard person, this saves you the trouble of clicking a tab whenever you want to view the contact information on a specific tab.

These shortcut keys are already assigned:

- Notes/History tab: Alt+N or Shift+F9
- Activities tab: Alt+A or Alt+F9
- Sales/Opportunity tab: Alt+A
- Groups tab: Alt+G or Ctrl+F9

To assign a shortcut key (press Alt+shortcut key) to any of the other tabs in the Contact window — Phone/Home, Alt Contacts, and Status — you must edit your layout from inside the Layout Designer. Here's how:

1. **Select Tools➪Design Layouts to open the Layout Designer.**
2. **Select Edit➪Tabs to open the Define Tab Layouts dialog box.**
3. **Highlight a specific tab, and click the Edit button.**

   The Edit Tab dialog box appears.

Here you enter, or modify, the tab's name and select the character that you want to use as a shortcut key. You can choose any of the letters in the name as the shortcut key. Editing ACT! layouts is discussed in detail in Chapter 26.

You must assign shortcut keys to the tabs of each layout individually.

Chapter 6

Defining ACT! Fields

• •

In This Chapter

▶ Selecting a record type to customize

▶ Customizing fields

▶ Creating drop-down menus

▶ Turning a field into a Trigger field

▶ Creating your own indexed fields

• •

*I*n this chapter, you discover how to customize the appearance of individual fields within your ACT! database. This flexibility enables you to customize ACT! to fit your individual work habits and work style and makes entering information into ACT! much easier.

After you have customized ACT! fields, you can change the layout of your ACT! fields on the contact layout. To change the layout, you use the Layout Designer, which you access by selecting Tools⇨Design Layouts from the menu bar. Customizing your ACT! layouts is discussed in Chapter 26.

The Define Fields dialog box is where you set the individual characteristics, or properties, for each field in an ACT! database. To edit a field's attributes, select Edit⇨Define Fields from the menu bar. The Attributes tab of the Define Fields dialog box is shown in Figure 6-1.

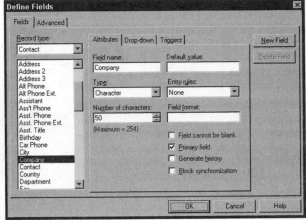

Figure 6-1:
The
Attributes
tab of the
Define
Fields
dialog box.

If you're using ACT! on a network, only the network administrator can access and change the field attributes.

Selecting a Record Type to Customize

Before you customize a specific ACT! field, you must first decide whether you want to change the contact fields or the group fields. You do this by choosing either Contact or Group in the Record type field. Next, you select the field that you want to define by highlighting the field in the Field list box. (The list of fields is displayed in alphabetical order.)

Any field in ACT! can be modified or changed.

To scroll through the list of ACT! fields, use your mouse, the up/down or left/right arrow keys, or the Page Up/Page Down keys. And you can press any letter of the alphabet to move to the first word in the list that begins with that letter. Ctrl+Home takes you to the first item in the list; Ctrl+End takes you to the last item in the list.

Customizing Fields

This section covers all of the different ways to customize ACT! fields. You'll learn how to change a field's name, create phone, date, and Web address fields, and more. So read on.

Changing a field name

Each field has a name that is displayed in an ACT! layout. For example, if you select User 1 in the List of Fields box, the word "User 1" appears in the Field Name box. By changing the name of a field, you change the field's name on the ACT! layout.

The number of characters that ACT! displays for a field's name is limited to the size of the Field Name. If the name is too long, the text will be truncated when it appears in the layout.

Deciding what type of data to enter in a field

The Type field's drop-down menu contains a list of the different types of data that you can enter into a field. This enables you to customize each individual field for a specific purpose.

- ✔ **Character:** A Character field accepts any character or number in the alphabet. The Company field is an example of a Character field.

- ✔ **Currency:** In a Currency field, ACT! inserts a dollar sign ($) in addition to commas.

  To record the dollar amount of a client's most recent order, designate one of your ACT! user fields as both a Currency field and a History field. When you enter the dollar amount of the order, the date and time are automatically recorded as a history item in the contact's Notes/History tab.

- ✔ **Date:** A Date field allows only dates. Click the field, and ACT! provides a drop-down calendar from which you select a date.

- ✔ **Initial Caps:** In an Initial Caps field, the first letter in each word is capitalized.

- ✔ **Lowercase:** In a Lowercase field, every character you type appears as lowercase text.

- ✔ **Numeric:** In a Numeric field, ACT! automatically inserts a comma after every third number. This field accepts only two decimal places unless you change the Windows default number settings.

- ✔ **Phone:** A Phone Number field accepts only numbers, and they appear in a phone-number format. You don't have to enter the dash between the area code or after the first three digits of the phone number.

Any field that you designate as a phone field — including fax numbers, beeper numbers, and cell phone numbers — appears in the list of telephone numbers in the Dialer dialog box, which pops up when you click the Dial Phone icon or select the Contact⇨Phone Contact command from the menu bar. If you have a modem, double-click the desired number, and ACT! dials the phone number for you.

✔ **Time:** In a Time field, all numbers are changed to a time format, like this: 5:00PM.

✔ **Uppercase:** In an Uppercase field, any character you type appears as uppercase text. For example, it makes sense to use the Uppercase data type in the State field, so that *il* is displayed as *IL*.

✔ **URL Address:** Specify a field as a URL (Uniform Resource Locator) Address field to record Web site addresses. With a URL entered, the field becomes an active link to the selected Web site. Click the Web site address and ACT! automatically launches your Web browser and goes to the specified Web site.

You change the Windows 95/98 Number, Currency, Date, and Time settings by opening the Regional Settings dialog box. The Regional Settings dialog box is in the Windows Control Panel. (Click Start⇨Settings⇨Control Panel.)

Working with Default Settings

Several settings apply specifically to what information ACT! adds to a new contact record in your database.

When you add a new contact to your ACT! database using the Contact⇨ New Contact command (or pressing the Insert key), ACT! uses the value (data) that has been entered in the Default Value field.

Many ACT! users use this feature to make life easier when adding a new contact to their ACT! databases. You can, for example, insert default values for your city, state, and so on. If the default value needs to be changed after you've created the new contact record, just delete it and enter the new contact information.

You have these three ways to add a new contact to your ACT! database:

✔ **Blank contact record:** To insert a new contact without copying any information from the contact whose record you're presently viewing, select the Contact⇨New Contact command. Any default values are inserted into this new contact record.

✔ **Duplicate contact from primary fields:** To add a new contact to the database by copying the data from the primary fields, select the Contact⇨Duplicate Contact command and select the Duplicate Contact From Primary Fields option. This option is useful if, for example, you are adding numerous contacts to the database who all work at the same company.

Choosing the Primary Fields command copies the information from the primary fields of the current contact's contact record into the new contact's record. (The default primary fields are the Company, Phone, Country Code, Fax Phone, Address 1, Address 2, Address 3, City, State, and Zip Code fields.)

✔ **Duplicate data from all fields:** To insert a new contact by copying all data from the current contact record, select Contact⇨Duplicate Contact and choose the Duplicate Data From All Fields option.

If you want to designate an additional field as a primary field — so that information in this field copies into a new contact's record — enable the Primary Field attribute for that field.

Automatically Recording Information in Fields as History Items

ACT! uses history items — part of the Notes/History tab — to maintain a record of all the things that have gone on with a particular contact. When you place a call, attend a meeting, perform a to-do, or send correspondence, including letters, memos, faxes, or e-mail messages, ACT! automatically makes a notation of this event and stores it in the contact's Notes/History tab. This notation includes the date and time that the event took place, the type of event, and a brief description of the event.

You can also designate specific fields as History fields. An example of this is the Last Results field. Enter information in the Last Results field — notes of a telephone conversation, for example — and ACT! automatically records that data as a history item. Another field designated as a History field is the ID/Status field.

Here's an example of how to put the history feature to use. Say that you designated the User 4 field as your "Last Sale" field and made it a History field. Whenever you close a sale, just type in the dollar amount of the sale, indicate what was purchased, and the notation is automatically entered as a history item. When you open the Notes/History tab, you see a complete listing of your sales activity — what the person bought, how much was spent, and when the purchase was made.

To designate fields as History fields, enable the Generate History option for that field in the Define Fields dialog box.

I maintain my mailing list for my *ACT! in ACTion* newsletter inside ACT!. I renamed one of my User Fields to "Expiration Date" and made it a History field. Then I created a drop-down menu listing the month and year of expiration and made this field a History field. When I add a new subscriber to my mailing list and enter the subscription's expiration date, the entry is automatically saved as a history item. This enables me to keep track of the length of time that someone has been a subscriber.

Additional ACT! Field Customization Options

Here are some more ACT! field customizing options:

- ✔ **Sizing a field:** In the Size field, you determine the number of characters that can be entered in each field.

- ✔ **Choosing a field format:** In the Field Format field, you specify how the data in certain fields (Character, Initial Capitals, Lowercase, or Uppercase) is automatically formatted. You use the following characters as placeholders:

    - **Alphabetic characters:** @

    - **Alphanumeric characters:** %

    - **Numeric characters:** #

      Use this feature to record contract or invoice numbers.

- ✔ **Applying rules to the field:** In the Entry Rules field, you select what options are available to a user when information is entered into an ACT! field. You choose the Entry Rule options from a drop-down list. You have the following choices:

    - **None:** Choose None if you do not want any entry rules to apply.

    - **Protected:** Choose Protected to keep the entries in the field from being modified.

    - **Only From Drop-Down:** Choose Only From Drop-Down to specify that information must be selected from the field's drop-down list.

Creating a new field

Click the New Field button in the Define Fields dialog box, and ACT! creates a new field. Give the field a name and assign to it any field attributes (such as Field Name, Default Value, or Type) that you like.

Deleting fields that you don't use

If you find that you no longer use certain fields and want to delete them, highlight the field in the Field List box of the Define Fields dialog box and click the Delete button.

When you delete an ACT! field, you lose any information in that field.

Setting block synchronization

If you do not want this field to be available for data synchronization, choose this option. Data synchronization is mentioned in Chapter 28.

Creating drop-down menus

When you select the Drop-down tab for a particular field — the Drop-down entries for the State field are shown in Figure 6-2 — you are provided the opportunity to enter information in a field from a drop-down menu.

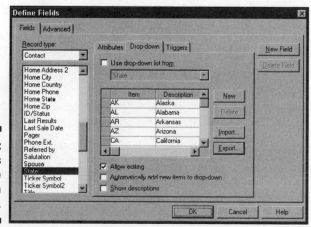

Figure 6-2:
The entries
of the State
drop-down
menu.

A drop-down menu contains lists of available entries for a specific field. Choosing an entry from a drop-down menu automatically inserts that entry into the field. This feature saves you lots of the time because you don't have to type the information for each contact. Entering information from drop-down menus is discussed in Chapter 7.

You can do the following in the Drop-down tab:

- **Name the drop-down item:** In the Drop-down item field, you enter the name of a drop-down item. This option is available by clicking the New button.

- **Provide a description:** In the Description field, you enter a description of the drop-down item. This option is available after you click the New button.

- **Add a new item:** To add a new item to the drop-down menu, click the New button.

- **Change an item:** To change an item, click the item and type your changes.

- **Delete an item:** Highlight the item by clicking the button on the left side of the item, and then click the Delete button.

- **Allow editing:** If you want to allow the database user — yourself or other users — to edit the items in the drop-down menu from the Contact window, choose the Allow Editing option.

- **Automatically add new items:** If you want each item that you type in this field to be added automatically to the field's drop-down menu, select this option.

- **Show the descriptions:** If you want the descriptions to be displayed in the drop-down menu, choose the Show Descriptions option.

Exporting and importing drop-down menu items

Putting in all the time and effort to create a drop-down menu is a tedious task that you don't necessarily want to do again and again. Fortunately, with ACT!, you don't have to. Just save (or export) your menu as a delimited file, and you can apply (import) it to another ACT! field in the current database or in any other database.

Turning a field into a trigger field

The Triggers tab turns ACT! into the center of your computing universe. Want to launch a program or run a macro when you enter or exit a selected field? Here are a few examples of ways to customize ACT! to suit your needs.

- ✔ Name an ACT! field "Excel," and every time you place the cursor in the field, ACT! opens a specific spreadsheet for you.
- ✔ Name a field "Word," and every time you get a new client or customer, you can create a form letter thanking him or her for doing business with you.

Creating your own indexed fields

Each time you enter contact information into ACT!, the program updates its index of all the contacts' first names, last names, company names, addresses, and so on. (The fields listed on the Lookup menu are all indexed.) When you perform a lookup, query, or sort, ACT! searches the index for the appropriate criteria. This is much faster than searching the entire database. These indexes are stored in separate ACT! files in the database directory.

The fields in an ACT! database are either indexed or non-indexed, and by choosing the Advanced tab in the Define Fields dialog box, you can add additional indexes to your ACT! database.

This is how you create a new index:

1. **Select your record type, either Contact or Group, in the Record type field.**

2. **Click the New Index button, and select the field to index from the drop-down list — which is a list of every field in the ACT! database — displayed in the Index On field.**

3. **Select the Then On field to determine the new index field's sort order.**

4. **Click OK.**

   ACT! re-indexes your database.

To perform a lookup on an indexed field, select Lookup⇨Other Fields from the menu bar, and the Lookup dialog box appears. Select the field on which you want to perform the lookup from the drop-down menu, enter the lookup criteria, and click OK. (Lookups are discussed in Chapter 10.)

To delete an indexed field (you're deleting the index, not the field), highlight the field in the Field List box and click the Delete button.

Part II

Using Your Database

In this part . . .

ACT! is nothing without a database full of information — information that you provide. Before ACT! can become a useful tool for you to use, you need to put some work into it. In other words, you need to fill up your ACT! database with the names, addresses, phone numbers, fax numbers, and e-mail addresses of everyone you know.

The chapters in this part show you how to use, abuse, and otherwise manipulate the information that you put into ACT!.

Chapter 7

Entering Information into Your Database

- -

- -

To enter information into a contact record — yours or anybody else's — the only thing you have to do is type in the information. It's that easy. Just place the cursor in a particular field and start typing.

My Record Is Your Record

The first piece of information you enter into an ACT! database is information about yourself, which you record in the My Record contact record. To locate the My Record contact record, select Lookup⇨My Record from the menu bar.

When you create a new database, ACT! copies the My Record information from the open database to the new database.

When you create a new empty database by copying an existing database — select File⇨Save Copy As, and then select the Create Empty Copy option — ACT! copies the information from the currently open database and displays it in the Enter "My Record" Information dialog box. Here, you can change the My Record information before creating the database.

If you're sharing ACT! with other users (a multi-user database), you entered information about yourself in the My Record contact record when you first signed on as a network user.

It's your database — while you're using it

The My Record contact record contains information about the owner, manager, or user of the ACT! database, and that's probably you. (If you're sharing a database on a network, the My Record contact record belongs to the person who is currently using the database.)

My Record information

ACT! also uses some of the information in the My Record contact record — such as your name and address — when you create letters, memos, faxes, and custom reports. So make sure that each entry, especially your name, company name, and title, is entered the way you want it to appear in all these formats.

If you plan to use one of the e-mail systems that ACT! supports, add your e-mail address to your contact record (My Record). (To learn more about ACT! e-mail capabilities, see Chapter 23.)

Your contact record is ACT!'s home base

When you turn on ACT!, the contact record that appears on-screen is always your own contact record. If you want to look up your contact record when someone else's contact record is displayed, select Lookup⇨My Record, and your contact record appears. The My Record contact record for yours truly is shown in Figure 7-1.

When you're using ACT! on a network, the program knows who is using it based on the logon ID. When you log on, ACT! knows which My Record contact record to activate and which activities are associated with it.

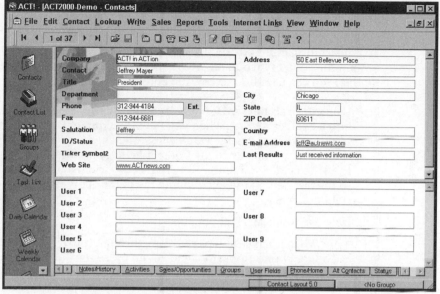

Figure 7-1:
Jeffrey
Mayer's
"My
Record"
contact
record.

Here are some My Record tips:

✔ Use your own contact record (My Record) to schedule activities that are not associated with other contacts. As you add more people to your ACT! database, you'll find that almost all of your activities will be associated with other contacts, and very few activities will be associated with your contact record. The My Record contact record can also be used to schedule activities for yourself.

✔ ACT! has a scheduling tool, SideACT!, that enables you to schedule activities — calls, meetings, and to-dos — without assigning them to a specific contact. You can even use SideACT! without using ACT!. I tell you all about SideACT! in Chapter 14.

✔ Many people find ACT! works much faster when they use the keyboard instead of pointing and clicking with the mouse. For example, to look up the My Record contact record, all you have to do is press Alt+L+M (Lookup⇨My Record). To look up a contact by the last name, press Alt+L+L (Lookup⇨Last Name), and the Lookup dialog box appears with Last Name selected in the Lookup field. To look up a contact by the first name, press Alt+L+F (Lookup⇨First Name).

✔ Whenever you delete a contact from your database, the date, time, and contact name are recorded in the History file of your contact record. This provides a record of each contact deleted from the database.

Navigating the Contact Record

To enter information into an ACT! contact record, you must be able to move around the contact layout, and ACT! offers you a number of different ways to do this. You can use the Tab key, the Enter key, or the mouse.

✔ **Using the Tab key:** ACT! has a predefined order for entering information into a contact record. When you're in the contact layout and the cursor is in the Company field, watch where the cursor goes when you press the Tab key. It moves to the Contact field. Press Tab again, and it goes to the Title field. Each time you tab, the cursor moves down; when you get to the last field in the left column, the cursor moves to the top of the right column.

Here are some ACT! tabbing tips:

- When you've tabbed your way through the fields in a User Fields tab, Phone/Home tab, and so on, press the Tab key again, and the cursor moves to the next tab — that is, it moves from the User Fields tab to the Phone/Home tab. This makes it easy for you to continue adding contact information.

- Pressing Shift+Tab moves your cursor backward.

- To change the predefined tab order, select Tools⇨Design Layouts from the Layout Designer menu bar. The Layout Designer is discussed in Chapter 26.

Having the tab sequence in an easy-to-follow and well-thought-out order makes entering contact information easy for you. To enter information in a specific field, just tab over to the field and type in the information.

✔ **Using the mouse:** You can use your mouse to move anywhere on the contact layout. Just place the cursor in the field into which you want to enter information, click once, and start typing. After you finish, press the Tab key to move to the next field, or use the mouse to move to another field.

✔ **Using the Enter key:** With the ACT! Group Stop feature, you can select specific fields to edit when you press the Enter key. You set Group Stops from within the Layout Designer. (Select Tools⇨Design Layouts from the menu bar.) The Layout Designer is discussed in Chapter 26.

The secret of the semicolon

When you enter the name of a company in a contact record, consider how you want ACT! to sort it. For example, if you have a company named "The ABC Manufacturing Company" and you enter it into ACT! just like that, ACT! sorts it alphabetically under the letter "T." You would probably prefer that it be filed under the letter "A."

If you type the name as "ABC Manufacturing Company, The" (note the comma), ACT! sorts it under "A," but when you create any word-processing document, the company name appears in the letter or other document as "ABC Manufacturing Company, The."

However, using a semicolon (;) after the word "Company" followed by "The" gives you the best of both worlds. ACT! sorts the company alphabetically under the letter "A" but inserts the name in your documents as "The ABC Manufacturing Company."

If you want to insert a person's name in the Company field, type the last name followed by a semicolon, and then the first name and the middle initial. For example, I type my name like this: Mayer; Jeffrey J. (Note the semicolon after Mayer.) This appears in an ACT! word processing document as Jeffrey J. Mayer, but it is sorted alphabetically under "M."

Getting Names Right So That ACT! Can Find People

When you enter a person's name into your database, ACT! needs to know the person's first and last names so that it can find that person when you perform a lookup. So when you enter a new contact into ACT!, the Contact Name dialog box (as shown in Figure 7-2) appears if the person has more than a first name and a last name entered, such as Jeffrey Joseph Mayer or Mitzi Bouffard Mayer, entered in the Contact field.

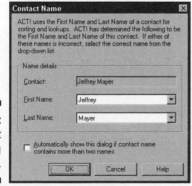

Figure 7-2:
The Contact Name dialog box.

From the Contact Name dialog box, you can tell ACT! which name is the First Name and which name is the Last Name. This guarantees that ACT! will find this contact when a First Name or Last Name lookup is performed or when the database is sorted.

You can have ACT! automatically bring up the Contact Name dialog box by selecting the option marked Automatically Show This Dialog If Contact Name Contains More Than Two Names on the Contact Name dialog box. This option can also be selected on the Names tab of the Preferences dialog box.

You can also bring up the Contact Name dialog box by clicking the gray button at the right side of the Contact field, or by pressing F2 when your cursor is in the Contact field.

First name prefixes, last name suffixes, and last name prefixes

ACT! also enables you to select name separators that tell ACT! what first name prefixes (Doctor, Dr., Mr., Ms., and Mrs.) or last name suffixes (Esq., Jr., Sr., J.D., Ph.D., and M.D.) to ignore when performing either a first name or last name lookup.

The last name prefix options (Del, Von, Van, de, and da) tell ACT! to use this last name prefix as the beginning of a person's last name when it sorts the database.

ACT! comes with many pre-installed name prefixes and suffixes, but if you need to add additional name separators to the list, just open the ACT! Preferences dialog box, select the Names tab, and click the Add button.

The name separator is an important feature because if you don't enter the correct name separator entries in the Name Separator lists before you enter the name, ACT! won't be able to accurately locate contact records when you perform a lookup.

If you enter a contact with a name separator that is not included in the Name Separator lists or if you don't identify the contact's First Name and Last Name in the Contact Name dialog box, the contact's name will not be found when you do a lookup.

Using the Salutation field

When you add a new contact to your ACT! database (adding contacts is covered in Chapter 9), ACT! automatically inserts the person's first name in the Salutation field. This is a nice feature if you send out lots of letters, memos, and other correspondence.

In the Names tab of the ACT! Preferences dialog box, you can have ACT! insert the person's first name or last name. And if you don't want ACT! to insert the person's name at all, choose the Do Not Fill Salutation option. You open the Preferences dialog box by selecting the Edit⇨Preferences command.

The Many Data Fields of ACT!

ACT! has different data types available for each field. This diversity allows you to customize each individual field. You can designate a field as a Character field, an Uppercase Only field, a Lowercase Only field, an Initial Caps field, a Date field, a Phone Number field, a Numeric field (ACT! inserts commas), a Currency field (ACT! inserts commas and a $ sign), a Time field, or a URL Address field (where you can enter Web sites). To change a field's data type, you open the Define Fields dialog box by selecting Edit⇨Define Fields from the menu bar. (Defining ACT! fields is discussed in Chapter 6.)

Working with drop-down menus and Edit List dialog boxes

The most time-consuming part of setting up and using a database comes when you have to enter information into individual fields. And because much of the information is repetitive, it is a big waste of time to retype the same basic information for one person after another, after another, after another. From my own experience, I can tell you that it gets mighty boring typing "Chicago, IL 60611" over and over. ACT! has a simple way of dealing with this problem. It uses drop-down menus and Edit List dialog boxes.

ACT! has a new feature that enables you to automatically add new items to specific drop-down menus. When you enter a new item into the field, the entry is automatically added to the list. This is how you turn the option on: Select Edit⇨Define Fields, click the Drop-down tab, and select the Automatically Add New Items to Drop-Down option.

Let me take a moment to explain what a drop-down menu does. A drop-down menu is a list of items that can be inserted in a field.

The beauty of the drop-down menu is that it enables you to select contact information from a list and have it automatically inserted into the field. ACT! offers enormous flexibility because any field in ACT! can be designated a drop-down menu field.

Let me give you an example. To enter information in the City field, you place your cursor in the City field, click the drop-down menu arrow that appears at the right edge of the field, and select a city from the list.

You can also select items from the drop-down menu by typing the first few letters of the item's name or by scrolling through the list by pressing the up- or down-arrow keys. Press Alt+DownArrow, and you can view an expanded list. Pressing F2 brings up the Edit List dialog box.

Customizing your drop-down menus

Every field in ACT! can have a drop-down menu that you can customize to display the specific words or phrases you use to describe your daily business activities. If you have data that you enter frequently, you can use a drop-down menu to automate the process of entering that information.

To edit a drop-down menu item, select the Edit List command, which is the last item on the drop-down menu, or press the F2 key, and the Edit List dialog box appears.

From the Edit List dialog box, you insert items into an ACT! field by highlighting the item and clicking OK. You can also add, delete, or modify existing drop-down menu items.

Here are some Edit List dialog box tips:

✔ While in an Edit List dialog box, just press the first letter of the name you want to insert; for example, in a City field dialog box, press **C** for Chicago, **N** for New York, **L** for Los Angeles, and so on, and ACT! moves to that letter of the alphabet. (To select an item that is not the first entry under that letter, press the same letter again until you find the city you want.) Then press Enter, and ACT! automatically inserts the city's name. This ACT! feature is called typing ahead.

✔ To select multiple entries next to each other in an Edit List box, hold down the Shift key while using the mouse or arrow keys to move up or down the list. To select multiple entries that are not next to each other, hold down the Ctrl key while you select the individual items by clicking them with your mouse.

✔ When you use drop-down menus or Edit List dialog boxes to enter information, you ensure that all of the entries in your database will be consistent and spelled correctly, thus enabling accurate database searches.

✔ You can export/import drop-down menu items for use in another ACT! field by clicking the Export or Import buttons that are located on the Drop-down tab of the Define Fields dialog box, which you open by selecting Edit⇨Define Fields. This ACT! feature is discussed in Chapter 6.

Utilizing drop-down menu descriptions

An ACT! drop-down menu can also insert items that are abbreviations of a word instead of the whole word. The State field is a good example of this feature. Put your cursor on the State field, press F2, and the State field's Edit List box appears. Click the Modify button, and the Modify dialog box appears where you can modify an item and its description.

If the description field isn't available or if you're unable to edit the drop-down menu items, go into the Define Fields dialog box and enable the Allow Editing and Show Description options. If you're using ACT! in a multi-user environment, only the administrator can make these changes.

Making drop-down menu fields

If a field doesn't have a drop-down menu available, you can enable the drop-down menu feature by selecting the Edit⇨Define Fields command and clicking the Drop-down tab. Defining ACT! fields is covered in Chapter 6.

Whenever you tab over to a field designated as a drop-down menu, the list is automatically available. Here's an example. After I enter a person's company, I press the Tab key and enter the person's name in the Name field. When I get to the City field, I press **ch** for Chicago, and Chicago appears in the City field. I press the Tab key once more, and the cursor moves to the State field; I type **il,** and IL is entered in the field. As you can see, this really makes the tedious process of entering information a breeze.

Customizing Individual Fields

The following is a list of fields that I suggest you customize with drop-down menus so you can make your ACT! database fit your own individual needs, desires, and preferences — but they should give you some ideas as to how powerful and easy ACT! really is to use.

- **Title field:** If it's important to note someone's position, title, or occupation, you should populate the Title field's drop-down menu with the appropriate list of positions, titles, and occupations.

- **City field:** This drop-down menu should contain frequently entered cities. You use this information in your written correspondence and when you look people up.

- **Last Results field:** The Last Results field is uniquely designed for you to write a quick note to yourself indicating the results of your last contact with a person. You can either type this information into the field or use a drop-down menu item to insert the details of your most recent exchange.

    Open the Define Fields dialog box, by selecting the Edit⇨Define Fields command, and select the Last Results field. I want to point something out to you.

    Please note that a check mark is in the Generate History box. Whenever you write anything in this field, the information is automatically entered as a History item that can be viewed by clicking the Notes/History tab. (Generating ACT! histories is discussed in Chapter 5.)

    If you have other fields whose information you would like ACT! to store as a history item, select the Generate History option for those fields.

- **ID/Status field:** This is the field that enables you to categorize your contacts. In theory, you can use any ACT! field to categorize your contacts, but the information in the ID/Status field is automatically indexed. This means that when you do a lookup in this field, ACT! gives you the results of your search in a fraction of a second. On the other hand, when you do a search in a field that is not indexed, ACT! must search the entire database. Depending upon the size of the database, this search can take some time. The indexed fields in ACT! are Company, First Name, Last Name, Phone, City, State, Zip Code, and ID/Status.

    Any ACT! field can become an indexed field. Just select the Advanced tab in the Define Fields dialog box. (Creating indexed fields is covered in Chapter 6.)

    To change the name of the ID/Status field from ID/Status to something like Category (that's what I did), open the Define Fields dialog box, and in the box that says Field Name, type **Category.**

Changing Information

Changing information in ACT! is easy. Just place the cursor in the field that you want to edit and start typing. When you tab to a field that already contains information, ACT! highlights the entire field, and you replace the old information when you begin typing in the new information.

ACT! offers you two ways to undo a change to a contact or field:

✔ **Undo command:** With the Undo command (Ctrl+Z or Edit⇨Undo), you can undo a change you have made to an ACT! field.

✔ **Revert command:** With the Revert command (Edit⇨Revert), you can undo all the changes you have made to an ACT! record.

After you execute another ACT! command, your changes are automatically saved. (You can also press Ctrl+S to save the changes you've made to the contact record.)

Editing several contact records at once

From time to time, you need to edit some of the information that appears in many contact records. A company has moved, and you must change the address for dozens of records, for example.

If you must make these changes one record at a time, you'll be frustrated by the time-consuming and time-wasting process. Fortunately, ACT! has a feature that enables you to change contact information for many contacts all at once.

Changing field information

The first thing to do is *group* your contacts together by performing a lookup. (ACT! lookups are discussed in Chapter 10.) After grouping your contacts, open the Replace window. To open the Replace window, select Edit⇨Replace from the menu bar.

Type the new information that you want to appear in the selected contact records in the appropriate fields. Using the preceding example, type the new address of the company that moved. After you finish inserting the new information, select the Replace⇨Apply command from the menu bar, and a message box appears asking:

```
This function modifies all records in the lookup.
Are you sure you want to continue?
```

Select Yes, and the new information is entered into each contact's record.

If you need to edit fields that do not appear in the currently selected layout, you must switch to the layout containing those fields. You can choose a different layout by clicking the Layout button at the bottom of the window and selecting a layout from the menu.

If you want to delete the contents of a field, place the cursor in the field and press Ctrl+F5, which inserts the <<BLANK> command.

Keep in mind that all the contacts in the current lookup are affected by this procedure. If the process is taking too long and you need to cancel it, press Esc. All changes already made will remain in effect.

Swapping or copying contact information between fields

You may from time to time want to move information between two fields (swap) or copy information from one field to another. You *swap* contact information between two fields by selecting the Replace⇨Swap Fields command from the Replace window's menu bar. You *copy* contact information from one field to another by selecting the Replace⇨Copy Fields command from the Replace window's menu bar.

Printing your address and phone book

In ACT!, you can print the names, addresses, and phone numbers of your ACT! database on various page sizes — full page, half page, large pocket, or small pocket — that are designed to fit in the most popular daily planning books.

To print your name-and-address book, choose File⇨Print or press Ctrl+P, and the Print dialog box appears. From this dialog box, you can print your calendars, as well as your address book, on pages that fit in your favorite organizer format. You can also print your ACT! reports and your mailing labels from the Print dialog box. I discuss printing calendars in Chapter 13 and printing reports in Chapter 24.

When printing your name-and-address book, you may want to experiment with different layouts, different formats, and different fonts before you decide which one you like best. So use regular printing paper, not your expensive custom paper, while you're experimenting. When you're fully satisfied with the appearance of your address book, put your good paper in the printer.

ACT! gives you the following printing options:

✔ **Selecting printout and paper options:** Select Address Book from the Printout, and the list of available address book forms appears. Just scroll through the list, and select the form you want. Select the Show Preview option, and ACT! previews the layout in the Preview window just to the right of the Paper Forms list.

✔ **Selecting your Address Book options:** Click the Options button, and the Address Book Options dialog box appears. You have these options:

- **Print options:** In the Print section, you select the information that you want printed on your name-and-address book. You can include: Primary Address, Secondary Address, Phone Numbers, Alternate Contacts, and E-mail Addresses, and up to three additional fields of your choice.

- **Print settings options:** From the Print Settings section, you select how you want your name-and-address book to be printed. You have these options: Double Sided Printing, Break Page On New Letter, Letter at Top of Page, Lines Between Contacts, or European Postal Format.

- **Sort order:** With the Sort Order option, you can have your address book sorted by Company or by Last Name.

- **Create printout for:** From the Create Printout For section, you can select the group of contacts whose names and addresses will appear in your name-and-address book. You can select the Current contact, the Current lookup, or All contacts.

- **Font options:** By clicking the Font button in the Address Book Options dialog box, you can select the specific font, font style, and font size that you want ACT! to use when it prints your name-and-address book.

After you've set up your printer and selected all of your Address Book options, it's time to print. From the Print dialog box, click the OK button. It doesn't get much easier than that.

Exporting Names and Addresses to a Palmtop Computer

If you're like most business people, you probably spend more than half of your time away from your office. But just because you're away from your desk doesn't mean you have to leave your ACT! information in the office.

Today many people prefer to use a palmtop computer, instead of lugging their laptop and notebook computers around. Palmtops are very powerful, yet weigh less than a pound, and are the size of a paperback book. Programs are now available that enable you to move ACT! information from your notebook and/or desktop PC to the most popular palmtop computers.

ACT! links are available for 3Com's Palm, Franklin's REX, Sharp's Mobilon, and other palmtop computers that utilize the Windows CE platform.

CompanionLink Software's CompanionLink is a fast and easy synchronization system that moves data from ACT! to your handheld organizer. CompanionLink supports the Palm, Windows CE Organizers, the REX PRO, the Royal daVinci, and other palmtop PC Organizers. For more information, visit CompanionLink Software's Web site at www.companionlink.com, or give them a call at 800-386-1623 or 541-412-0300. You can write to them at CompanionLink Software, P.O. Box 1660, 340 Pacific Avenue, Brookings, OR 97415.

Chapter 8

Viewing Your Contacts as a List

● ●

In This Chapter

▶ Viewing contact information

▶ Changing contact information

▶ Scheduling activities

▶ Doing all sorts of useful stuff from the Contact List

● ●

A CT! gives you two ways to view your contact data. From the Contact window, you can see your contact information in a field-by-field format; in the Contact List window, you can view and edit your contact information in spreadsheet form.

To open the Contact List window, select View⇨Contact List from the menu bar, click the Contact List button on the status bar, or press the F8 key. The Contact List window is shown in Figure 8-1.

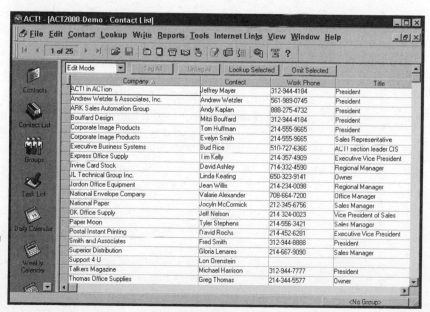

Figure 8-1:
The Contact
List window.

Viewing Contact Information

With the Contact List, you can change the way you view contact information. You can add or remove columns, change their position, change their sort order, and refine your lookups.

You can do these things within the Contact List window:

✔ **Change from Edit Mode to Tag Mode:** To edit contact information, you need to be in Edit Mode. To refine your lookups, you can be in either Edit Mode or Tag Mode. You can switch from one mode to the other by clicking the Edit/Tag Mode box, by selecting View⇨Edit/Tag Mode from the menu bar, or by pressing Shift+F8.

✔ **Select the information that you wish to view:** In the Contact List window, you can change the way contact information is displayed. You have the following options:

- **Add a column:** To add a column, right-click a blank portion of the window and select the Add Columns command from the subsequent menu. The Add Columns dialog box appears. Select the column that you want to add, and click OK.

  Right-click a label on the column heading to get a shortcut menu that you can use to add columns.

- **Change column positions:** To change the position of a column, click the column's heading and drag the cursor (which turns into a fist) to where you want the column; then release the mouse.

- **Remove a column:** To remove a column, click the column's heading and drag it up and off the Contact List.

- **Change column width:** To change the width of a column, place the cursor on the line between two column headings or on the grid line if displayed. The cursor turns into a sizing tool, which you move left or right to make the column wider or smaller.

- **Show grid lines:** To display grid lines between your columns, select the Show Grid Lines option for the Contact List in the Colors and Fonts tab of the Preferences dialog box.

- **Lock columns:** To lock your columns in place, click the small bar located at the left edge of the column heading and drag it to the right of the column(s) that you want to lock. The columns to the left of the column lock remain in place when you scroll left or right.

✔ **Change the appearance of the Contact List window:** To change the font (size, style, color), and/or the background color of the Contact List window, open the Preferences dialog box, select the Colors and Fonts tab, and then select the Contact List. (You open the Preferences dialog box by selecting Edit⇨Preferences from the menu bar.)

✔ **Change the sort order:** Click a field label in the column heading, such as Contact, Company, City, and so on, and ACT! re-sorts the data in the column based on the information in that column. A little arrow appears in the selected field to indicate which field ACT! is sorting. Another way to change the sort order is to right-click a label on the column heading. A shortcut menu appears from which you select your sort order — ascending or descending. You can also sort contacts by selecting Edit⇨Sort from the menu bar. (Sorting ACT! contacts is discussed in Chapter 10.)

Changing Contact Record Information

To change contact information in the Contact List, select Edit Mode and put your cursor in the desired cell — a cell is where a row and a column meet in a spreadsheet — and enter the new information. If a drop-down menu is available, you can enter information from that menu.

Right-click the text in the cell, and you find some basic Windows editing tools that are available. Highlight the text in the cell, and you can cut, copy, paste, or delete the text with just a click of your right mouse button. With the Select All command, you can highlight all the text in the cell. If you want to undo your changes to a single cell, select the Undo (Edit⇨Undo) command. If you want to undo your changes to the contact record itself, select the Revert (Edit⇨Revert) command.

You can do these additional things from within the Contact List window:

✔ **Schedule activities from the Contact List:** Scheduling activities — calls, meetings, and to-dos — directly from the Contact List is a breeze. Select Contact⇨Schedule (Call, Meeting, or To-do) from the menu bar, or select one of the Schedule commands (Call, Meeting, or To-do) when you click the right mouse button. The Schedule Activity dialog box appears. Scheduling activities is covered in detail in Chapter 13.

You can also schedule an activity for several contacts at once. You do this by selecting the contacts that you want to schedule the activity with and then selecting a scheduling command.

In Edit Mode, you select contacts that appear in sequence, holding down the Shift key and selecting the first and last contacts in the list by clicking on the Contact button at the left edge of the Contact List window. If the contacts are not in order, hold down the Ctrl key while clicking on each contact's Contact button individually. In Tag Mode, just "tag" the desired contacts. (Tagging contacts is covered at the end of this chapter.)

✔ **Attach a file to a contact's record:** With the Attach File command (Contact⇨Attach File), you can attach a file to a single contact or to multiple contacts, if several contacts have been selected. Attaching files is covered in Chapter 5.

✔ **Record a history item:** With the Record History command (Contact⇨Record History), you can record a history item for a single contact or for multiple contacts, if several contacts have been selected. Recording history items is covered in Chapter 5.

✔ **Copy contact name and address information to other applications or documents:** To copy a contact's name, address, and telephone number to other applications or documents, highlight a contact (or several contacts) in the Edit Mode and press Ctrl+C to copy the contact information. Press Ctrl+Tab to toggle over to another application, such as your word processor or e-mail software; then press Ctrl+V to paste the contact's name, address, and phone number into this other application.

✔ **Phone a contact from the Contact List:** You can phone a contact directly from the Contact List window. Just select the Contact⇨Phone Contact command from menu bar, or right-click to access that same command. ACT!'s telephone and dialing features are covered in Chapter 20.

✔ **Write a letter from the Contact List:** To write a letter to a contact from the Contact List window, just select the letter, memo, or fax that you wish to send from the Write pull-down menu, or right-click to access the same command. Chapter 21 discusses correspondence.

✔ **Send a fax from the Contact List:** To send a fax to a contact from the Contact List, just select the WinFax PRO icon from the toolbar. See Chapter 22 for more on sending faxes from ACT!.

✔ **Send e-mail from the Contact List:** To send an e-mail to a contact or multiple contacts from the Contact List, just highlight the contact(s) and select the Write⇨E-mail command. ACT! creates the e-mail messages and inserts the contact's e-mail address in the To field. See Chapter 23 for more information about sending e-mail from ACT!.

✔ **Print your Contact List:** You print your Contact List by selecting File⇨Print⇨Contact List from the menu bar. ACT! prints your Contact List just as it appears on your screen.

✔ **Add and delete contacts:** You can add new contacts to your ACT! database and remove unwanted contacts. Adding and deleting contacts are covered in Chapter 9.

Refining Your Lookups Using the Tag Mode

The easiest way to refine your lookups is to use the Contact List's Tag Mode. In the Tag Mode, you refine your lookups by tagging or untagging your contacts. First, create your lookup, and then go through the list and tag the contacts by clicking them — a plus (+) sign appears in the left column — one by one. (You can also tag a contact by pressing the space bar.)

After you select the contacts, you can refine your lookup in one of two ways.

- ✔ **Lookup Tagged:** Click the Lookup Tagged button, and you create a lookup of only the tagged contacts.

- ✔ **Omit Tagged:** Click the Omit Tagged button, and you create a lookup of the contacts that were not tagged.

The Tag All, Untag All, Lookup Tagged, and Omit Tagged commands are also available from the menu that appears when you right-click in the Contact List window.

After you've refined your lookup, double-click on one of the contacts in the Contact List, and ACT! opens the lookup in the Contact window and displays the chosen contact's record.

Chapter 9

Adding and Removing Contacts

*I*n this chapter, I show you how to add new contacts to your ACT! database, how to remove contacts, find duplicates, and more.

Adding New Contacts to Your ACT! Database

ACT! offers several ways to add new people to your ACT! database from either the Contact window or the Contact List window. The commands are the same in both windows. Here are some of the things you can do:

✔ Insert a new contact without copying any information from the record of the currently displayed contact into the new contact record (also referred to as *default values*).

✔ Insert a new contact by copying some information from the record of the currently displayed contact into the new contact record (also referred to as *Primary Fields*).

✔ Insert a new contact by copying all the information from the record of the currently displayed contact into the new contact record (also referred to as *All Fields*).

The ACT! software designers sometimes get rather technical and use a phrase such as *default value* without explaining what a value is. A *value* is anything that you enter in a specific field. When you enter someone's name in the Contact field, the person's name is the value. When you enter a phone number in the Phone field, that number is the value.

Using the New Contact command

When you add a new contact to your ACT! database by selecting Contact⇨New Contact from the menu bar, ACT! uses the default values that are selected in the Define Fields dialog box in creating the new contact record. Defining ACT! fields is discussed in Chapter 6. To open the Define Fields dialog box, select Edit⇨Define Fields.

You can also insert a new contact by pressing the Insert key or by selecting the New Contact command after clicking the right mouse button.

By entering default values in the Default Value field, you can enter contact information that you want ACT! to insert in every new contact record that you create using the New Contact command. To enter default information, just highlight the field (City, for example) in the List of Fields field and type the desired default value (Chicago) data in the Default Value field.

If you have repetitive information that you enter for almost every new contacts, such as city, state, or zip code, you can insert this specific information into the respective Default Value fields, and it will appear in every new contact record that you create using the New Contact command. When the default information isn't applicable to the contact record you're about to add to your ACT! database, just highlight the text, press Delete, and enter the new information.

Using the Duplicate Contact command

When you add a new contact to your ACT! database by using the Contact⇨Duplicate Contact command, the Duplicate Contact dialog box appears, as shown in Figure 9-1. You can also access the Duplicate Contact command by clicking the right mouse button and selecting Duplicate Contact from the shortcut menu.

Figure 9-1:
The
Duplicate
Contact
dialog box.

The Duplicate Contact dialog box gives you two choices:

✔ Duplicate data from primary fields

✔ Duplicate data from all fields

I describe these two choices in the following sections.

Duplicating data from primary fields

When you select the Duplicate Data from Primary Fields option to create a new contact record, ACT! copies the information from the primary fields of the current contact — Company, Phone, Address, and so on — into the new contact. You can specify which fields are primary fields in the Define Fields dialog box.

When you select the Primary Fields attribute in the Define Fields dialog box, you specify that you want the information in a particular field to be copied into a new contact's record whenever you create a new contact by using the contact's primary fields.

Select the Duplicate Data from Primary Fields option when you want to create a contact record for a person who works for the same company or organization as another contact. This way, you have to type only the new person's name and phone number because the other information remains the same.

Duplicating data from all fields

When you add a new contact to your ACT! database by selecting the Duplicate Data from All Fields option, ACT! inserts all the information that's entered in the displayed contact record, except for the contact's name, into the new contact record.

Select the Duplicate Data from All Fields option when you want to copy all the information from an existing contact to a new contact.

Saving your new contact record

After you've entered the information for the new contact into the individual fields, ACT! automatically saves your new contact's record when you execute another command. You can also press Ctrl+S to save your new contact record.

Adding new contacts with the Add Contact dialog box

ACT! has made it easy to add new contacts from different places within ACT! so that you don't have to go back to the Contact window when you're scheduling an activity for a person who isn't already in your ACT! database, when you receive e-mail from someone who isn't in your database, or when you locate someone using ACT!'s Internet Directory Lookup feature.

Here are the ways you can add a new contact to your ACT! database from the Add Contact dialog box:

✔ **When you're scheduling an activity:** When you've opened up the Schedule Activity dialog box and are about to schedule an activity for a person who isn't already in your ACT! database, just click the Contacts button, and select New Contact from the drop-down list. The Add Contact dialog box, shown in Figure 9-2, opens and enables you to enter the person's name, address, and other information. Scheduling activities is covered in Chapter 13.

✔ **When you receive an e-mail message:** When you receive an e-mail message from someone and want to add that person to your ACT! database, just select the E-mail⇨Create Contact from Sender command, and the Add Contact dialog box opens. Using ACT! to send and receive e-mail is covered in Chapter 23.

✔ **From the Internet Directory Lookup:** ACT!'s Internet Directory Lookup enables you to find people over the Internet. To find someone, just select Lookup⇨Internet Directory, type in a person's name, and select which directory service you want to use — Bigfoot, WhoWhere, or Yahoo!. ACT! logs onto the Internet, accesses the directory, and displays a list of names. To add a person to your ACT! database, just highlight the name and click the Add Contact button. The Add Contact dialog box opens. I just happen to cover the subject of how to find people in ACT! in Chapter 10.

Figure 9-2:
Add Contact
dialog box.

Removing Contacts from ACT!

From time to time, you'll need to remove people from your ACT! database. People move away or change jobs. Or you may have a person in your ACT! database whom you don't plan to call again, so you decide that this name needs to be removed from the database.

In ACT!, you can easily delete a contact record. Just bring up the contact's record in the Contact window and select Contact⇨Delete Contact from the menu bar. You can also select the Delete Contact command from the menu that appears after clicking the right mouse button, or you can press Ctrl+Delete. Any of these actions brings up the Delete Contact dialog box. Here, you are warned that:

```
Deleting contacts cannot be undone. Would you like to
delete the current contact or the entire contact lookup?
```

To delete the current contact, click the Delete Contact button.

When you select the Delete Contact button, a message box appears stating:

```
Are you sure you want to delete:
[contact's name and company name is inserted]?

NOTE: This action CANNOT be undone!
```

If you click Yes, the contact's record is permanently removed from your ACT! database and cannot be retrieved. (The default setting is No so that you can't accidentally delete a contact.)

Deleting a lookup

In addition to being able to delete an individual contact record, you can also delete an ACT! lookup, which is a group of contact records. When you perform a lookup in ACT!, you can group a number of contacts together — for example, everybody who lives in Chicago or everybody who has the last name of Smith.

When you select the Contact⇨Delete Contact, the same dialog box that I describe in the preceding section opens, and you are warned that:

```
Deleting contacts cannot be undone. Would you like to
delete the current contact or the entire contact lookup?
```

Click the Delete Lookup button, and a message box appears stating:

```
Are you sure you want to delete:
The [number of contacts is inserted] in this lookup?
NOTE: This action CANNOT be undone!
```

If you do, click Yes.

Stopping the deletion of lookups

As the contacts in the lookup are being deleted, a status box appears that displays the progress of the deletion and shows you the name of each contact as it is being deleted. The Record Counter begins counting as ACT! removes contacts from the database.

To stop the deletion process, click the Stop button on the status box.

Deleting contacts from within the Contact List window

If you want to delete more than one contact from within the Contact List window, you must first highlight, or *tag,* the contacts before you select the Delete command.

To highlight contacts that appear in sequence in the Edit Mode, hold down the Shift key while clicking the first and last contacts in the sequence. To highlight contacts that do not appear in sequence, hold down the Ctrl key while you highlight each contact individually.

To delete contacts in the Tag Mode, you go through the Contact List and tag the contacts by clicking them — a plus (+) sign appears in the left column — one by one. (You can also tag a contact by pressing the space bar.)

After you've tagged your contacts, select the Contact⇨Delete Contact command to delete the tagged contacts or lookup.

Avoiding disaster

Over the past few years, I've received a number of telephone calls from ACT! users who were having a problem. Why were they calling? They had deleted a large portion of their entire ACT! database by mistake.

This is what they had done: They deleted a lookup instead of deleting a single contact, and the lookup just happened to be a very large portion of the database. Before they knew it, ACT! deleted every contact record in the lookup.

Most experienced ACT! users understand the difference between deleting a contact and a lookup. But many inexperienced users may not — your assistant or people who have just recently joined your organization, for example.

Today, many users across large networks may use the same ACT! database. That is why every ACT! user needs to know the difference between deleting a contact and deleting a lookup.

A *lookup* — lookups are discussed in Chapter 10 — is a collection of contact records within the database that are grouped together after a database search. Although only one contact record is displayed at a time in the Contact window, you can make a lookup of a single contact record, many contact records, or the entire database.

When you perform a lookup — first name, last name, company, city, and so on — you search your ACT! database for contact records with similar or identical information, such as everybody who has a last name of Smith or everybody who lives in Chicago. When ACT! finds these records, it groups them together.

The type of lookup that you're performing is shown at the bottom-left corner of the Contact window.

Undeleting deleted contacts

ACT! has a utility — ACTDIAG.EXE — that enables you to undelete deleted contacts. This utility restores all deleted contacts since the database was last compressed and reindexed.

ACTDIAG.EXE does not have a help file or other documentation. I suggest that you call your ACT! Certified Consultant or ACT! technical support at 541-465-8645 and have them walk you through the undelete process. (For information on the services of ACT! Certified Consultants, turn to Chapter 30.)

I explain ACTDIAG's features in Chapter 29.

Getting rid of duplicate records

When you have many contact records in your database, you may find that you have accidentally entered the same contact more than once. Now you have two or more records for the same person. With ACT!'s Scan for

Duplicates command, you can scan your database for duplicate contact or group records. When ACT! finds duplicates, you decide which of the contact records to keep.

If you have useful information in a duplicate record, use the Copy and Paste commands to transfer the information to the record that you plan on keeping. You can also use the Copy and Paste commands to move notes, histories, and attachments from one contact record to another.

Setting your criteria

To set your duplicate search criteria, you must open the Advanced tab in ACT!'s Define Fields dialog box. Select Edit⇨Define Fields, click the Advanced tab, and select Contact or Group as your Record Type.

The default search criteria for finding duplicate contact records are Company, Contact, and Phone. The default search criteria for finding duplicate Group records are Group Name and Record Creator. (If duplicate groups were created by two different people, the Record Creator is different, and ACT! can't locate the duplicate records.)

Enabling duplicate checking for contact and group records

To enable duplicate checking, you must first select either Contact or Group as your Record type and then select the Enable Duplicate Checking option.

Scanning for duplicates

To scan your database for duplicates, select the Tools⇨Scan For Duplicates command, and ACT! creates a lookup of all the contacts that meet the selected criteria.

Part III
Working with ACT! Contacts

The 5th Wave — By Rich Tennant

"NIFTY CHART, FRANK, BUT NOT ENTIRELY NECESSARY."

In this part . . .

1 explain how you find people in your ACT! database, and I also show you how to create groups of contacts, a great feature that will make your life much easier.

Chapter 10

Finding People in ACT!

● ●

In This Chapter

▶ Understanding the basics of lookups

▶ Performing ACT! lookups

▶ Using ACT!'s Lookup dialog box

▶ Finding people over the Internet

▶ Sorting your database

▶ Searching by keyword

▶ Viewing your lookup in the Contact window

▶ Refining lookups

▶ Saving lookups

● ●

*O*ne of the most important — and most powerful — features in ACT! is its lookup feature. With the lookup feature, you can find anyone in your ACT! database in just a fraction of a second. (You can also search your ACT! database for any piece of information or keyword, but searching can take a lot longer than a fraction of a second if you have a large database.) When you perform a lookup, you're searching your ACT! database for contact records that contain similar or identical pieces of information.

Finding people in ACT! is a key concept from my *Growing Your Business with ACT!* program. My programs are ideal for entrepreneurs, corporate executives, sales professionals and anyone else who wants to grow their business. Call 312-944-4184 for more information.

Lookup Basics

When you use the Lookup command, you're actually creating a *collection* of contacts from within your ACT! database. For example, if you do a lookup of Chicago by selecting Lookup⇨City and typing **Chicago,** you create a collection of contact records of people who live or work in Chicago. Or if you do a lookup of Smith by selecting Lookup⇨Last Name and typing **Smith,** you create a collection of contact records of people who have the last name of Smith.

Here are some lookup tips:

✔ A lookup remains active until you do another lookup.

✔ You can create specific groups of ACT! contact records while keeping your ACT! database intact. (I discuss how to do this task in Chapter 12.)

✔ The type of lookup that was last performed is displayed on the bottom-left side of the Contact window on the status bar.

✔ To see your entire ACT! database after you've performed a lookup, select Lookup⇨All Contacts.

✔ To view your lookup as a list, click the Contact List icon (or press F8, or select View⇨Contact List) to open the Contact List window.

If you can't remember how a person's name is spelled, just type the first few letters of the name when you do a lookup, and ACT! creates a list of all your ACT! contacts whose names have those letter combinations. Then press the PageUp or PageDown buttons to scroll through the list, or click the Contact List icon to open the Contact List window where you can scroll through the list until you find the name that you're searching for.

Many people find that it's much faster to perform a lookup by using the keyboard instead of the mouse. To look up a person by first name, just press Alt+L+F (Lookup⇨First Name), type in the first few letters of the first name, and press Enter. To look up a person by last name, press Alt+L+L (Lookup⇨Last Name), type the first few letters of the last name, and press Enter. If your computer is connected to your telephone line, have ACT! dial the phone for you. As a result of the conversation, you'll probably have to schedule some type of activity with that person. So schedule that activity now, before you move on to your next task.

Performing ACT! Lookups

On the next few pages, I explain how to find people within your ACT! database. You access ACT!'s Lookup commands by selecting Lookup from the menu bar. The Lookup menu is shown in Figure 10-1.

Make ACT! your electronic Rolodex

Add the names, addresses, and phone numbers of everybody you speak to or meet with, to your ACT! database. You just don't know if — or when — you'll need to speak with that person again.

When you do need to find someone's phone number, just look up the person's first or last name, and the contact record is displayed before you can blink your eye.

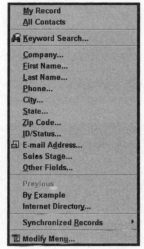

My Record
All Contacts
Keyword Search...
Company...
First Name...
Last Name...
Phone...
City...
State...
Zip Code...
ID/Status...
E-mail Address...
Sales Stage...
Other Fields...
Previous
By Example
Internet Directory...
Synchronized Records ▶
Modify Menu...

Figure 10-1:
The Lookup
menu.

Three of the Lookup menu's commands are predefined. Just make your selection. This is how they work:

- **My Record:** Select Lookup⇔My Record when you want to find *your contact record.*

  The My Record contact record contains information about the owner or main user of the database, who is you when you're using it. If you're sharing a database, the My Record contact record displays the contact information of the person who is currently using the database.

  When you're using ACT! on a network, you tell ACT! that you're the user when you enter your name and password. After you enter your name and password, ACT! knows which My Record contact record to activate.

- **All Contacts:** Select Lookup⇔All Contacts to find everyone in your ACT! database.

  When you want to scroll through your entire database, just look up everyone and then press F8 to open the Contact List. Refining your lookups with the Contact List window is discussed later in this chapter. (I discuss the features of the Contact List in Chapter 8.)

- **Previous:** Select Lookup⇔Previous, and ACT! displays your previous lookup.

  Use the Previous command when someone needs a phone number or address. Say, for example, that you're talking to Jane on the phone, and she asks you for Tarzan's address. Do a lookup for Tarzan, and after you give Jane the information, use the Previous command to return to Jane's contact record.

Using ACT!'s Lookup Dialog Box

When you perform a lookup for Company, First Name, Last Name, Phone, City, State, Zip Code, ID/Status, E-mail Address, Sales Stage, or Other Fields, the Lookup dialog box (shown in Figure 10-2) opens. From the Lookup dialog box, you search your database.

From the Lookup dialog box's Lookup field, you can search any field in your ACT! database by selecting the field from the drop-down list.

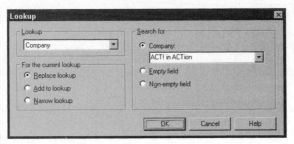

Figure 10-2:
The Lookup
dialog box.

This is how you perform a lookup for all the contacts who live or work in a city — Chicago, for example:

1. **Select Lookup⇨City from the menu bar.**

   The Lookup dialog box opens, and the City field appears in the Lookup field.

2. **Type** Chicago **in the Search For field, or select Chicago from the drop-down menu.**

3. **Click OK.**

   ACT! finds everybody in your database who is located in Chicago.

If you wanted to send a letter to everybody that you know who lives or works in California, just select Lookup⇨State, and enter **CA** in the Search For field. Then run your mail merge. (Performing ACT! mail merges is covered in Chapter 21.)

Here are some ACT! lookup tips:

✔ When you want to find all of the contact records of people who work for the same company, choose Lookup⇨Company.

✔ When you do a lookup for a field that has been designated as a drop-down menu field, you can access the same drop-down menus that are used in the respective fields in the Contact window. (To read more about defining ACT! fields, turn to Chapter 6.)

✔ When you can't remember how a person's last name is spelled, perform a First Name lookup and then open the Contact List (press F8) so you can scroll through the list. After you locate the person, double-click the Contact button to the left of the name, and ACT! brings up the contact record.

✔ To sort your ACT! database alphabetically, select the Lookup command that you want (such as Company, First Name, Last Name, and so on), leave the Search For field blank, click OK, and your lookup is sorted in alphabetical order.

✔ When you want to find a person's contact record, just press Alt+L+L (Lookup⇨Last Name) to bring up the Lookup Last Name dialog box; type in the first three or four letters of the person's last name and press Enter, and ACT! groups all the people together who have those letters in their last names. Then use the Page Up/Page Down buttons to scroll through the list.

✔ When you want to call someone but can't remember the exact spelling of either his or her first or last name, perform a lookup of the person's city, and then open the Contact List (by pressing F8) and scroll through the list.

The next time you plan an out-of-town business trip, search for all the people who work in the cities you'll be visiting to see whether you have any additional people who you need to meet with. You can then group-schedule a call, instead of scheduling a call one contact at a time. You can also send out a mass mailing to these people.

Using the ID/Status field

The ID/Status field is an ACT! field that enables you to assign your own categories to your contacts. For example, you may want to identify the people in your ACT! database as customers, prospects, clients, vendors, friends, family, relatives, and so on.

For myself, I do much of my own public relations work and use the ID/Status field to categorize people by the industries in which they work, such as radio, television, newspaper, or magazine. I also enter a person's position or title in ACT!'s Title field so that I know whether this radio person is a producer, station manager, or talk show host.

When you want to search for people who have the same ID/Status, choose ID/Status from the Lookup menu and enter your search criteria in the Lookup dialog box's Search For field.

When you perform a lookup for contacts by their ID/Status, use the drop-down menu. This ensures that you're using the correct search criteria.

Searching for sales stages

Sales forecasting is a new ACT! feature, and it's so important that I've given it an entire part in this book. So if you want to read about it right now, turn to Part V.

Searching for empty and non-empty fields

From time to time, you may want to search for fields that are empty or fields that are not empty — they have data entered in them. Here are a few examples:

✔ You want to send a mailing to several hundred people, so you must be sure that each contact record has a complete mailing address. The easiest way to check that a field has an entry is to use the Lookup dialog box's Empty Field option. You then search the Company, Contact, Address 1, City, State, and Zip Code fields to find records that are empty. Then you can call these people to get current addresses.

✔ You want to send out a fax or e-mail broadcast announcing the release of a new product, so you select Lookup, and choose Fax or E-mail Address in the Lookup box's Lookup field and the Non-Empty Field option. ACT! will find each contact that has either a fax number or e-mail address.

To search your database for contact records in which a field is empty, select the field from the Lookup dialog box's Lookup drop-down menu and select the Empty Field option.

To search your database for contact records in which a field contains data, select the field from the Lookup dialog box's Lookup drop-down menu and select the Not-Empty Field option.

Refining Your Lookups

ACT! enables you to narrow your lookup or refine it. Or you can expand your lookup by adding the results of a new database search to the results of the previous search. After you've created your lookup, you can use the Contact List window to further refine your lookup by selectively removing individual contacts from the lookup. (I discuss this ACT! feature in just a moment.)

You can also use ACT!'s very powerful Query window (select Lookup⇨ By Example), where you can perform very sophisticated database searches. This is covered in the next chapter.

Narrowing your lookups

When you narrow your lookup, you are refining the number of contacts that match certain search criteria. Some people refer to this process as *drilling down*. For example, say that you're going on a business trip and want a list of all your customers in Boston. This is what you do:

1. **Select Lookup⇨City, type** Boston, **and click OK.**

   ACT! creates a lookup of everybody who is in Boston.

2. **Select Lookup⇨ID/Status and type** Customer.

   This step assumes that you use the ID/Status field to categorize your contacts and that one of your categories is Customer.

3. **Select the Narrow Lookup option.**

   This option tells ACT! to search the previous lookup list (people who live or work in Boston) for contacts matching the current lookup criteria (people who are also customers). This option creates a smaller and more refined lookup.

4. **Click OK.**

   ACT! creates a lookup of all your customers in Boston.

Expanding your lookups

When you expand your lookups, you're adding the results of two or more lookups together. For example, say that you're going to California and want a list of all your contacts in Los Angeles and San Francisco. This is how you can compile your list:

1. **Select Lookup⇨City, type** Los Angeles, **and click OK.**

   ACT! creates a lookup of everybody who is in Los Angeles.

2. **Select Lookup⇨City and type** San Francisco.

3. **Select the Add to Lookup option.**

   This option tells ACT! to add the contacts found using the lookup criteria to the current lookup.

4. **Click OK.**

   ACT! creates a lookup of everybody you know in both Los Angeles and San Francisco.

Here's another example of how you could use ACT!'s Add to Lookup feature. Say that you wanted to send a mailing to everybody in the Chicago metropolitan area. The easiest way to find everybody would be to search by area codes — the Chicago metropolitan area now has five area codes — and add each one to the lookup.

Adding queries to your lookup menu

If you have lookups that you perform frequently, you can add them to the Lookup menu. This is how you do it:

1. **Select Lookup⇨By Example.**

   The Query window opens.

2. **Enter your search criteria.**

3. **Select File⇨Save to save your query.**

4. **Close the Query window and return to the Contact window.**

5. **Select Lookup⇨Modify Menu.**

   The Modify Menu dialog box opens.

6. **Click the Add Item button to add your query to the Lookup menu.**

Finding People over the Internet

From ACT!'s Internet Directory dialog box (select Lookup⇨Internet Directory), you are able to search for people by using several Internet directory services: Bigfoot, WhoWhere, and Yahoo!.

You must have an Internet service provider (ISP) in order to use the powerful Internet Directory feature.

This is how you search the Internet:

1. **Enter a person's name in the Enter Name to Be Found field.**

2. **Select the directory in which you want to look.**

3. **Click the Search button.**

ACT! logs onto the Internet, goes to the selected directory, and displays the search results.

From the Internet Directory dialog box, you've some additional options:

- ✔ **Narrow your Internet searches:** If your search results are too large, you may want to narrow your search. You do this by clicking the Narrow Search button. From the Narrow Search dialog box, you can narrow your search by selecting City, State, Country, Organization, or All.

- ✔ **Add, remove, and edit Internet directories:** Click the Directory Options button, and the Directory Options dialog box appears. Here, you can select the Add, Edit, or Remove options to search directories from your Internet Lookup directory.

- ✔ **Add contacts to your database:** After you find a contact, you can add it to your ACT! database by highlighting the person's name and clicking the Add Contact button. The Add Contact dialog box appears, and you enter the person's name, address, and so on. Adding contacts to your ACT! database is covered in Chapter 9.

- ✔ **Send an e-mail message:** If you want to send an e-mail message to someone you just located, highlight the person's name and click the Send Message button. Sending e-mail is covered in Chapter 23.

From the Internet Links menu you can access Yahoo! Search and Yahoo! People Search. To find out all about ACT!'s Internet links, check out Chapter 25.

Sorting Your Database

After you've created an ACT! lookup, you may want to change the sort order. You can this in two ways.

Using the Sort Contacts dialog box

To change the ACT! sort order, select Edit⇨Sort from the ACT! menu bar, and the Sort Contacts dialog box, shown in Figure 10-3, appears.

Figure 10-3:
The Sort
Contacts
dialog box.

You use the Sort Contacts dialog box to sort the database in ascending or descending order. You can use three fields to customize the sort:

- ✓ In the **Sort Contacts By** section, you specify the first field (criteria) by which you want to sort your lookup. You can also choose whether to perform the sort in ascending (A to Z) or descending (Z to A) order.

- ✓ In the **And Then By** section, you specify the second-level criteria by which you want to sort your lookup. You can also choose whether to perform this sort in ascending or descending order.

- ✓ In the **And Finally By** section, you specify the third-level criteria by which you want to sort your lookup. You can also choose whether to perform this sort in ascending or descending order.

To sort by one set of criteria, choose None as the second and third sort criteria.

Sorting contacts from the Contact List window

You can also sort your contacts from within the Contact List window. Click the Contact List icon, or press F8, to open the Contact List window. Then click on any column heading, and ACT! sorts your database in ascending or descending order.

Searching Your Entire Database by a Keyword

In addition to having the ability to search the contact fields of your ACT! database, you can perform a search for a keyword or key phrase within your entire database. Select Lookup⇨Keyword Search, and the Keyword Search dialog box appears, as shown in Figure 10-4.

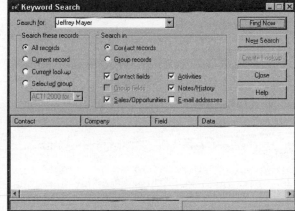

Figure 10-4: The Keyword Search dialog box.

From within the Keyword Search dialog box, you have several choices:

✓ **Which records do you want to search?** In the Search These Records section, you can select All Records, Current Record, Current Lookup, or a Selected Group.

✓ **Do you want to search for contacts or records?** In the Search In section, you tell ACT! where you want it to search. You can select Contact or Group records, and then you can select Contact (or Group) fields, Sales/Opportunities, Activities, Notes/History, or E-mail addresses.

Enter the keyword or string of words (a phrase), and ACT! creates a group of all the people in your database who have that keyword or phrase somewhere within their contact records.

Keep in mind that a keyword search can take a long time, and if you have a large database, it can take a very long time.

Finding keywords and key phrases

When ACT! finds a key word or phrase in a Sales/Opportunity, Activity, or Notes/History search, it brings up the contact record in which that key word or phrase appears. It doesn't locate the specific word within the contact record.

ACT! displays a list of the instances of the keyword you specified. If the keyword was found more than once in a contact's record, the contact will be displayed multiple times. ACT! also displays the Contact , Company, Field Type and Data. In the Field column, ACT! indicatea the type of field the keyword was found in. In the Data column, ACT! shows you the entire text of the field where the keyword was found.

If you double-click the record you wanted to find, ACT! returns to the contact view. The keyword will be highlighted so you can easily find it.

You can enter the word or phrase that you want ACT! to find in a keyword search in any of the following ways:

- ✔ You can have ACT! search for a single word, such as "price."

- ✔ You can use wild cards (*) to search for an incomplete word. See the sidebar "Wild cards, you make my heart sing" for more information on using wild cards.

- ✔ You can use operators to look for two or more words. For example, you can search for Chicago AND Detroit, Chicago OR Detroit, or Chicago AND_NOT Detroit.

- ✔ You can search for complete phrases, such as "price list enclosed."

Keyword lookups are not case sensitive. For example, if you do a search for the keyword "National," ACT! includes the words "National" (first letter capitalized), "NATIONAL" (all caps), and "national" (all lowercase) in the search results.

Viewing Your Lookup in the Contact Window

When ACT! completes your lookup, you see the first contact record of the lookup on-screen.

To determine the position of the contact record that's presently displayed in the Contact window within the current lookup, check the numbers that are

Wild cards, you make my heart sing

When you want to look up words that have specific groups of letters in them, you use wild cards. You denote a wild card search by placing an asterisk (*) before or after a group of letters. The following is an explanation of how to use wild cards:

✔ **An asterisk at the end of the group of letters:** If you want to do a search for all the words that begin with the letters *con,* type **con*.** When your search is complete, you will find such words as contest, conversation, convoluted, and conversion.

✔ **An asterisk at the beginning of a group of letters:** If you want to do a search for all the words that end with the letters *con,* type ***con.** After your search is completed, you will find such words as falcon, lexicon, and icon.

✔ **An asterisk at the beginning and ending of a group of letters:** If you want to do a search for all the words that have the letters *con* in the middle of the word, type ***con*.** After your search is completed, you will find such words as intercontinental, economy, economical, and iconoclast.

displayed in the status area on the toolbar (see Figure 10-5). For example, 7 of 15 means that this contact record is the 7th record out of a total of 15 records; 125 of 327 means that this contact record is the 125th record out of a total of 327 records.

Figure 10-5:
The status area on the toolbar.

Here are ACT! lookup tips for moving through a lookup one record at a time:

✔ **The Previous/Next Contact buttons:** Click the Previous/Next Contact buttons, located on the toolbar (they're the buttons with the single arrows) to move to the prior or next contact in the lookup. Refer to Figure 10-5 to see these buttons.

✔ **Ctrl+PageUp/Ctrl+PageDown keys:** The Ctrl+PageUp and Ctrl+PageDown keys move you to the prior or next contact in the lookup.

✔ **PageUp/PageDown keys:** The PageUp and PageDown keys move you to the prior or next contact in the lookup (if you selected the Move Between Records Using ACT! 2.0 Shortcut Keys command in the General tab of the Preferences dialog box).

Here are ACT! lookup tips for moving to the first or last record in a lookup:

- **The First/Last Record buttons:** Click the First/Last Record buttons (they're the buttons with the arrow facing a line) to move to the first or last record in the lookup. Refer to Figure 10-5 to see these buttons.

- **Alt+Home/Alt+End:** You can move to the first record in your lookup by pressing Alt+Home, and you can move to the last record in your lookup by pressing Alt+End.

- **Ctrl+Home/Ctrl+End:** You can move to the first record in your lookup by pressing Ctrl+Home, and you can move to the last record in your lookup by pressing Ctrl+End (if you selected the Move Between Records Using ACT! 2.0 Shortcut Keys command in the General tab of the Preferences dialog box).

Another great feature of the status bar is the Lookup indicator. The Lookup indicator, which is on the status bar at the bottom of the Contact window, tells you the type of lookup — Everyone, First Name, Last Name, City, State, and so on — that you have performed. This indicator helps you keep track of how you grouped your contacts.

For example, if the Lookup indicator says "All Contacts," all the contacts in the current group have been selected. (I cover grouping contacts in Chapter 12.)

Refining Your Lookup in the Contact List Window

With the Contact List window (shown in Figure 10-6), you can see the results of your database search as a list. You can then use the Edit Mode or Tag Mode to further refine your lookup. In the Edit Mode, you can edit contact information, and in the Tag Mode, you cannot. You can use either mode for refining your ACT! lookups.

You can switch from one mode to the other by clicking the Edit/Tag Mode box with your mouse, by selecting View⇨Edit/Tag Mode from the menu bar, or by pressing the Shift+F8 keys.

To open the Contact List window, press F8 or click the View Contact List button. I discuss ACT!'s Contact List in Chapter 8.

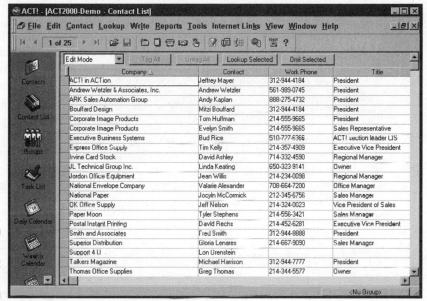

Figure 10-6:
The Contact
List window.

Refining your lookup in the Edit Mode

1. **Select the people by clicking their Contact buttons (the gray button at the left edge of the window).**

   To select records that are in sequence, hold down the Shift key, click the Contact button of the first person, and then click the Contact button of the last person. To select more than one person, hold down the Ctrl key and click each person's Contact button.

2. **Click the Lookup Selected button to keep these records in the lookup, or click the Omit Selected button to remove these records from the lookup.**

Refining your lookup in the Tag Mode

1. **Select the people by clicking on them or by pressing the space bar.**

   A plus sign (+) appears in the left column.

2. **Click the Lookup Selected button to keep these records in the lookup, or click the Omit Selected button to remove these records from the lookup.**

Finding People in the Lookup

To scroll through the Contact List from the keyboard, you can use the up- and down-arrow keys or the PageUp and PageDown keys. To scroll through the Contact List with your mouse, click and hold the scroll buttons with your mouse pointer. Pressing Ctrl+Home takes you to the first item on the list; pressing Ctrl+End takes you to the last item on the list.

ACT! has a feature that's called typing ahead. To find people in any Contact List column — Company, Contact, State, City, and so on — just click on the specific column and begin typing. For example, to find people in your Contact List by name, click the Name column and begin typing the person's last name. ACT! highlights the first person whose name begins with those letters.

Saving Your Lookups

After you've gone through the effort of creating a lookup, you may want to save it so that you don't have to go through the process a second time. With ACT!'s Group feature, you can save your lookups. I cover creating, using, and managing groups in Chapter 12.

Chapter 11

Performing Advanced Database Queries

• •

In This Chapter

▶ Performing advanced contact lookups from the Query window

▶ Performing advanced Query Lookups

▶ Using the Query Helper

• •

*1*n ACT!, you're able to perform advanced database searches that go way beyond the commands that are available from the Lookup menu. (Performing ACT! lookups is discussed in Chapter 10. If you haven't read that chapter already, you should do so now because this one is a bit more technical.)

Performing Advanced Lookups from the Query Window

To perform an ACT! advanced query, select Lookup⇨By Example from either the Contact or Groups window. The Query window appears, as shown in Figure 11-1.

From the Query window, you can instruct ACT! to search for contacts who match specific search criteria. When you perform a lookup for all the people who live or work in a particular city, such as Chicago, that's a criterion. When you perform a lookup for a person by his or her first name, last name, or anything else, that's also a criterion. If you combine these two criteria, for example, to lookup everyone who has the last name of Smith and who lives in Chicago, you create an advanced query.

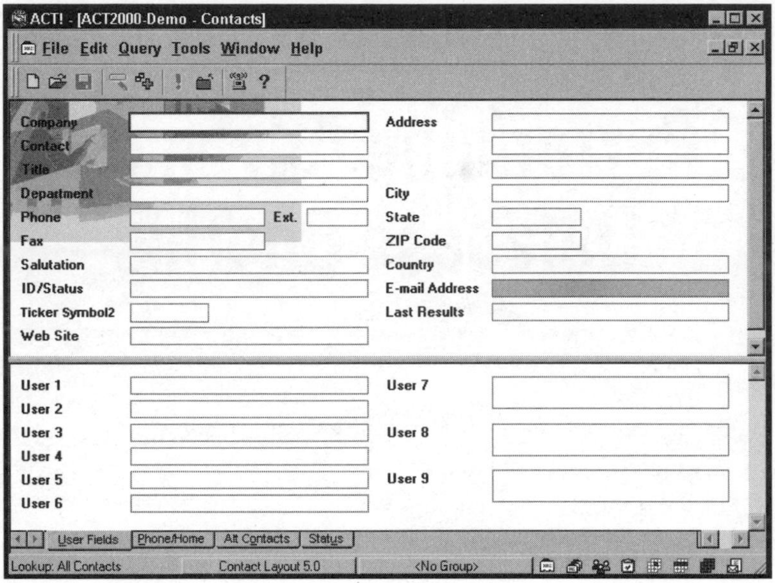

Figure 11-1:
The Query
window.

From the Query window, you can perform lookups for contacts who meet all sorts of criteria. You can, for example, perform a lookup of all your clients (as opposed to prospects) who live in Dallas, Detroit, or Los Angeles and who have placed an order with you within the last 90 days. (This assumes that you set up your ACT! fields in such a way that you store this type of information.)

Here are some advanced query commands that can help you get more out of your advanced queries:

✔ **Saving a query:** After you've created an advanced query, you can save it by selecting the File➪Save command or by pressing Ctrl+S. If you want to save an existing query with a new name, select the File➪Save As command or press F12. Queries are saved in ACT!'s queries directory. Saving your queries has several useful benefits, such as the following:

  • When you want to perform the same query in the future, you won't have to re-create the query.

  • If you're creating a complex query, you may want to save it so you can use it again. (ACT! automatically erases search criteria after it performs a search.)

  • You can use a previous query as the foundation for another query.

✔ **Add frequently used queries to the Lookup menu:** If you have frequently used queries, add them to the Lookup menu so they're easy to execute. You do this by selecting the Lookup➪Modify Menu command from within the Contact window.

✔ **Clearing a query:** If you've started creating a query and want to erase it and start over, select Query⇨Clear Query. You can also create a new query by selecting File⇨New or pressing Ctrl+N.

✔ **Checking your query:** After you've created your query, select the Query⇨Check Query Syntax command, and ACT! checks your query for errors.

✔ **Sorting your query:** After you've created your query and checked it for errors, you can select the field on which to sort the database search. You begin this sort function by selecting Query⇨Specify Query Sort. You may want to do this when you're creating a report, for example. Or, when you perform a lookup for clients who live in Texas but not in Dallas, you can tell ACT! how you want it to sort that database search — by last name, company, city, zip code, and so on.

✔ **Executing a query:** When you're ready to execute a query from the Query window, choose Run Query from the Query menu, or press Ctrl+R, and ACT! executes your query.

All the drop-down menus and Edit List boxes that you use within your ACT! contact layouts are accessible from the Query window. Your ACT! layouts are also available. To change layouts in the Query window, click the Contact Layout button at the bottom of the window and select the layout from which you want to perform your query.

Using Operators in Your Lookups

When you want to perform a lookup on an ACT! field, you can use operators within the field to expand the power of your lookup. (I go into a more detailed explanation of operators in the section on "Using the Query Helper" later in this chapter.)

Here are some examples:

✔ You want to perform a lookup for people who live and work in one of two cities — say Dallas or Houston. You would enter this search string in the City field: `Dallas || Houston`. The double bar (||) is the symbol for the `OR` operator.

✔ You've a field named Expiration Date and want to search for all of your 2001 expirations, you would enter `*2001*` to search for records that CONTAIN 2001 in that field. The double asterisks (*___*) is the symbol for the `CONTAINS` operator.

✔ You want to search your database for people that you haven't contacted since January 1, 1999. You would click on the Status tab and enter `<1/1/99` in the Last Reach field. The (<) symbol is the `LESS THAN` operator.

On the Status tab are fields for Last Reach, Last Meeting, Last Attempt, Create Date, Edit Date, Merge Date, and Letter Date. You can perform this type of query on all of these fields. I go into more detail about searching ACT! dates in the section titled "Example 4: Searching for contacts based on dates" later in this chapter.

- ✔ You want to search your database for people that you have contacted since January 1, 1999. You would click on the Status tab and enter >1/1/99 in the Last Reach field. The (>) symbol is the GREATER THAN operator.

- ✔ You've a field named Products Of Interest, and in this field, you enter multiple items. You would enter Thingamagigs && Whatchamacallits in the Products Of Interest field to find Thingamagigs and Whatchamacallits. The double ampersand (&&) is the AND Operator.

- ✔ To search for a BLANK, or empty field, place your cursor in the field and press F5. ACT! inserts these symbols, <<>>, in the field. This is BLANK operator.

- ✔ You can also use the STARTS WITH (___*) and ENDS WITH (*___) operators.

Performing Advanced Query Lookups

With ACT!, you can perform very powerful searches that enable you to find contacts who meet complex search criteria. In this section, I give you some examples of how you can search your ACT! database. The more you explore ACT!'s advanced query features, the better you'll get at performing database searches. In these examples, I use operators, which I explain after these examples. My purpose in writing this part of the chapter in this manner is to give you the examples first and then explain how ACT! performs these custom lookups.

Example 1: Looking for clients in Dallas

Say that you want to perform a lookup for all your clients who live in a specific city; for illustrative purposes, I'll use Dallas. This is what you do:

1. **From the Query window, enter the criteria that you want ACT! to use to perform an advanced query.**

   In this example, you enter the city's name — that is, Dallas — in the City field and the word Client in the ID/Status field of the Query window. (This assumes that you categorize your contacts in the ID/Status field and that one of the categories is "Client.") Remember to use your drop-down menus or Edit List boxes (press F2) to enter information.

2. **To run a query, select Query⇨Run Query.**

   Because I want to give you a more thorough explanation of what ACT! does to create this advanced query, I'm going to suggest that you not run the query just yet. After you enter the basic criteria, choose the Convert to Advanced Query command from the Query menu, and the Advanced Query window appears. ACT! has taken the entries that you made in the Query window and made the phrase ((("City" = "Dallas"*)) AND (("ID/Status" = "Client"*)) out of it.

Proper spacing and the insertion of quotation marks are very important to an ACT! query. The word "City" (note the quotation marks) identifies the ACT! field in the statement. The equal sign (=) is the EQUAL operator, and the word "Dallas" (note the quotation marks) is the value, which is the data that you enter into a field. (Values are not case sensitive.) The word AND that connects the two statements in the phrase is the AND operator.

The asterisk (*) after the value — ("City" = "Dallas"*) — is the BEGINS WITH operator.

Example 2: Looking for clients who live in Texas but not in Dallas

To modify the previous example a bit, suppose that you want to look for all your clients who live in Texas but not in Dallas. Your search string looks like this: (((("State" = "TX"*) AND ("City" <> "Dallas"*))) AND ("ID/Status" = "Client"*).

Note the triple parentheses around the first part of this search string: (((("State" = "TX"*) AND ("City" <> "Dallas"))). The triple parentheses tell ACT! that you want it to look for everybody who is a client and who lives in Texas except for those who live in Dallas.

Example 3: Searching for birthdays

Many people like to keep a record of the birthdays of their important customers, clients, family, and friends so that they can remember to send them a card, buy them a gift, or take them out to dinner. Here's an easy way to set up your ACT! Birthday fields.

1. **Designate a field as a Birthday field.**

   Creating new ACT! fields and renaming existing ACT! fields are covered in Chapter 6.

2. **Create a drop-down menu, including Descriptions, with the 12 months of the year (that is, January, February, March, and so on; and their abbreviations Jan., Feb., Mar., and so on) as the item.**

You create drop-down menus from within the Define Fields dialog box. Open the Define Fields dialog box by selecting Edit⇨Define Fields. (I discuss defining ACT! fields and creating drop-down menus in Chapter 6.)

Using a drop-down menu makes the entry of the birth month easy and keeps all your entries consistent. January is abbreviated as Jan., for example.

3. **To find everyone who has a January birthday, choose Lookup⇨ By Example to bring up the Query screen.**

4. **Type Jan.* in the Birthday field.**

5. **Select Query⇨Run Query, and ACT! searches for everybody who has a January birthday.**

That was easy, wasn't it?

If you convert your query to an advanced query before you click OK, your search string looks like `(("Birthday" = "Jan."*))`.

When you type `Jan.*` in the Birthday field, it becomes `(("Birthday" = "Jan."*))`. The asterisk (*), which is called a wild card, after the word `"Jan."` tells ACT! to look for a string of characters that starts with the word `"Jan."` The asterisk (*) is the `STARTS WITH` operator.

If you want to perform a lookup of your clients who have a January birthday, you type **Jan.*** in the Birthday field and **Client** in the ID/Status field. This is how your search string looks: `(("Birthday" = "Jan."*)) AND ((ID/Status = "Client"*))`.

Example 4: Searching for contacts based on dates

You can also search for contacts based on a date or range of dates. On the bottom of the Status tab, ACT! records the following:

- ✔ **Last Meeting:** The date of your last meeting with a person.
- ✔ **Last Reach:** The date you last reached a person on the phone.
- ✔ **Last Attempt:** The date you last attempted to reach a person on the phone.

✔ **Letter Date:** The date you last sent the person a letter, memo, or fax; and the date the contact record was created, merged, or edited. (This is why clearing your activities and logging your correspondence into the contact's History file is so important.)

✔ **Create Date:** The date a contact record was created.

✔ **Edit Date:** The date a contact record was last edited.

✔ **Merge Date:** The date a contact record was merged into this database.

To perform a search of all the people to whom you haven't spoken on the phone since, let's say, July 1, 1999, just enter **<7/1/1999** in the Last Reach field. ACT! searches your database for every contact that has a Last Reach date that is less than July 1, 1999.

To find everybody you spoke with on the phone during the month of July 1999 (the period of time from July 1, 1999, through July 31, 1999), just enter **7/*/1999** in the Last Reach field. ACT! searches your database for every contact that has a Last Reach date is any day in July.

To find everybody you spoke with on the phone during the months of July 1999 and August 1999(the period of time from July 1, 1999, through August 31, 1999), just use the range (..) operator. In the Last Reach field, enter **7/1/1999 .. 8/31/1999.**

When you're replacing an existing operator with a new operator in the Advanced Query window, it's best to use ACT!'s Query Helper dialog box, which is shown in Figure 11-2. (You open the Query Helper dialog box by selecting Query⇨Show Query Helper. This ACT! feature is discussed in greater detail in the next section.) Highlight the operator that you want to replace in the search string, and then double-click the operator that you want to replace it with from the list of operators displayed in the Query Helper dialog box. The new operator overwrites the old operator. When you replace operators in this manner, you eliminate the possibility of typing the wrong characters in the search string.

Figure 11-2:
ACT!'s
Query
Helper
dialog box.

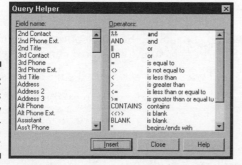

To find everybody with whom you had some type of contact during the month of July 1999 (the period of time from July 1, 1999, through July 31, 1999), your search string would look like this: `(("Edit Date" >= "7/1/99"*)) AND (("Edit Date" <= "7/1/99"*))`.

Whenever you make any changes to a contact's information, ACT! automatically enters the date of that change into the Edit Date field. The next time your boss asks you for a list of everybody you spoke with on the phone, had a meeting with, or sent a letter, memo, or fax to during the past week (or any period of time), perform your advanced database search on the Edit Date field. ACT! searches your database based upon the range of dates that you select in the Edit Date field, and you have your list in just a few moments.

Using the Query Helper

You use the Query Helper dialog box (refer to Figure 11-2) to create a new query or edit an existing query. The Query Helper dialog box spares you the trouble of entering the information from the keyboard, thus reducing the possibility of making a mistake. The Query Helper dialog box is also the easiest way to insert field names and operators into a query.

ACT! places operators in the Query Helper dialog box. They can also be inserted from the keyboard.

To insert ACT!'s field names and/or operators into a query, highlight the field name or operator that you want to insert and click the Insert button.

Insert as much search criteria as you can into your query by first entering information into the fields of the Query window. After you've entered this information, convert your query to an Advanced Query by selecting Query⇨Convert to Advanced Query. Then you just make changes to the operators. If you need to move, copy, or rearrange the statements or phrases within the query, use the Cut, Copy, and Paste commands. This method spares you the trouble of typing in the search statements and reduces the possibility of entering a statement incorrectly.

To hide the Query Helper dialog box, click the Close button, and the dialog box disappears. To show the Query Helper dialog box, choose Query⇨ Show Query Helper, and it reappears.

Using Operators

Operators are words and symbols that show the relationship between a specific field and its value. In the example `(("City" = "Dallas"*)), "City"` identifies the ACT! field, the equal sign (=) is the operator, and "Dallas" is the value. (Note the quotation marks.) Table 11-1 is a list of operators.

Table 11-1	Operators
Symbol	*Meaning*
&&	And
AND	And
||	Or
OR	Or
=	Equal to
<>	Not equal to
<	Less than
>	Greater than
<=	Less than or equal to
>=	Greater than or equal to
CONTAINS	Contains
<<>>	Blank (The field is empty.)
BLANK	Blank
*	Begins/ends with
..	Range
!	Not
NOT	Not

The following list explains how to use an asterisk (*) to perform a wild card search:

✔ **Starts With:** The field that you are searching contains data that starts with a specific letter, number, word, or part of a word. Type ___* in a Query field, and it becomes ___* in the Advanced Query window. For example, if you wanted to search for all the zip codes in Atlanta, you type **303*** in the Zip Code field.

✔ **Ends With:** The field that you are searching contains data that ends with a specific letter, number, word, or part of a word. Type *___ in a Query field, and it becomes *___ in the Advanced Query window. For example, if you want to search for all your contacts who have contracts that are up for renewal in 2000, you type ***2000** in the Contract Expiration field.

✔ **Contains:** The field that you are searching contains a specified combination of letters and/or numbers. Type ***___*** in a Query field, and it becomes *___* in the Advanced Query window.

For example, say that you've designated a specific ACT! field as your "Products of Interest" field. In this field, you insert the names of the products — Widgets, Thingamajigs, and Whatchamacallits — that your customers have indicated they may be interested in purchasing.

The next time that you have a sale on Widgets, you search your database for everybody whose "Products of Interest" field contains Widgets. To perform this search, you type ***Widgets*** in the "Products of Interest" field, and in a few moments, ACT! creates a group of everybody in your database who has indicated that they may be interested in buying Widgets. Now all you have to do is call them.

To find a field that is empty — that is, one that contains no information — position the cursor in the field that you want to check, press Ctrl+F5 to insert the blank characters `<<>>` in the field. Select Query➪Run Query, and ACT! finds every contact in the active lookup or active group in which this field is empty. If, for example, you're looking up contacts that have an empty Zip Code field, your search string looks like this: (`"ZIP" <<>>`).

To find a field that contains some information — that is, one that's not empty — position the cursor in the field you want to check and place an asterisk (*) in the field. Click OK, and ACT! finds every contact in the active lookup or active group in which this field is not empty. If, for example, you want to look up contacts that have a fax number, place an asterisk (*) in the Fax field, and select Query➪Convert to Advanced Query. Your search string looks like this: (`"Fax Phone" ! <<>>`). The statement reads "User 1 is not empty."

Chapter 12

Grouping Your Contacts

● ●

In This Chapter

▶ Different ways to use ACT! groups

▶ Setting your group preferences

▶ Knowing the features of the Groups window

▶ Adding members to an ACT! group automatically

▶ Viewing group information

▶ Changing the appearance of your Groups window

▶ Performing group lookups

● ●

ACT!'s Groups feature is another reason why ACT! is such a powerful tool. When you have all your contacts in an ACT! database, you may find it useful to group some of them together so that you can quickly bring up a collection of records based on a certain criterion. Groups also make managing sets of contacts easier.

A group can have an unlimited number of members, and a person can be a member of an unlimited number of groups.

You may want to categorize some of your contacts as personal and some as professional so that you can quickly print an address book for one of the two sets of contacts at a time. Or you may want to set up distinct categories for your contacts based on their business or profession so that you can send bulk mailings to certain categories of contacts. You can also create groups of contacts to help you manage your accounts, company contacts, or any other collection of contacts who have something in common.

Different Ways to Use ACT! Groups

ACT!'s Groups feature gives you a lot of power. You can create your own group layouts; associate specific contacts, activities, note/history, and sales/opportunity items to a group; and insert your own group notes.

The following list shows a few examples of how you can use groups to manage information in your ACT! database:

- **Collections of contacts:** Groups are great when you need to view a bunch of diverse contacts at the same time. Your groups can contain the contact records of your customers, friends, vendors, and so on.

- **Project records:** When you're working on projects, use groups to keep track of all the people involved by recording notes, histories, activities, and the like.

- **Account records:** As with projects, you can create groups for all the people related to your accounts. Again, doing so helps you to keep track of notes, history, and activities.

- **Sales opportunities:** Groups are a big help when you need to keep track of sales and business opportunities. By customizing the User fields, you can record revenue forecasts, the salesperson for the account, the closing date, and so on.

- **Company records:** It is often useful to create a group to record information about the companies with which you do business. You can keep track of all the notes, history, and activities that pertain to the company, instead of for each individual contact who is associated with that company.

- **Saved lookups of contacts:** You can use groups to act as saved lookups of contacts that you need to access often. For example, if you're a team leader for a project at work, you probably need to schedule meetings with other team members, send e-mail messages, or schedule calls. By creating a group for the team, you can quickly access all their records.

- **Group your committees and organizations:** If you're on a committee or involved in a charitable organization, you may want to create a specific group for the members of that committee or organization.

- **Manage your projects:** If you're working on a large project or program, you may want to create a group of the specific contacts who are part of the project or program. (A friend of mine who is a journalist has grouped his contacts by subject areas: the telecommunications industry, the auto industry, the computer industry, the media industry, and so on.)

- **Business trips:** For each of your business trips, create a group that has only one record: your own. Then assign all of the calls, meetings, and to-dos that pertain to this trip to the ACT! group. This enables you to see everything that you need to do in preparation for this trip.

- **Business meetings:** Create a group by the name of the subject of your regular business meetings, and include the contact records of the people who attend those meetings. When you schedule a meeting for that group, just pull up a member's contact record, schedule the appointment, and associate the appointment with a group. After the meeting, you can put the meeting's notes in the group notes section. This enables you to maintain a record of who attended each meeting and a record of the results of each meeting.

✔ **Seminar participants:** Create separate groups for each seminar or meeting that you're conducting. As people R.S.V.P., you add them to the group, and if someone cancels, you just remove him or her. From this list, you can send out mailing pieces; create welcome letters, agendas, and name tags; and even provide a complete list of participants to the person who is conducting the seminar or meeting.

✔ **Create separate groups for people to whom you send things:** If you mail or send things to specific groups of people, such as company presidents, human resource people, purchasing agents, engineers, or sales managers, create specific groups for each of them.

✔ **Products or services purchased:** Create a group for each product or service that you sell. When you make a new sale, add the customer to the appropriate group. When you announce a new and improved product or service, you have a complete list of all your customers.

✔ **Mailing pieces and holiday mailing lists:** Create separate groups for things that you mail out to people. You can have separate groups for monthly mailers, weekly e-mail newsletters, holiday party invitations, holiday cards, Thanksgiving cards, or anything else that comes to mind.

With ACT!'s grouping capabilities, you have lots of different ways to improve your productivity.

Setting Your Group Preferences

Two preference settings apply specifically to ACT! groups. To open the Preferences dialog box, choose Edit⇨Preferences from the menu bar and then select the Startup tab.

The Startup tab offers you these group startup selections:

✔ **Default Group Layout:** With the Default Group Layout option, you can choose a group layout to use as the default every time you start ACT!.

✔ **Make New Groups Private:** With the Make New Groups Private option, you can choose whether you want to make new groups public or private.

The Features of the Groups Window

To open the Groups window, where you can create, modify, and delete your groups, choose View⇨Groups from the menu bar or click the Groups button. The Groups window appears, as shown in Figure 12-1.

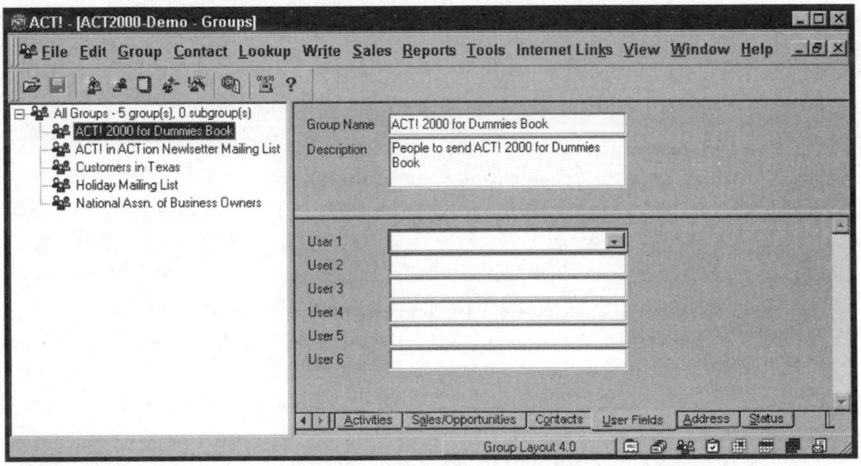

Figure 12-1: The Groups window.

Creating a new group

ACT! offers several ways to create a new group. You can use the following methods:

- ✔ Create a new group without copying any information from the currently displayed group (also referred to as *default values*).
- ✔ Create a new group by copying some information from the currently displayed group into the new group (also referred to as *primary fields*).
- ✔ Create a new group by copying all the information from the currently displayed group into the new group (also referred to as *all fields*).

Using the New Group command

You create a new group by choosing Group⇨New Group from the menu bar, or by selecting New Group from the menu that appears after you click the right mouse button, or by pressing the Insert key within the Groups window. When you use one of these methods for creating a new group, ACT! uses the default values that are selected in the Define Fields dialog box. (I discuss defining ACT! fields in Chapter 6.) To open the Define Fields dialog box, choose Edit⇨Define Fields from the menu bar.

By entering default values in the Default Value field, you can enter group information that you want ACT! to insert in every new group that you create with the New Group command. To enter default information, just highlight the field (City, for example) in the List of Fields field and type the desired default value data (Chicago) in the Default Value field.

If you have repetitive information that you enter for almost every new group (such as city, state, or zip code), you can insert this specific information into the respective Default Value fields, and it will appear in every new group that you create. When the default information isn't applicable to the contact record that you're about to add to your ACT! database, just highlight the text, press Delete, and enter the new information.

Using the Duplicate Group command

When you create a new group by choosing Group⇔Duplicate Group from the menu bar, or by right-clicking and choosing Duplicate Group from the menu that appears, the Duplicate Group dialog box appears. The Duplicate Group dialog box gives you two choices:

The Duplicate Data from Primary Fields option

When you select the Duplicate Data from Primary Fields option to create a new group, ACT! copies the information from the primary fields of the current group — Company, Phone, Address, and so on — into the new group.

You can specify which fields should be primary fields in the Define Fields dialog box. (I discuss defining ACT! fields in Chapter 6.) To open the Define Fields dialog box, choose Edit⇔Define Fields from the menu bar.

When you select the Primary Field attribute in the Define Fields dialog box, you specify that you want ACT! to copy the information from this field into a new group whenever you create a new group by using the group's primary fields.

Use the Duplicate Data from Primary Fields option when you want to create a new group for the same company or organization. This way, you have to type only the new group's name because the other information remains the same.

The Duplicate Data from All Fields option

When you create a new group by selecting the Duplicate Data from All Fields option, ACT! inserts all the information that's entered in each group field into the new group.

Creating a new subgroup

After you've created a group, ACT! enables you to create subgroups within the group. This allows you to streamline the information that you want to manage. With this feature, you can further categorize or refine the members of a group. Here are some examples of how you can use subgroups:

- **Account Management:** Suppose that you have a large account and want to break this down into distinct territories. You can create subgroups for the East, Midwest, Southwest, and West Coast.
- **Project Management:** If you work on several projects for a single customer or client, you can create a group for the customer and then create subgroups for each of the projects that you are working on.
- **Committees:** If you belong to an industry or trade organization and are involved in several committees, you can create a group for the organization and then create subgroups for each of the committees of which you are a member.

Moving groups to subgroups and vice versa

Choose the Group➪Move Group command, and the Move Group dialog box opens. From this dialog box, you can make a group a subgroup of another group, and you can promote a subgroup to a group.

Deleting groups from ACT!

From time to time, you may find that you want to remove a group. (You're removing the group, not the contact records that make up the group.) In ACT!, deleting a group is very easy. You just highlight the group, and then choose Group➪Delete Group from the menu bar, or choose Delete Group from the right-mouse-button menu, or press Ctrl+Delete. The Delete Group dialog box appears, warns you that deleting groups cannot be undone, and asks you whether you want to delete this specific group. Click Yes, and ACT! deletes the group.

Entering group information

You enter group information in the same way that you enter information into an ACT! contact record. (I discuss entering information into ACT! in Chapter 2.)

Defining group fields

You can customize each of the fields in a group. This flexibility enables you to customize each group to fit your individual work habits and work style and makes entering group information much easier.

The Define Fields dialog box is where you set the individual characteristics, or *properties,* for each field in an ACT! group. To edit a field's attributes, choose Edit⇨Define Fields.

The features for defining fields for ACT! contacts and groups is the same (and I discuss this in Chapter 6). You select which record type you want to modify — Contact or Group — from the Record Type drop-down menu.

After you customize your Group fields, you may want to change the layout of the group fields. To change the layout, you use ACT!'s Layout Designer by choosing Tools⇨Design Layouts from the menu bar. (I discuss customizing your contact and group layouts in Chapter 26.)

Adding members to a group

To add a member to an ACT! group, choose Group⇨Group Membership, and select Add/Remove Contacts from the submenu bar or right-click and select Group Membership, Add/Remove Contacts from the submenu that appears. The Add/Remove Contacts dialog box appears, as shown in Figure 12-2.

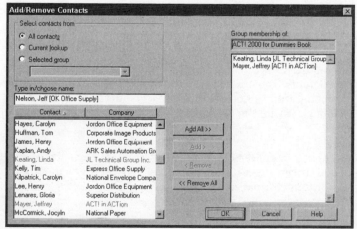

Figure 12-2:
The
Add/Remove
Contacts
dialog box.

You use the Add/Remove Contacts dialog box to add members to a new group or to edit — add or remove — the membership of an existing group.

This section tells you how to use the Add/Remove Contacts dialog box:

- **Selecting contacts for group membership:** You can select contacts to become members of a group from three sources:

  - **All Contacts:** Choose the All Contacts option to make all contacts in the database available for selection.

  - **Current Lookup:** Choose the Current Lookup option to select contacts from the current lookup only.

  - **Selected Group:** Choose the Selected Group option to select contacts from a specific group.

- Adding people to a group: After you select the source of your contacts — All Contacts, Current Lookup, or Selected Group — ACT! displays a list of all the contacts. To add new members to a group, highlight the names of the people that you want to add, and click the Add button. ACT! adds the names to the list of members of the selected group.

  To add all the available contacts to a specific group, click the Add All button, and ACT! adds all the names to the list of members of the selected group.

  You can add a contact to a group by clicking the contact record and dragging it into the group window.

- **Removing people from a group:** To remove people from a group, just select the members that you want to remove, and click the Remove or Remove All buttons.

Adding a contact to a group from the Contact window

From within the Contact window, you can add specific contacts to or remove specific contacts from an ACT! group. You do so by choosing Contact⇨ Group Membership from the menu bar, or from the menu that appears when you right-click within the Group tab. The Group Membership dialog box opens.

From the Group Membership dialog box, you can see a list of all the available groups and the groups of which a person is presently a member.

Adding Members to an ACT! Group Automatically

With ACT!'s Group Membership Rules commands, you can automatically add contacts to a group when they meet certain criteria. This saves you the time, trouble, and effort of manually adding contacts to a group. When you select ACT!'s Run Group Membership Rules command, ACT! searches the database for records that have selected values in certain fields and adds them to their respective groups.

Let me give you an example of how you can use this new ACT! feature. Say that you do lots of business on the East Coast and that you have a group named East Coast Customers. This is how you can use ACT!'s Group Membership Rules to automatically add new customers to this group:

1. **Choose Group⇨Group Membership, and then choose View Group Membership Rules from the submenu.**

   The Group Membership Rules dialog box, shown in Figure 12-3, appears.

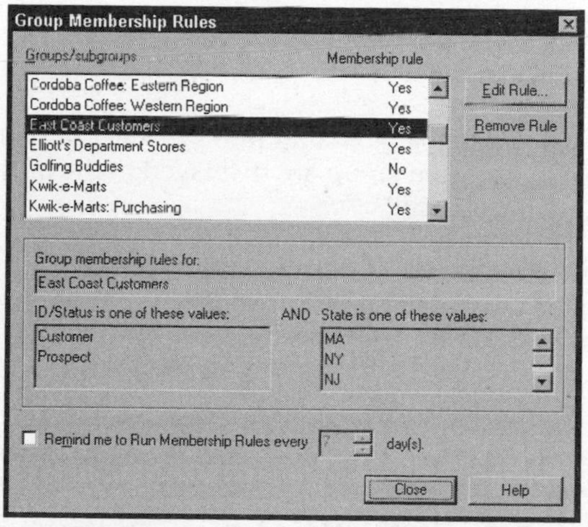

Figure 12-3:
The Group Member-
ship Rules dialog box.

2. **Select a group or subgroup (in this example, it's East Coast Customers), and click the Edit Rules button.**

   The Group Membership Rules Wizard Method dialog box opens. From the Method dialog box, you define your rules based upon Field Values (data that is entered in specific ACT! fields) or a Saved Query, a previously saved ACT! query. (I discuss defining rules by using a saved query in the next section.)

3. **Select Field Values and click the Next button.**

   The Wizard's Rule 1 dialog box opens. From this Wizard dialog box, you define the first membership rule condition that will be used to assign contacts to this group.

4. **Select the field that you want to use from the Contact Field drop-down menu.**

   In this example, we'll use the ID/Status field.

5. **Click the Add Value button, and the Add Value dialog box opens.**

   Here you enter a value, which will be CUSTOMER, and click OK. (You can select your value from the drop-down menu, or press F2 to bring up the Edit List dialog box.) If you would like to enter multiple values, such as CLIENT or PROSPECT, click the Add Value button again.

6. **Click the Next button after you've completed adding your values.**

   The Wizard's Rule 2 dialog box opens. From this Wizard dialog box, you can define a second membership rule condition that will be used to assign contacts to this group. So click the Add Value button, and insert some states like MA, NY, NJ, and PA.

7. **Click Finish.**

   ACT! saves your membership rules and returns you to the Group Membership dialog box.

Select a group within the Group Membership Rules dialog box, and the group membership rules for the selected group are displayed in the bottom half of the Group Membership Rules dialog box.

When you run your group membership rules, ACT! adds every contact record that is a customer and is located in Massachusetts, New York, New Jersey, or Pennsylvania to your East Coast Customers group.

Using a previously saved ACT! query to create group membership rules

In addition to creating group membership rules with the Group Membership Rules Wizard, you can also use an ACT! query that you have created and saved. This enables you to create very sophisticated group membership rules. (Creating ACT! queries from the Query window, which is opened by choosing Lookup⇨By Example, is covered in Chapter 10.) This is how you do it:

1. **Choose Group⇨Group Membership, and then choose View Group Membership Rules from the submenu.**

   The Group Membership Rules dialog box, shown in Figure 12-4, appears.

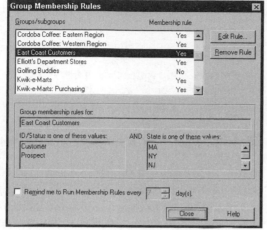

2. **Select a group or subgroup, and click the Edit Rules button.**

   The Group Membership Rules Wizard Method dialog box opens.

3. **Select Saved Query and click the Next button.**

   The Select Query Wizard opens.

4. **Click the Browse button.**

   ACT!'s query folder opens where you select your previously saved query.

5. **Click the Next button, and the Finish Wizard opens.**

6. **Click Finish.**

   You return to the Group Membership Rules dialog box.

Editing or removing membership rules

To edit a group's membership rule, just highlight the group and click the Define Rule button. The Group Membership Rules Wizard Method dialog box opens, and you can make your changes by going through the process that is described in the preceding section.

To remove a group's membership rule, just highlight the group and click the Remove Rule button.

Running group membership rules

You have several ways to run your group membership rules:

✔ **Using the Run Group Membership Rules dialog box:** From the Run Group Membership Rules dialog box (choose Group⇨Group Membership⇨ Run Group Membership Rules), you can search your entire database and apply the membership rules to all of your groups or to selected groups.

✔ **ACT! reminds you to run your rules:** If you want ACT! to remind you to run your rules, select the Remind Me to Run Membership Rules Every ___ Days option in the Group Membership Rules dialog box. (This option is also available in the Run Membership Rules dialog box.)

When you turn on your computer, a message box appears and reminds you that it has been a certain number of days since you last ran your group membership rules. Click Yes if you want to run the group membership rules now.

Using the Define Group Membership Rules command

You can also define and run group membership rules by selecting a group from within the Groups window. This is how you do it:

1. **Select a group from within the Groups window.**

2. **Choose Group⇨Group Membership, and then choose Define Group Membership Rules from the submenu.**

   The Group Membership Rules Wizard Method dialog box opens and allows you to follow the steps that have been described in this section to either create a new set of membership rules or edit an existing set of membership rules.

3. **Click the Finish button when you've completed creating or editing your membership rules.**

   ACT! asks whether you want to run the group membership rules for the selected group. Click Yes, and ACT! searches your database and adds every contact record that matches your selected criteria to the group.

Viewing Group Information

You can view information about each of your groups by clicking the tabs at the bottom of the Groups window.

The Contacts tab

Click the Contacts tab, and ACT! displays a list of all the members of the selected group.

Highlight a contact by clicking the Contact button to the left of the contact's name; then double-click the Contact button, and ACT! brings up the person's contact record in the Contact window and creates a lookup of everybody who is a member of the group. You can also select the Create Lookup command on the menu that appears when you click the right mouse button.

In the Contacts tab, you can change the information that ACT! displays, and you can change the look and feel of your columns. You can do the following things:

- ✔ **Add columns:** Click the right mouse button and choose Add Columns from the menu. The Add Columns dialog box appears. Select the column that you want to add and click OK.

- ✔ **Change the position of columns:** To change the position of a column, click the column's heading and drag it to its new position. (The cursor turns into a hand.)

- ✔ **Remove a column:** To remove a column, click the column's heading, and drag it up and off the Contacts tab.

- ✔ **Change the sort order:** Click a column heading, and ACT! changes the sort order.

- ✔ **Change the width of a column heading:** To change the width of a column heading, place the cursor on the line between two column headings — it turns into a sizing tool — and move it left or right to make the column wider or smaller.

- ✔ **Show grid lines:** To display grid lines between your column headings, select the Show Grid Lines option in the Colors and Fonts tab of the Preferences dialog box.

- ✔ **Print your list of group members:** You can print your list of group members by choosing the Print Group Members command from the menu that appears when you click the right mouse button.

The Activities tab

Click the Activities tab, and you can see a list of all the activities that are scheduled for members of this group.

With the Filtering command, you can choose which activities to display in the Activities tab. You can view your activities by user, activity type, activity priority, and activity dates.

You can also view the activities for the Current group, where you see all the activities associated with the current group; the Contacts in Group, where you see all the activities scheduled with the members of the current group; Subgroups, where you see all the activities associated with the subgroups of the current group; and Contacts in Subgroups, where you see all the activities scheduled with contacts in the current group's subgroups.

Additional options include:

- **The Show Only Timeless option** enables you to display only the activities that you have scheduled for a particular day, but at an unspecified time.
- **The Show Cleared Activities option** enables you to display activities that have been cleared.
- **The Show Outlook Activities option** enables you to display Outlook appointments and tasks. To display Outlook appointments, you must select the Meetings option. To display Outlook tasks, you must select the To-dos option. (You do need to have Microsoft Outlook 98 or Outlook 2000 installed on your computer. I cover ACT!'s integration with Microsoft Outlook in Chapter 13.)

You can view and change your filtering options by clicking the Filter button at the top of the Activities tab. Or you can change your filtering options by opening the Filter Activities dialog box. You do this by choosing View➪ Filter Activities from the menu bar or by choosing Filter Activities from the menu that appears when you right-click in the Activities tab.

The Notes/History tab

Click the Notes/History tab, and you can see a list of all the notes, history items, attachments, and e-mail messages that are part of a group.

The Sales/Opportunities tab

Click the Sales/Opportunities tab, and you can see a list of all sales opportunities that have been associated with this group.

ACT!'s sales opportunities feature is so powerful and important that I've devoted an entire part of my *ACT! 2000 For Windows For Dummies* book to it. So if you want to read about it now, turn to Part V.

Other Groups window tabs

You find these additional tabs in the Groups window:

- ✔ **The User Fields tab:** Here, you can record information in User Fields 1 through 6.
- ✔ **The Address tab:** Here, you record basic group information, such as the group's mailing address.
- ✔ **The Status tab:** Here, you have group status information, such as Create Date, Edit Date, Record Manager, and so on.

Writing group notes

To enter notes of meetings or conversations that pertain to a group, choose Group⇨Insert Group Note from the menu bar, press the F9 key, click the Insert Note button on the Notes/History tab, or choose the Insert Group Note command from the menu that appears after you click the right mouse button. Here are a couple of group note tips:

- ✔ **Entering a note:** After you select the Insert Note command, ACT! automatically inserts the date in the Date column and inserts "Note" in the type column. All you have to do is type the note.
- ✔ **Modifying a note:** To modify the date that a note was entered, click the Date column with your mouse; then click the drop-down menu and pick a new date from the calendar. To modify the note itself, just place your cursor in the Regarding field and make your changes.

Attaching files to a group

You can attach files to both ACT! contact records and to ACT! groups. Attaching a file to a group is very easy. This is what you do:

1. **Select the group to which you want to attach the file.**

2. **Choose Group⇨Attach File from the menu bar.**

   The Attach File dialog box appears. You can also press Ctrl+I or choose the Attach File command from the menu that appears after you right-click.

3. **Select the file you want to attach and click OK.**

   The file is attached to the contact record.

You can attach any file to a contact record by dragging it from the desktop or from Windows Explorer and dropping it onto the Notes/History tab in the Groups window. For example, you may have created a spreadsheet to track orders from a specific contact, or you may have written a custom presentation in your word processor. Just drag and drop the file to the group's Notes/History tab, and that file will always be part of the group's record.

After you've attached a file to a group record, you can open it and/or view its details.

✔ **Opening an attached file:** To open an attached file, double-click the attached file icon with your mouse. ACT! launches the program that created the file and opens the file.

✔ **Viewing the details of a note, history entry, or attachment:** To view the details of a note, history entry, or attachment, highlight the specific item by clicking its icon. Click the Details button, and the Details dialog box appears.

Changing the Appearance of Your Groups Window

You can change the appearance of your Notes/History, Activities, Sales/Opportunities, or Contacts tabs and your group layouts. This section tells you how to do it.

✔ **Changing the appearance of the Notes/History, Activities, Sales/Opportunities, or Contacts tab:** To change the appearance — font, font size, font style, font color, and background color — of the Notes/History, Activities, Sales/Opportunities, or Contacts, open the Preferences dialog box by choosing Edit⇨Preferences from the menu bar. Then click the Colors and Fonts tab. To read more about how to change ACT! window and tab appearances, turn to Chapter 27.

✔ **Changing the appearance of group layouts:** To change group layouts, select a layout from the Group Layout button at the bottom of the Groups window and then choose Tools⇨Design Layouts. With the Layout Designer, you can create your own custom group layouts. I cover the features of the Layout Designer in Chapter 23.

Performing Group Lookups

You perform lookups on ACT! groups in the same way that you perform lookups on ACT! contact records. To perform an ACT! group lookup, select Lookup from the menu bar. You can then choose from the following lookup options:

- ✔ All Groups
- ✔ Other Fields
- ✔ Previous
- ✔ Key Word
- ✔ By Example
- ✔ Internet Directory
- ✔ Contact
- ✔ Synchronized Records

I cover lookups in Chapter 10.

Part IV

Scheduling: A Play in Four Acts

The 5th Wave   By Rich Tennant

"IT'S ANOTHER DEEP SPACE PROBE FROM EARTH, SEEKING CONTACT FROM EXTRATERRESTRIALS. I WISH THEY'D JUST INCLUDE AN E-MAIL ADDRESS."

In this part . . .

This part is really the centerpiece of the book because scheduling is probably the most important and most used ACT! feature. In the next four chapters, I cover all of the ways that you can schedule activities. I walk you through the Schedule Activity dialog box and integrate your ACT! database with Microsoft Outlook 98 or Outlook 2000; I show you how to use SideACT!; and I explain how to get the most out of ACT!'s calendars and Task List.

Chapter 13

Scheduling Your Activities

. . . .

In This Chapter

▶ Setting your default scheduling preferences

▶ Understanding the art of scheduling activities

▶ Scheduling activities with several people

▶ Adding details to your activity

▶ Scheduling recurring activities

▶ Rescheduling activities

▶ Clearing and erasing activities

▶ Viewing your ACT! and Microsoft Outlook activities

. . . .

*A*CT! offers you many ways to schedule an activity — a call, meeting, or to-do. You can schedule activities from the Contact window, the Contact List window, and the Task List window, in addition to the Daily, Weekly, and Monthly calendars. Because we all have different work styles and work habits, ACT! provides many ways to schedule and view our activities. I'm leaving it up to you to find the ones that work best for you.

Here are some ACT! scheduling tips:

✔ Add everybody you know to your ACT! database. In ACT!, an activity is always associated with a specific contact. And before you can schedule an activity for a specific contact, he or she must be in the database. That's why it's important for you to get as many people into your database as quickly as you can.

✔ Don't list your calls, meetings, and to-dos under your own My Record contact record. Instead, you should list your activities under the contact record of the person with whom you're doing the activity.

✔ Use SideACT! to schedule activities that aren't associated with a particular contact. SideACT! is an ACT! scheduling tool that enables you to schedule activities and keep them as a list. I explain SideACT! in Chapter 14.

Setting Your Default Scheduling Preferences

Before I go into the specifics of how to schedule activities, I want to spend a moment explaining ACT!'s scheduling preferences. The scheduling options in ACT!'s preferences are some of the most important components of setting up your ACT! database. These settings allow you to customize how ACT!'s scheduling features will act when you schedule a new call, meeting, or to-do.

To open the Preferences dialog box, choose Edit⇨Preferences either from the menu bar or from the right-mouse-button menu, and then select the Scheduling tab. ACT!'s scheduling preferences are shown in Figure 13-1.

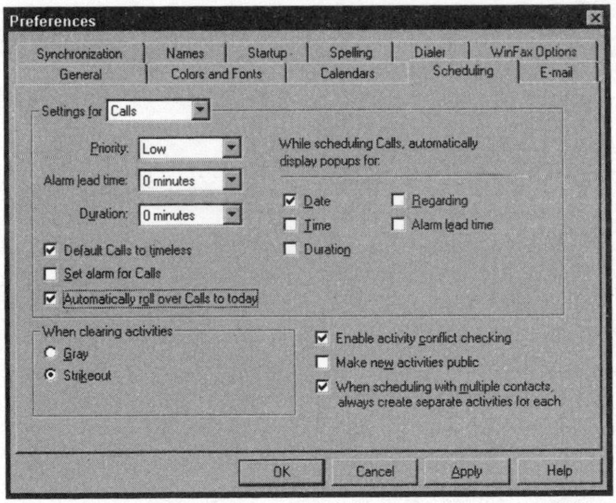

Figure 13-1:
ACT!'s
scheduling
preferences.

Setting your activity defaults

With the activity defaults settings, you can have separate settings for your calls, meetings, and to-dos. In the Settings For drop-down box, choose the type of activity for which you want to set preferences: Calls, Meetings, or To-dos. You have the following scheduling options:

✔ **Priority:** The Priority option enables you to choose a High, Medium, or Low default priority for the selected activity.

✔ **Alarm Lead Time:** The Alarm lead time is the amount of time before the activity that you want the alarm to sound. You can choose a default alarm lead time anywhere from 5 minutes to 30 days.

The Set Alarm option must be selected for the Alarm Lead Time option to work.

✔ **Duration:** You can choose a duration default from 5 minutes to 30 days.

✔ **Default to Timeless:** Use this option if an activity type can be completed at any time during the day and doesn't need to be scheduled for a specific time.

✔ **Set Alarm For [Activity Type]:** When the alarm is turned on, ACT! reminds you of the activity for which you set the alarm — as long as ACT! is running — even if you're using another Windows application.

It's my suggestion that you set alarms only for activities that are really important; otherwise, every activity becomes really important.

Rolling over unfinished activities automatically

If you want ACT! to automatically roll over your unfinished calls, meetings, and/or to-dos, select the Automatically Roll Over to Today option.

Basically, if you didn't get something done yesterday, ACT! moves the unfinished task(s) forward to today.

With this feature, you never forget about or lose track of any of your calls or to-dos. When you start ACT!, a pop-up message box asks if you want to roll over these unfinished tasks to today's calendar.

You click either the Yes button or the No button. If you click Yes, all of your unfinished activities are rolled over to today's date. If you click No, the date of the activities remains unchanged.

Select this option only for your unfinished calls and to-dos. It makes no sense — at least to me — to roll over your previously scheduled meetings.

If you are synchronizing activities with another user or database, you should not use the rollover feature.

When the Task List window opens, click the Filter button at the upper-left edge of the Task List window to change the Task List's view. (You can also choose Edit➪Filter from the menu bar or right-click the Task List to access the Filter command.)

From the Filter Activities dialog box, select the Past option, and all your past activities — activities that have not been completed or activities that have been completed but not cleared — are displayed.

Adding Auto Pop-Ups

When scheduling activities, ACT! makes it easy for you to enter information. It does this by giving you the option to have calendars and lists pop up automatically when you move to the next field in the Schedule Activity dialog box.

If you want any of the calendars or lists that are available in the Date, Time, Duration, Regarding, and/or Alarm Lead Time fields to pop up automatically when you schedule a call, meeting, or to-do, just make a selection from the check boxes in the While Scheduling [Activity Type], Automatically Display Pop-Ups For section.

Dealing with cleared activities

You choose how you want cleared activities to appear on a contact's Activities tab, the Task List, and the calendars. You have these choices:

- **Remove:** This choice deletes the activity.
- **Gray:** This choice colors the activity gray.
- **Strikeout:** This choice displays the activity in the strike-through format.

Making your scheduled activities public or private

When you schedule activities, ACT! gives you the option of making these activities public (which means that everybody on the network or shared database can view the activities) or private (which means that you are the only person who has access to your scheduled activities). If you want your default selection to be public, check the Default Activities to Public check box.

Configuring conflict checking

This feature instructs ACT! to notify you when you are scheduling an activity that conflicts with a previously scheduled activity. When you do this, the Conflict Alert dialog box appears.

If you accept the conflict, ACT! goes ahead and schedules the activity. If you don't want this new activity to conflict with the previously scheduled activity, click the Reschedule button to access the Schedule Activity dialog box, where you can change either the date or the time of the new activity.

To disable conflict checking, select the Disable Activity Conflict Checking option in the Conflict Alert dialog box.

Scheduling multiple activities

When you schedule an activity with more than one person, you can have ACT! schedule a single activity so that it applies to each person. If you modify or clear the activity for one person, the changes are made for each person.

If, on the other hand, you want ACT! to schedule separate activities for each person, select the When Scheduling with Multiple Contacts, Always Create Separate Activities for Each option.

Understanding the Art of Scheduling Activities

In ACT!, you schedule activities from the Schedule Activity dialog box, shown in all its glory in Figure 13-2.

To access the Schedule Activity dialog box, do one of the following:

- ✔ Click the appropriate [Call, Meeting, or To-do] button (see Figure 13-3).
- ✔ Choose Contact⇨Schedule [Call, Meeting, or To-do] from the menu bar, or choose a schedule command after right-clicking with your mouse.
- ✔ Press Ctrl+L for a call, Ctrl+M for a meeting, or Ctrl+T for a to-do, if you prefer to use the keyboard.
- ✔ Drag and drop a contact from the Contact window to the Daily, Weekly, or Monthly calendar or to the Task List.
- ✔ Drag and drop a contact record from the Contact window to the Mini-calendar.

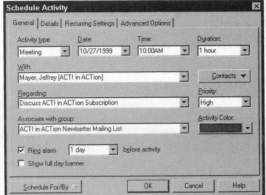

Figure 13-2:
The
Schedule
Activity
dialog box.

Scheduling activities from the Daily, Weekly, and Monthly calendars is discussed in Chapter 15. Scheduling activities from the Task List is discussed in Chapter 16.

You modify a previously scheduled activity by highlighting the activity and selecting the Reschedule Activity command. Rescheduling activities is discussed later in this chapter.

Figure 13-3:
The Call,
Meeting,
and To-do
buttons.

What type of activity would you like to schedule?

When you schedule an activity with the Schedule [Call, Meeting, or To-do] commands, ACT! automatically selects the call, meeting, or to-do as the activity in the Activity Type field. If you want to change an activity, just make a selection from the drop-down menu.

With FindersKeepers! Pro from Practical Sales Tools, you have a practical way to manage multiple databases. FindersKeepers! lets you effectively use more than one database to manage your contacts better. You no longer have to open and close databases to look for your scheduled activities, task lists, and contact information. It's like having two or more databases open at once. FindersKeepers! Pro is available from Practical Sales Tools, Inc.; phone 888-433-2891; Web site: www.pstools.com.

What is the activity's date?

The Date field identifies the date selected for an activity. You select a date from the drop-down calendar.

Right-click the displayed month's name — January, February, or March, for example — and a menu appears that enables you to move to today's date or to select a month that is two months in the past or up to six months in the future.

You can change the date that is displayed in the Date field, forward or backward one day at a time, by pressing the equal (=) key or the hyphen (-) key respectively. To move forward or backward a month, press Shift+Equal (=) or Shift+Hyphen (-) respectively. If the calendar is already displayed, you can change the year by pressing Shift+PageUp or Shift+PageDown.

To insert a date manually, just type in the numbers, and ACT! automatically inserts the slash marks (/) between the day, month, and year. ACT! is very intuitive, so you don't even have to type in the entire date. For example, to insert 9/3/99, just type **93**, and ACT! displays the date as 9/03/99, assuming that you're in the calendar year 1999. (To enter a January date, always enter it as 01; otherwise, ACT! may confuse it with October, November, or December.)

ACT! makes it extremely easy for you to select dates with the calendar. Whenever the calendar appears, the current date is always highlighted. If you're rescheduling an activity, the date of the scheduled activity is highlighted.

What is the activity's time?

You should always select a starting time for your meetings, though you may or may not want to select a time for either a call or a to-do. ACT! makes it easy to schedule times for all of these activities.

When scheduling a new activity, the Drop-Down Time Selector, shown in Figure 13-4, aids you in selecting a time and duration for the activity. To help prevent conflicts, currently scheduled activities are displayed.

To make an activity timeless (that is, not associated with a particular time), select the Timeless bar at the bottom of the Drop-Down Time Selector, or type the letter **N**, and the word NONE appears in the Time field.

Figure 13-4:
The Drop-
Down Time
Selector.

Here are some tips for using the Drop-Down Time Selector:

- The length, or duration, of an activity is automatically displayed in the Duration field.

- ACT! makes it easy for you to insert times into the Time field directly from the keyboard. To insert 9:15 a.m., just type **915a**. Press the Tab key to move to the next field, and ACT! displays 9:15AM in the Time field. Type **115a,** and ACT! displays 11:50AM in the time field; **150p** appears as 1:50PM.

To set the increments of the Drop-Down Time Selector's time slots, go to the Calendars preferences by choosing Edit⇨Preferences from the menu bar and then selecting the Calendars tab. In the Daily Calendar Increments box, you can select time increments, which range from 5 minutes to an hour. You can also select the starting time that you want to appear on your calendar.

What's the activity's duration?

The Duration field displays the length of time that an activity is scheduled to take. When you use the Drop-Down Time Selector to schedule an activity, the duration of that activity is automatically displayed in the Duration field. You can also select the duration of an activity from the Duration drop-down menu.

Duration times can also be entered from the keyboard. For example, when you type **4h**, ACT! displays it as 4 hrs; **35m** becomes 35 min.

What are your priorities?

You can assign each of your tasks a priority of High, Medium, or Low, depending upon the level of importance. On the Activities tab, the Task List, and the Daily, Weekly, and Monthly calendars, all high-priority activities appear in red, medium-priority activities appear in blue, and low-priority activities remain in black.

What is the activity regarding?

As long as you're scheduling an activity, you should make a notation to your-self as to the purpose or nature of the activity. You make this notation in the Regarding field by typing it in from the keyboard, or you can choose a nota-tion from the drop-down menu. (You should never leave the Regarding field empty.)

To add an item to, modify an item in, or remove an item from the Regarding drop-down menu, press F2 or select the Edit List option at the bottom of the drop-down menu. The Edit List dialog box appears. Modifying drop-down menu items is discussed in Chapter 7.

Type the first letter of the entry that you're looking for, and ACT! automati-cally highlights the first item in the list that starts with that letter. Use the arrow keys to highlight the specific item that you're searching for and then click OK, and that item is inserted into the Regarding field.

To enter more than one item from the Edit List dialog box into the Regarding field, open the Edit List dialog box and hold down the Ctrl key while you high-light the individual items with your mouse. Then click OK.

With whom are you scheduling the activity?

ACT! gives you two ways to select or change the person with whom you're scheduling an activity. You can select from the drop-down list in the With field, or you can click the Contact button and select from the Select Contacts dialog box.

In the With field, just click the down arrow with your mouse, or place your cursor in the With field and press Alt+down arrow, and the list of contacts in the database opens. This list is shown in Figure 13-5.

Scroll through the list until you find the name of the person with whom you want to schedule the activity. You can also locate people by typing the letters of the person's last name.

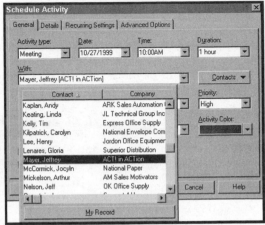

Figure 13-5:
The list of contacts with whom you can schedule an activity.

You can sort your list by last name or by company name by clicking the Contact or Company button located at the top of the window. To quickly locate your "My Record" contact record, click the My Record button.

Adding a new contact

From time to time, you'll find yourself attempting to schedule an activity with a person only to discover that he or she isn't in your ACT! database. To solve that problem, ACT! enables you to add contacts directly from the Schedule Activity dialog box. To add a new contact, just choose Contact⇨New Contact, and the Add Contact box appears, as shown in Figure 13-6.

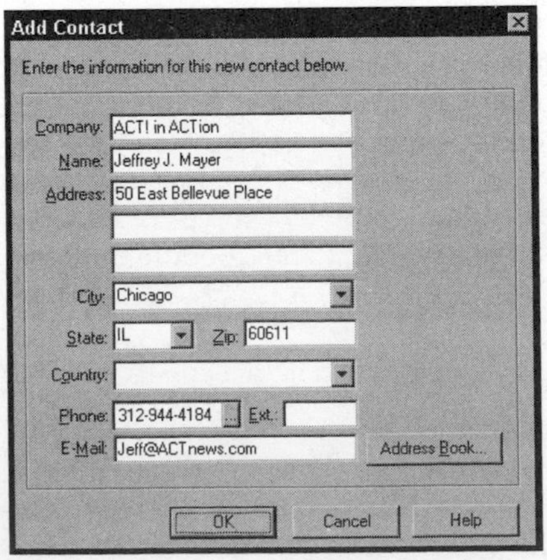

Figure 13-6:
The Add Contact dialog box.

Enter the contact information, click OK, and continue scheduling your activity.

 You can also add a new contact to your ACT! database by clicking the New Contact button from inside the Select Contacts dialog box. (This scheduling feature is discussed later in the chapter.)

Associating an activity with a group

To associate an activity with a group so that the activity can be viewed in the group's Activities tab, choose the group from the drop-down menu in the Associate with Group field.

Setting the Alarm

One of the neat things you can do in ACT! is to use its alarm to remind you to do something. When the alarm goes off at the appointed time, ACT!'s Alarms dialog box appears. To turn on the alarm, click the Ring Alarm check box in the Schedule Activity dialog box.

Here are some ACT! alarm tips:

✔ As long as ACT! is open, you will receive your activity alarms — a beep sounds every 15 seconds — even when you're using another application.

✔ Use the alarm to remind yourself to make telephone calls. When you really want to reach someone, go to the Time field, select the time you want the alarm to go off, and turn on the alarm by clicking it with your mouse.

✔ When someone says, "Call me in 20 minutes," turn on the alarm.

✔ Don't set an alarm for every activity you schedule. Do it only for the important ones.

Setting the alarm's lead time

When you turn on ACT!'s alarm, you need to select the lead time so that ACT! knows how far in advance you want to be reminded of the upcoming activity. In the Schedule Activity dialog box's Ring Alarm [number of minutes or days] Before Activity field, you select how far in advance of an activity you want ACT! to remind you of the activity. To insert a lead time, select it from the drop-down menu or enter it from the keyboard.

When an ACT! alarm goes off, the activity still appears on your to-do list for the day that it's scheduled, not the day you were reminded of the activity.

With HeadsUp! Pro from Practical Sales Tools, you can see alarms from all your ACT! databases without running ACT!. You'll never miss another call, meeting, or to-do. You can get alarms from one database while working in another. And with the dialer, you can call the contact right from the alarm window. With HeadsUp! Pro, you no longer have to open and close databases just to see your scheduled alarms. HeadsUp! Pro is available from Practical Sales Tools, Inc.; phone 888-433-2891; Web site: www.pstools.com.

Using the Alarms dialog box

When an ACT! alarm goes off, the Alarms dialog box appears, as shown in Figure 13-7. ACT! provides you with this information:

- ✓ A list of the alarms that have gone off
- ✓ The type of activity that the alarm or alarms represents
- ✓ The name of the contact, the phone number, and the activity's date and time

Figure 13-7:
The Alarms
dialog box.

When an ACT! alarm appears, you can select individual activities by highlighting them individually. Or you can select all the activities by clicking the Select All button.

You have the following alarm options:

- ✓ **Snooze:** When you click Snooze, the Snooze Alarm dialog box appears. Just like your favorite feature on your bedside alarm clock, ACT!'s snooze enables you to silence the alarm associated with the current contact record for a specific period of time, such as 5 minutes, 10 minutes, and so on. When your time's up, the alarm goes off again.

To move within the Snooze Alarm dialog box, you can use the mouse or the arrow keys, or just press the underlined numbers or letters. For example, press 5 for 5 minutes, 1 for 10 minutes, H for hour, D for day, and so on.

✔ **Clear Alarm:** When you select Clear Alarm, the alarm is turned off, but the activity remains on your schedule.

✔ **Clear Activity:** When you select Clear Activity, the Clear Call, Clear Meeting, or Clear To-do dialog box appears, and you can clear the activity from your schedule. The information is then recorded in that contact's history. ACT! doesn't let you get away with anything. It sure is a vigilant task master. (Clearing activities is covered later in this chapter.)

✔ **Reschedule:** When you choose to reschedule the activity, the Schedule Activity dialog box pops up, enabling you to change the activity's date, time, or anything else about the activity.

If you have more than one contact who has a critical alarm, you can go through the list of alarms, one contact at a time. After you make a decision as to what you want to do with this contact's alarm — by selecting Snooze, Clear Alarm, Clear Activity, or Reschedule — you can then decide what you want to do with the next person's alarming activity.

✔ **Go To:** When you select Go To, you go to that contact's record. If there is more than one critical alarm, select the contacts whose records you want to go to, or click the Select All button before you click the Go To button.

How much lead time would you like?

The Alarm lead time setting is very important when you want to be reminded of a call, meeting, or to-do in advance. (Remember, the alarm must be on.) Here are some examples:

✔ You may want a 15-minute lead time to remind yourself of your next appointment.

✔ Perhaps you have an important project that's due on the 10th of the month and you want to get started on it early, so you set the lead time for 10 days. The alarm goes off when you turn on your computer 10 days prior to the activity's scheduled date and time.

✔ You want to be reminded to make a telephone call in an hour.

✔ If you want to be reminded of someone's birthday or anniversary, schedule that important day into ACT! as either a call or a to-do, and give it a lead time of 7 to 14 days (and set the alarm) so that you can be reminded to purchase a gift or card.

✔ **Select All:** Click the Select All button to highlight all your alarms. You can then select any command and that command will be applied to each of the activities.

Scheduling activities for another ACT! user

If you're using ACT! on a network or sharing your ACT! database with other ACT! users, you can schedule activities for your colleagues. This is how you do it:

1. **Click the Scheduled For/By button at the bottom of the Schedule Activity dialog box.**

   The Scheduled For and the Scheduled By boxes appear.

2. **Select the user for whom you want to schedule the activity from the list of available users in the Schedule For field.**

   The Scheduled By field shows the user scheduling the activity.

Adding banners and colors to your activities

Two additional scheduling features are available from the General tab of the Schedule Activity dialog box. This section explains those features.

✔ **Displaying a banner:** If you've scheduled an activity whose duration is longer than eight hours, click the Show Full Day Banner option, and ACT! displays a full banner in the Month Calendar window.

✔ **Adding color to your activity:** You can select colors for your activities. By default, a high-priority item is red, a medium-priority item is blue, and a low-priority item is black. The activity's color is displayed in the contact's Activities tab and the Task List. When you view activities in the Daily, Weekly, or Monthly calendars, a colored bar appears that shows the duration of the activity. If the activity is scheduled for more than one day, the bar spans the scheduled days when viewed on the Weekly or Monthly calendars.

Making activities public or private

If you're using ACT! within a multi-user database, you have the option of designating your activities as either public or private. You do this from the Advanced Options tab of the Schedule Activity dialog box.

Selecting Public in the Schedule Activity dialog box enables other ACT! database users to view your scheduled activities. By leaving the Public activities box empty, you ensure that all of your activities remain private.

Confirming an activity via e-mail

After you've scheduled an activity with someone, ACT! offers you the option of sending that person an e-mail message confirming the scheduled activity. To send an e-mail message, just click the Advanced tab of the Schedule Activity dialog box and select the Send E-Mail Message to Activity Participants option. You can also send the activity as an attachment in the ACT! activity format, the Internet Standard Format (which makes it compatible with Microsoft Outlook), or in both formats.

When you click OK, the Create E-Mail window opens. The activity's particulars — the type of activity and what it's regarding — are automatically inserted in the e-mail message's subject line; and the Regarding, Date, Time, and Duration information is inserted in the message body.

The activity is also included as an attachment in either the ACT! activity format, the Internet Standard Format, or in both formats. When the recipient receives the e-mail message, it is added to his or her ACT! database or Outlook calendar. Using ACT!'s e-mail features is covered in Chapter 20.

Scheduling an Activity with Several People

ACT!'s Schedule Activity dialog box can also be used to schedule a single activity for several people at once. You do this from within the Select Contacts dialog box (see Figure 13-8), which you open by clicking the Contacts button and then choosing Select Contacts.

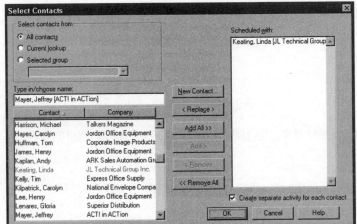

Figure 13-8:
The Select
Contacts
dialog box.

This is how you use the Select Contacts dialog box to schedule a meeting (it can also be a call or to-do) with two or more people:

1. **From the Schedule Activity dialog box, bring up the Select Contacts dialog box.**

2. **Choose the list of contacts from which you want to select your contacts.**

   You can select from All Contacts, the Current Lookup, or a Selected Group, and the list of contacts is displayed in the Select Contacts From box.

3. **Highlight the contacts with which you want to schedule the activity.**

4. **Click the Add button, and their names are added to the list of names in the Scheduled With box.**

5. **Click OK, and you return to the Schedule Activity dialog box.**

You can use your mouse to highlight several contacts. To select contacts whose names are next to each other, highlight the name of the first contact and drag your mouse pointer up or down to highlight the names of the additional contacts. (You can also hold down the Shift key and use the Up and Down arrow keys.) If the names are not next to each other, hold down the Ctrl key and highlight the individual names with your mouse. Then click the Add button.

Another way to schedule an activity for a group of contacts is to perform a lookup so that you can group the contacts together before you schedule the activity. Then when you open the Select Contacts dialog box, choose the Select Contacts from Current Lookup option, click the Select All button, and then click the Add button. (If you're not familiar with ACT!'s lookup features, see Chapter 10.)

Removing a person from an activity

If you want to remove a person from a scheduled activity, just highlight the person's name in the Scheduled With box and click the Remove button.

Creating a separate activity for each contact

When you schedule an activity with more than one person, you can have ACT! schedule a single activity that will be applicable for each person. When the activity is modified or cleared for one person, the changes will be made for everyone.

If, on the other hand, you want ACT! to schedule separate activities for each person, select the Create Separate Activity for Each Contact option.

Adding Details to Your Activity

If you would like to add additional details to your activity, click the Details tab. In the Details tab, you can write very descriptive and lengthy notes (up to 30,000 characters) about the specifics of this activity.

Here are some additional Activity Details features:

- **Print:** To print the notes that you have entered in the Details tab, click the Print button.
- **Copy:** You can copy text from another ACT! record or document and paste it here. This can even include directions to the contact's office.
- **Use Details from Previous Activity:** When you're clearing one activity and scheduling a follow-up activity, you can have ACT! insert the details from the previous activity into this activity by selecting the Use Details from Previous Activity option in the Details tab. (This option is available only when you are scheduling a follow-up activity.)

You have several ways to view an activity's details:

- **The View/Edit Details command:** When you are in the Activities tab or the Contact List window, you select an activity by clicking the Activity button at the left of the tab or window. Then you select the View/Edit Details command that is available from the Contact menu or from the menu that appears when you click the right mouse button.

- **Click the Details button:** If you have added the Details column to the Activities tab or Contact List window, you can view an activity's details by clicking the Details button.

Scheduling a Recurring Activity

The Recurring Activity dialog box appears when you select the Recurring Settings tab in the Schedule Activity dialog box. From the Recurring Activity tab, you can schedule activities that occur on a repeated basis. The frequency of these activities can be specified for as often as daily or as rarely as once per year. The duration can be set for as little as one day or for as far into the future as you wish.

You have the following options:

- **Daily:** With the Daily option, you specify the number of days between occurrences of the activity and the date on which the activity is to end.

- **Weekly:** With the Weekly option, you specify the number of weeks between occurrences of the activity, the day of the week on which the activity is to be repeated, and the date on which the activity is to end.

- **Monthly:** With the Monthly option, you specify the number of months between occurrences of the activity, the day of the week on which the activity is to be repeated, the weeks in which the activity is to be repeated, and the date on which the activity is to end.

- **Custom:** With the Custom option, you specify the time between occurrences of the activity, select the specific day(s) of the month on which the activity is to be repeated, and the date on which the activity is to end.

When you're viewing your activities on the Daily, Weekly, or Monthly calendars, you can schedule additional activities by using the Copy and Paste commands. Just highlight the activity that you want to copy, and press Ctrl+C to copy the activity to the Windows Clipboard. Then place the cursor on the new date and time, and press Ctrl+V to paste the activity into your calendar.

Here are some ways to use ACT!'s recurring activity feature:

✔ If you have a weekly or monthly staff or sales meeting, schedule it as a recurring meeting.

✔ If you have a regularly scheduled conference call, schedule it as a recurring call.

✔ If you're a member of an organization that holds regularly scheduled meetings, schedule these as recurring meetings.

✔ If you want to take your important customers and clients out to lunch on their birthdays, schedule their birthdays as recurring activities.

✔ If you want to take your best customers out for a special day once a year — to play golf, go to a sporting event, attend the opera, enjoy the symphony, or whatever — schedule a recurring activity.

Rescheduling an Activity

Modifying or changing the particulars — the date, time, or what it's regarding, for example — of a scheduled activity is easy.

Highlight the activity on the Activity tab in the Contact window, the Task List, or one of ACT!'s calendars, and you can do any of the following to bring up the Schedule Activity box:

✔ Double-click the activity.

✔ Right-click with your mouse and choose the Reschedule Activity command from the menu that appears.

✔ Choose Contact⇨Reschedule Activity from the menu bar.

✔ Press the Ctrl+Shift+D keys.

When you finish making your changes, click OK.

Clearing and Erasing Activities

In ACT!, you can clear an activity, clear multiple activities, and erase activities.

Clearing a single activity

To clear an activity, you must first highlight the activity on the Activity tab in the Contact window, the Task List, or one of ACT!'s calendars; then choose

Clear Activity from the Contact menu or the right-mouse-button menu, and the Clear Activity dialog box appears. You can also press Ctrl+D. The Clear Activity dialog box for a call is shown in Figure 13-9.

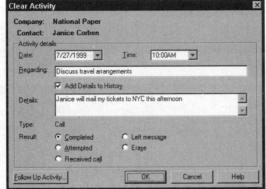

Figure 13-9:
The Clear
Activity
dialog box
for a call.

The Clear Activity dialog box enables you to select any of the appropriate results for clearing a call, meeting, or to-do. When the activity is cleared, it is added as a history item in the contact's Notes/History tab. The following sections discuss the result selections for clearing a call, meeting, or to-do.

You have the following Result choices for clearing a call:

✔ **Completed:** This choice clears a call that you've successfully made (you spoke with the contact) and updates the contact's history to indicate that this call was completed. The date of the call is also recorded in the Last Reach field.

✔ **Attempted:** This choice clears a call that you made, even though you did not get through to the contact. ACT! updates the contact's history to indicate that the call was attempted and also records the date in the Last Attempt field.

✔ **Received Call:** This choice clears a call when the contact called you. ACT! updates the contact's history to indicate that the call was received.

✔ **Left Message:** This choice clears a call for which you have left a message. ACT! records a notation in the contact's history indicating that you left a message.

✔ **Erase:** This choice completely erases a scheduled call. ACT! clears the previously scheduled call and does not record it in the contact's history.

You have the following Result choices for clearing a meeting:

- ✔ **Held:** If the meeting was held, ACT! clears the meeting and makes a notation in the contact's history stating that the meeting was held.
- ✔ **Not Held:** If the meeting was not held, ACT! clears the meeting and makes a notation in the contact's history stating that the meeting did not take place.
- ✔ **Erase:** This choice completely erases a scheduled meeting. ACT! clears the previously scheduled meeting and does not record it.

You have the following Result choices for clearing a to-do:

- ✔ **Done:** ACT! clears the to-do and makes a notation in the contact's history stating that the to-do was completed.
- ✔ **Not Done:** ACT! clears the to-do and makes a notation in the contact's history stating that the to-do was not completed.
- ✔ **Erase:** This choice completely erases a scheduled to-do. ACT! clears the previously scheduled to-do and does not record it.

Always clear your completed activities. When you clear an activity, it's recorded as a history item in the contact's Notes/History tab. This information becomes extremely valuable when you want to gauge or analyze your relationship with a person — especially when you're preparing for an upcoming meeting.

The items in the History file provide you with lots of useful information about the quality of your relationship. It shows you, for example, how many times you attempted to call a person or how many times you left messages for a person that weren't returned. It also shows you how many meetings you scheduled that were not held, and much more.

Adding details to your history

If you would like to add additional details about the activity that you are about to clear, select the Add Details to History option.

Scheduling a follow-up activity

Many times, the clearing of one activity will necessitate the generation of another activity. For example, when someone asks you to send him something, you schedule a to-do item as a reminder that something needs to be sent. After that something has been sent, the to-do item needs to be cleared and a follow-up call needs to be scheduled (because you want to know the response to the item you sent).

Click the Follow Up button, and you bring up the Schedule Activity dialog box where you schedule your follow-up activity.

Clearing multiple activities

To clear multiple activities, highlight the activities in the contact's Activity tab or in the Task List and press the Delete key, or choose Clear Multiple from the menu that appears when you click the right mouse button. ACT! gives you three clearing choices: Completed, Not Completed, and Erase.

Unclearing cleared activities

From time to time, you may find that you want to unclear a cleared activity. Unclearing activities can be done from within the Activities tab, the Task List, or any of the ACT! calendars. First, you must open the Activities filter by clicking the Filter button in the Activities tab or the Task List, or by choosing the Filter Calendar command from the menu that appears when you click the right mouse button.

When the cleared activity appears, click the Completed Activity check mark. A message box opens asking if you want to unclear this activity. Click Yes.

Erasing activities

To erase an activity, highlight the activity in the contact's Activity tab, in the Task List, or in the Daily, Weekly, or Monthly calendar. Then choose the Erase command from the menu that appears when you click the right mouse button, or press Ctrl+X, and ACT! erases the activity.

Viewing Your ACT! and Microsoft Outlook Activities

ACT! 2000 offers complete integration with Microsoft Outlook 98 or Outlook 2000. This new feature enables you to do these things:

- View your ACT! activities in Outlook
- View your Outlook activities in ACT!

You can view your Outlook activities in the Activities tab, the Task List window, or on any of ACT!'s calendars. To view these activities, you must select the Show Outlook Activities option, which is on the Filter dialog box. (You open the Filter dialog box by choosing the Filter command from the right-mouse-button menu.) You must select Meetings to view your Outlook appointments and To-dos to view your Outlook tasks.

After you've selected the Show Outlook Activities option, you have to update your ACT! and/or Outlook calendars. You do this by choosing Tools➪ Outlook Activities and then choosing Update from the submenu. The Update Calendars dialog box opens, which is shown in Figure 13-10.

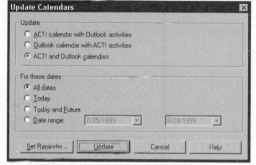

Figure 13-10:
The Update
Calendars
dialog box.

From the Update Calendars dialog box, you have the following ACT!/Outlook calendar options:

- ✔ **Which calendars do you want to update?** You can update your ACT! cal-endar with Outlook activities, update your Outlook calendar with ACT! activities, or update both calendars.

- ✔ **For what dates do you want these activities to appear?** You can select All Dates, Today, Today and Future, or a range of dates.

- ✔ **When do you want to be reminded to update your ACT! and/or Outlook calendars?** You can have ACT! remind you to update your ACT! and/or Outlook calendars when you start ACT! or at specific times during the day.

Click the Update button, and ACT! updates your ACT! and/or Outlook calendars.

Choose Tools➪Outlook Activities and then choose Remove All from the sub-menu. The Remove Activities dialog box opens. Select the Remove All ACT! Activities from Outlook option, or the Remove All Outlook Activities from ACT! option, or both options, and click OK. Your activities are removed from ACT! and/or Outlook.

Chapter 14

Scheduling Activities with SideACT!

● ●

In This Chapter

▶ Finding creative uses for SideACT!

▶ Using SideACT!

▶ Moving or copying SideACT! activities into ACT!

▶ Dragging and dropping

▶ Using SideACT!'s right-mouse-button menu

● ●

S ideACT!, shown in Figure 14-1, is an ACT! utility whose sole purpose is to make it easy for you to maintain lists independently of ACT!. It gives you a place to store lists of things to do or people to call. You open SideACT! by clicking the SideACT! icon or pressing Ctrl+Q.

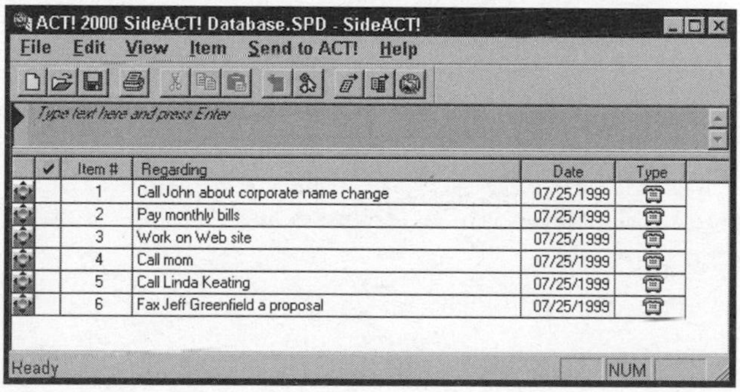

Figure 14-1: SideACT!

SideACT! makes it easy for you to maintain lists because all you have to do is begin typing. When you're finished, just press Enter. After you've entered some items, you have the ability to change the order in which new items appear on the list, change the activity type, and change the create date. You can even rearrange the items on the list by dragging them up or down on the list, or by pressing the Ctrl+Up arrow and Ctrl+Down arrow.

One of the features that makes SideACT! such a powerful utility is that you can move or copy activities — even completed ones — to specific contacts within your ACT! database. You can even copy activities to a contact's record by just dragging the activity from SideACT! and dropping it onto a contact record.

Creative Uses for SideACT!

These are some of the ways people are using SideACT!:

✔ **As a replacement for sticky notes:** How many sticky notes do you write to yourself and then attach to the wall or computer monitor? And how long do they stay there? As an alternative to sticky notes, use SideACT!. When something crosses your mind, just jot down a brief SideACT! note and keep working. When you need a reminder to make a call or you want to jot down someone's number, put it into SideACT!. In no time at all, you'll eliminate sticky notes and reduce your desktop clutter.

And best of all, you can't lose your list. Papers can get lost or buried, but your SideACT! database is inside your computer. When you're finished, you can transfer the task into ACT!.

✔ **As an interruption reducer:** Suppose that you're working on a project and someone comes in or calls and asks you to do something. Instead of writing the task on a piece of paper, jot down the task inside SideACT! and keep working.

✔ **For tracking ideas:** As ideas cross your mind, jot them down inside SideACT!. Think of SideACT! as a replacement for your pen and pad of paper. (You can even create separate SideACT! databases for each of your subjects.)

✔ **To keep track of good news:** We all have a tendency to remember every bad thing that happens during a day. But how do you keep track of the good things? Create a SideACT! database, and name it Great Things That Happened to Me. When you're feeling down, read through it, and it will brighten up your day.

✔ **For goal setting:** If you like to set goals for yourself, you can keep track of them within SideACT!. You can create a separate SideACT! database for your daily, weekly, monthly, and annual goals, and they're always at your fingertips.

✔ **To organize your thoughts and plan your day:** SideACT! offers a way to organize and plan your day/week and keep track of tasks for people who aren't in your ACT! database.

✔ **To keep your personal to-do lists:** If you're in the habit of writing lists of personal things you need to do, such as going to the doctor or renewing your driver's license, keep them in SideACT!.

✔ **To keep a grocery list:** You can use SideACT! to keep your grocery list and all the things you need to get done over the weekend.

✔ **To maintain a daily to-do list:** Use SideACT! as a daily to-do list for items that you don't want to schedule inside ACT!.

✔ **As a travel checklist:** When you're going on a business trip or planning a vacation, use SideACT! to maintain a list of everything you need to do, or take with you, in preparation for your trip.

✔ **For project management:** When you're working on a large project, you can use a SideACT! database to maintain a complete list of all the tasks that are associated with the project, as well as the objectives and the desired outcomes. You can create a new SideACT! database for every project that you're working on. When you've finished a task, just mark it as completed, and you have a complete listing of everything that you did.

✔ **To keep track of Web addresses:** Here are several suggestions of how you can use SideACT! to keep track of Web site addresses:

  • When someone suggests that you visit a Web site, where do you write down the address? On a scrap of paper? As an alternative, write down the address inside SideACT!.

  • Use SideACT! as an alternative to bookmarking your sites — where they usually get lost deep inside the Favorites subdirectories. Enter them into SideACT!, and write a note to yourself as a reminder of why you're interested in the site.

  • When you receive e-mail and someone suggests that you visit a Web site, just copy and paste the address, along with a brief note, into SideACT!. When you want to visit the site, just copy and paste the address into your Web browser. This makes it easy to keep track of sites to visit.

✔ **To keep track of Internet passwords:** Where do you keep all of your Internet passwords? Why not create a SideACT! Internet password database?

✔ **As a voice mail notepad:** When you listen to your voice mail or answering machine, use SideACT! as an alternative to writing your notes on a piece of paper.

✔ **As a thought organizer:** Use SideACT! as a place to keep track of the things you want to do or accomplish during the week. And when you've finished them, print out a copy and put it in a folder so that you have a record of the things you did during the week.

✔ **To assign tasks to your assistant:** Use SideACT! to keep track of all the tasks that you delegate to your assistant. You can even create separate SideACT! databases for everybody you work with.

- ✔ **So that your assistant can also leave tasks for you:** As an alternative to leaving lots of messages of people who called, your assistant can record them inside SideACT! and place the file on your Windows desktop.

- ✔ **To keep track of office supplies:** If you're in charge of keeping track of all the office supplies, use SideACT! to maintain the list. When you're running low on fax paper, just write it down. Then when you go to the office supply store, press Ctrl+P to print a copy of your list, and walk out the door.

- ✔ **To store temporary names and phone numbers:** When you want to keep someone's name and number for a short period of time and don't want to add that person to your ACT! database, enter the information into SideACT!.

Create as many SideACT! databases as you like — to keep track of all of these types of information. SideACT! database are kept in ACT!'s database directory. They have the .SPD extension.

For ease of use, you can attach a SideACT! database to an ACT! contact record. This enables you to create lists of things to do that are associated with a specific person, task, or project. To open your SideACT! database, just double-click the attachment icon.

Working with SideACT!

Now that you've read about some of the creative ways people have been using SideACT!, here's how you can make it work for you:

Opening SideACT!

You can open SideACT! several ways:

- ✔ Click the SideACT! icon on your Windows desktop.

- ✔ Click the SideACT! icon on your Windows menu bar (if SideACT! is in your Startup folder).

- ✔ Click the SideACT! icon on your ACT! toolbar.

- ✔ Choose Tools⇨SideACT! from the ACT! menu bar.

- ✔ Press Ctrl+Q.

Setting your SideACT! preferences

SideACT! gives you several default preference settings. You open the preferences by choosing Edit➪Preferences or pressing Ctrl+E. You have the following choices:

- ✔ **Which activity do you want as your default?** With this selection, you make your default setting for new SideACT! activities, calls, meetings, or to-dos.

- ✔ **What happens to completed items?** With this setting, you choose whether SideACT! moves a completed item to the bottom of the list or leaves it in the current position.

- ✔ **Where are new activities placed?** This setting determines whether SideACT! places new activities at the top or the bottom of the list.

- ✔ **Where do these activities go when they're sent to ACT!?** SideACT! either automatically sends each activity to your My Record contact record or prompts you to select a contact.

- ✔ **Would you like SideACT! to display a confirmation box?** Select the Display Confirmation Dialog before Transferring Activities to ACT! option if you want to be reminded before you transfer the activity.

- ✔ **Add SideACT! to Windows Taskbar?** Select this option if you want the SideACT! icon automatically added to the Windows taskbar.

Performing various functions in SideACT!

Here's how to do lots of basic things in SideACT!:

- ✔ **Entering activities:** To enter an activity, just begin typing the activity's specifics and press the Enter key. You can enter up to 256 characters. When you transfer the SideACT! activity to ACT!, the Activity Regarding field will accept only the first 70 characters. If you enter more than 70 characters, your SideACT! activity will appear in its entirety in the Details field.

- ✔ **Modifying a single activity:** To modify an activity, click any of the activity's fields — Item #, Regarding, Date — and begin typing. To change a call, meeting, or to-do to a different type of activity, click the Type field and select a new activity type.

- ✔ **Changing the activity type for several activities:** To change the activity type for more than one activity, highlight the activities (by holding down the Shift or Ctrl key and clicking the activities with your mouse) and then choose Item➪Set Item Type from the menu bar.

✔ **Clearing an activity:** To clear a SideACT! activity, click the Cleared Activity column. The Cleared Activity column is the one with the check mark in it. You can also mark an item as completed by highlighting the item and choosing Item⇨Mark as Completed or by pressing Ctrl+M.

✔ **Unclearing activities:** To unclear a cleared item, just click the Cleared Activity column. You can also unclear a cleared item by highlighting the item and choosing the Item⇨Unmark Item command, or by pressing Ctrl+Shift+M.

✔ **Deleting activities:** To delete an activity, or several activities, highlight the activity and choose Edit⇨Delete Selected, or press the Delete key.

✔ **Changing an activity's position:** To move an activity higher or lower on the list, just highlight the item and choose Item⇨Move Item Up or Item⇨Move Item Down. You can also press Ctrl+Up arrow or Ctrl+Down arrow.

✔ **Saving a SideACT! database:** Choose File⇨Save to save your SideACT! database.

You can have more than one SideACT! database. This enables you to create different SideACT! lists. (SideACT! databases have the .SPD extension.) Place the database on your Windows desktop, and then just double-click it to launch SideACT! and open the selected SideACT! database.

✔ **Printing your list of SideACT! activities:** To print your list, choose File⇨Print or press Ctrl+P.

Moving or Copying SideACT! Activities into ACT!

SideACT!'s real power comes from its ability to move and copy items from SideACT! into ACT!. This is how you move a SideACT! activity to ACT!:

1. **Highlight the activity (or activities).**

2. **Choose Send to ACT!⇨Move to Database.**

   (To copy an activity from SideACT! to ACT!, choose the Send to ACT!⇨Copy to Database command.) The Associate with Contact dialog box appears, as shown in Figure 14-2.

3. **Select the contact to which you want to assign this activity.**

Type the first letter of the contact's last name or of the company's name, and ACT! locates the contact. To change the lookup from Contact to Company, click the Contact or Company bar.

4. Click OK.

ACT! moves the activity from SideACT! to the selected contact's activity tab within ACT!.

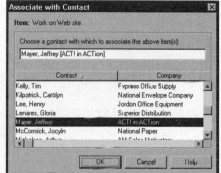

Figure 14-2:
The
Associate
with Contact
dialog box.

Here are some SideACT! moving and copying tips:

- After the activity moves into ACT!, you may want to modify the activity's particulars, such as duration, priority, and so on.
- Cleared activities move to the selected contact's Notes/History tab.
- Choose the Send To ACT!⇨Select ACT! Database command if you want to send the SideACT! activity to a different database than the one that is presently selected.

Dragging and Dropping

You can also copy an activity from SideACT! to ACT! by using the drag-and-drop technique. Just highlight the SideACT! activity and drag it over to ACT!. ACT! adds the activity to the contact's Activity tab or places a cleared activity in the contact's Notes/History tab.

SideACT! activities can be dragged and dropped onto any of the following ACT! windows:

- **The Contact window:** Select the ACT! contact with which you want to associate the activity, and drop the activity on the Contact window or any of the tabs.
- **The Contact List window:** Drop the SideACT! activity on the ACT! contact to whom you want to assign the activity from the list displayed in the Contact List window.

- **The Task List window:** Drop the SideACT! activity on ACT!'s Task List window, and the Associate with Contact dialog box appears. From this box, you select the contact to which you want to assign the activity.

- **The Calendar window:** Drop the SideACT! activity on ACT!'s Daily, Weekly, or Monthly calendars, and the Associate with Contact dialog box appears. From this box, you select the contact to which the activity should be assigned.

All activities are assigned as timeless activities.

Using SideACT!'s Right-Mouse-Button Menu

Many SideACT! commands can be selected by highlighting an activity, clicking the right-mouse-button, and choosing from the menu that appears. From this menu, you can do any of the following:

- Cut, copy, or paste an activity within SideACT!.

- Delete the selected activity.

- Mark an item as completed.

- Unmark a completed item.

- Send the activity to ACT!.

- Change the activity type.

Chapter 15

Using ACT!'s Calendars

In This Chapter
▶ Setting your calendar preferences
▶ Viewing your activities a day at a time
▶ Using ACT!'s Mini-calendar
▶ Using the Weekly and Monthly calendars
▶ Customizing the look and feel of your calendars
▶ Printing your calendars

*I*n ACT!, you can view your activities in a daily, weekly, or monthly calendar by just clicking an icon. In this chapter, I explain how to use each of these views.

Your activities are displayed in color when you view them in any of ACT!'s calendars, in the Activities tab, or in the Task List. High-priority activities are displayed in red, medium-priority activities in blue, and low-priority activities in black.

Setting Your Calendar Preferences

ACT!'s specific preference settings enable you to customize the look and feel of your ACT! calendars. To open the ACT! calendar preference settings, choose Edit⇨Preferences from the menu bar and select the Calendars tab, or choose Preferences from the right-mouse-button menu.

The Calendar preferences are shown in Figure 15-1.

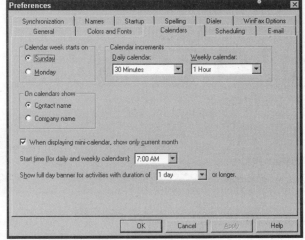

Figure 15-1:
ACT!'s
Calendar
prefer-
ences.

The Calendars tab offers these options:

- **Sunday or Monday:** You can choose to have your Mini-, Weekly, and Monthly calendars start on either Sunday or Monday.

- **Calendar Increments:** You can choose separate time increments for your Daily and Weekly calendars of 5, 10, 15, 30, 45, or 60 minutes.

- **Contact or Company Name:** You can choose to display either the contact name or the company name.

- **Show Full Day Banner:** If you want ACT! to show a full-day banner for activities that are displayed on the Monthly calendar, select the Show Full Day Banner for Activities with Duration Of option.

- **Mini-calendar display:** The Mini-calendar, which is discussed later in this chapter, normally displays the current month, the past month, and the next month. If you want it to display only the current month, choose the When Displaying Mini-calendar, Show Only Current Month option.

Viewing Your Activities a Day at a Time

To activate the Daily calendar, click the Daily Calendar icon with your mouse, choose View⇨Calendar⇨Daily Calendar from the menu bar, or press Shift+F5. The Daily calendar appears, as shown in Figure 15-2.

The commands for using the Daily, Weekly, and Monthly calendars are the same, so I'll explain them all here.

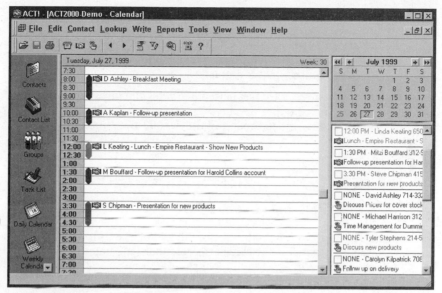

Figure 15-2:
The Daily
calendar.

When you activate the Daily calendar, the activities you've scheduled for today are displayed. You use the same toolbar icons to schedule an activity and to display the type of activity you've scheduled. The contact's name, the regarding information, and the activity icon are displayed. A colored bar, or band, shows how long each activity is scheduled to last.

Any activity that you schedule with yourself does not show your name; instead, it shows what the activity is regarding.

Scrolling through the calendar

Depending upon the size of your monitor and the time increment you've chosen, the Daily calendar may display only a portion of the work day. If you need to view times of the day that are not displayed, you can use the up-arrow key or the Scroll Up button to view early morning hours and use the down-arrow key or the Scroll Down button to view late-afternoon or evening hours.

In the Daily calendar, the activities that you assigned to a specific time of day are displayed. All of your activities — those to which you have assigned a specific time of day, and the ones that have no specific time associated with them (your timeless activities) — appear in the activity box at the right of the Daily calendar window.

Here are some Daily calendar tips:

✔ If you have activities scheduled prior to the earliest time shown on the calendar, the calendar displays an up arrow in the upper-right corner of the calendar, just to the left of the Scroll Up button.

✔ If you have activities scheduled after the latest time shown on the calendar, the calendar displays a down arrow in the lower-right corner of the calendar, just to the left of the Scroll Down button.

Viewing activities scheduled for a specific date

To see what your scheduled activities look like on any specific date, just select that date on the Navigator calendar (the calendar displayed in the upper-right corner of the Daily calendar).

Right-click a date, and ACT! opens a window that displays a list of all your scheduled activities for the selected date. This Activities List is shown in Figure 15-3.

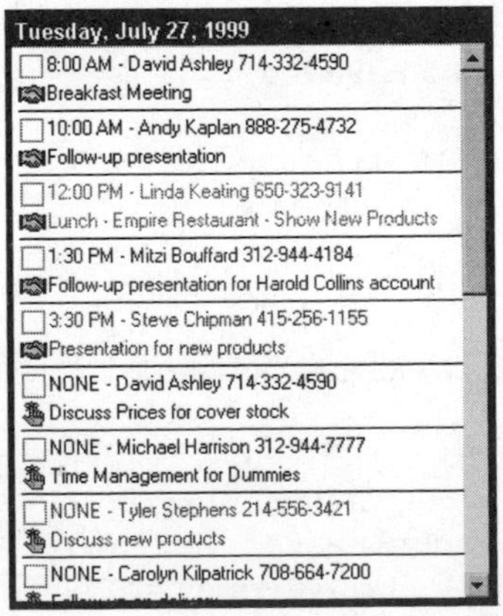

Figure 15-3:
The
Activities
List.

Tuesday, July 27, 1999
- 8:00 AM - David Ashley 714-332-4590 — Breakfast Meeting
- 10:00 AM - Andy Kaplan 888-275-4732 — Follow-up presentation
- 12:00 PM - Linda Keating 650-323-9141 — Lunch - Empire Restaurant - Show New Products
- 1:30 PM - Mitzi Bouffard 312-944-4184 — Follow-up presentation for Harold Collins account
- 3:30 PM - Steve Chipman 415-256-1155 — Presentation for new products
- NONE - David Ashley 714-332-4590 — Discuss Prices for cover stock
- NONE - Michael Harrison 312-944-7777 — Time Management for Dummies
- NONE - Tyler Stephens 214-556-3421 — Discuss new products
- NONE - Carolyn Kilpatrick 708-664-7200 — Follow-up on delivery

You can move within the Daily calendar by using the keyboard: To move one day at a time, use the left- and right-arrow keys. To move one week at a time, use the up- and down-arrow keys. To move one month at a time, use the Page Up and Page Down keys.

Changing your views

If you want to change your view from the Daily calendar to either the Weekly or Monthly calendar, you can do it with the click of your mouse:

- ✔ To change to the Weekly calendar, click the Weekly Calendar icon or press F3.

- ✔ To change to the Monthly calendar, click the Monthly Calendar icon or press F5.

- ✔ To change to the Daily calendar, click the Daily Calendar icon or press Shift+F5.

Printing your calendar, and taking it with you

To print your calendar, choose File⇨Print from the menu bar or press Ctrl+P, and the Print dialog box appears. From this dialog box, you can print your calendar and address book in any one of several popular daily-planning book formats, including full page, half page, large pocket, or small pocket calendar/address book. (All the details of printing your calendars are discussed later in this chapter.)

Viewing activities

You can choose which activities you want to view by using the Filter Calendar dialog box. Choose View⇨Filter Calendar from the menu bar, or right-click in the Daily calendar and choose the Filter Calendar command from the menu that appears.

The Filter Calendar dialog box offers the following options:

- ✔ **Users:** In the Users box, you can view the activities of selected users or all users.

- ✔ **Activity Type:** In the Activity Type box, you can choose to filter out calls, meetings, or to-dos.

- ✔ **Activity Priority:** In the Activity Priority box, you can choose to filter out all activities with a high, medium, or low priority.

- ✔ **Show Cleared Activities:** If you want your cleared activities to appear on your calendar, select the Show Cleared Activities option.

✔ **Show Outlook Activities:** The Show Outlook Activities option enables you to display Outlook appointments and tasks. To display Outlook appointments, you must select the Meetings option. To display Outlook tasks, you must select the To-dos option. (You do, of course, need to have Microsoft Outlook 98/2000 installed on your computer. I cover ACT!'s integration with Microsoft Outlook in Chapter 13.)

Scheduling a new activity

You have several ways to schedule a new activity from the Daily calendar. Any of the following actions opens the Schedule Activity dialog box:

✔ Click the time on the left edge of the Daily calendar.

✔ Highlight a time on the Daily calendar and choose Contact⇨Schedule [Call, Meeting, or To-do] from the menu bar. You can also access the Schedule commands from the right-mouse-button menu, or press Ctrl+L, Ctrl+M, or Ctrl+T, to schedule a call, meeting, or to-do, respectively.

✔ Click an activity's starting time and drag the mouse pointer down to the ending time.

✔ Double-click the activity's starting time.

✔ Click a blank portion of the Contact window and drag the contact from the Contact window onto the calendar.

Scheduling activities with the Schedule Activity dialog box is covered in Chapter 13.

Modifying a previously scheduled activity

To modify a previously scheduled activity, highlight the activity with your mouse and double-click the activity. You can also select Contact⇨Reschedule Activity, choose the Reschedule Activity command from the right-mouse-button menu, or press Ctrl+Shift+D. The Schedule Activity dialog box appears, enabling you to modify your previously scheduled activity.

To change the date of a timeless activity, highlight the activity, drag it onto the Navigator calendar, and drop it on the desired day.

Dragging and dropping

If you're really into using your mouse, you can even change the date and time of an activity by using the drag-and-drop technique. To do so, highlight the activity, drag it to a new time, and then release the mouse button. Be sure to hold down the left mouse button as you drag the text. Here are some more ACT! mousing tips:

- To change a timeless activity to a timed activity, highlight the activity, drag it to the desired time, and release the mouse button.

- To change the date of a specific activity, highlight the activity and, while holding the left mouse button, move the pointer to the right of the border of the calendar. This action moves the calendar forward one day at a time. Move the mouse pointer to the left of the calendar's border to go backward one day at a time. To move forward or backward more than one day at a time, keep the mouse pointer outside the border of the calendar; the date changes every second.

- When you view your activities on the Daily, Weekly, or Monthly calendar, you can schedule recurring activities by using the Copy and Paste commands. Highlight the activity that you want to copy, and press Ctrl+C to copy the activity to the Windows Clipboard. Then place the cursor on the new date and time, and press Ctrl+V to paste the activity into your calendar.

- Use the Cut and Paste commands to move an activity from one date to another. Highlight the activity that you want to move, and press Ctrl+X to remove it from your calendar and copy the activity to the Windows Clipboard. Place the cursor on the new date and time, and press Ctrl+V to paste the activity into your calendar. Presto! Your activity has been rescheduled.

You can change the duration of an activity by highlighting the activity and dragging the colored activity bar to an ending time.

Clearing, unclearing, and erasing activities

After you've completed an activity, you can clear or erase it from the Daily calendar. You can also unclear a cleared activity. Here's how you do it:

✔ **Clearing an activity:** After you complete an activity, you can clear it directly from the Daily calendar. To do so, highlight the activity that you want to clear and choose Contact⇨Clear Activity from the menu bar; or choose the Clear Activity command from the right-mouse-button menu; or press Ctrl+D. The Clear Activity dialog box appears.

You can also clear an activity by clicking the box just to the left of the activity's time in the Activity List field. The cleared activity will then have a check in the box.

When you clear an activity, ACT! makes a record of this activity in the contact's History file.

✔ **Unclearing a cleared activity:** To unclear a cleared activity, click the cleared activity check box described in the preceding bullet. A message box appears stating, "The activity is currently cleared. Do you want to unclear it?" To unclear the activity, click Yes. (To view your cleared activities, open the Filter dialog box by choosing View⇨Filter Calendar and selecting the Show Cleared Activities option.)

✔ **Erasing an activity:** To erase an activity, highlight the activity and select the Erase Activity command from the right-mouse-button menu or press Ctrl+X.

When you erase an activity, ACT! does not make a record of this activity in the contact's History file.

Creating lookups and going to contacts

To create a lookup of your scheduled activities, highlight any portion of the calendar, right-click, and choose Create Lookup from the menu that appears. ACT! brings up the Contact window with all the contacts that have an activity scheduled for that day.

From the Weekly calendar, you can create a group of everyone with whom you have an activity scheduled for that week. From the Monthly calendar, you can create a group of everyone with whom you have an activity scheduled for that month.

To view a complete list of the contacts that are included in this group, choose View⇨Contact List from the menu bar or press F8.

If you want to go to a specific contact's record, highlight the contact, right-click, and choose Go to Contact from the menu that appears. ACT! brings up the Contact window, and the highlighted contact's record is displayed.

Using ACT!'s Mini-Calendar

ACT!'s Mini-calendar is a small calendar that you can use to schedule new activities or to modify previously scheduled activities. To bring up the Mini-calendar, shown in Figure 15-4, choose View⇨Mini-Calendar from the menu bar or press the F4 key.

Figure 15-4:
The Mini-
calendar.

In ACT!'s Calendar preferences, you can select whether you want to view a one- or three-month Mini-calendar. (To open the Calendar preferences, choose Edit⇨Preferences and then click the Calendars tab.)

Here are some Mini-calendar tips:

- ✔ **Opening the Daily calendar:** To view your scheduled activities for a specific date, double-click the date. The Daily calendar appears.

- ✔ **Viewing your scheduled activities:** To view a list of your scheduled activities for a specific date, right-click the date, and the Activities List appears (refer to Figure 15-3). From the Activities List, you can modify or clear an activity.

Scheduling a new activity in the Mini-calendar

To schedule a new activity from the Contact window with the Mini-calendar, follow these steps:

1. **Locate the contact with whom you want to schedule the activity.**

2. **Click the contact layout with your mouse.**

   Don't click a field.

3. **Drag the mouse pointer onto the Mini-calendar, and drop it onto the desired date.**

   The Schedule Activity dialog box appears so that you can schedule your activity.

Scheduling activities for more than one contact

With the Mini-calendar, you can schedule activities for one or more contacts. This is how you do it:

1. **Open the Contact List window.**

2. **Highlight the contacts.**

3. **Drag the mouse pointer onto the desired date on the Mini-calendar.**

   The Schedule Activity dialog box appears and lets you enter the activity's particulars.

Modifying an activity for more than one contact

With the Mini-calendar, you can also change the date of several activities at once. This is how you do it:

1. **Open the Task List window.**

2. **Highlight several activities.**

3. **Drag the mouse pointer onto the new date on the Mini-calendar.**

   ACT! changes the date for all the activities.

You can also change an activity's date from the Activities tab. Just select the activity and drag it onto the Mini-calendar.

Using the Weekly and Monthly Calendars

When you select the Weekly calendar, all your scheduled activities for the current week appear. The Weekly calendar displays either the contact's first initial and last name or the company name (depending upon whether you selected the Show Contact Name or Show Company Name option in ACT!'s calendar preference settings), and the activity's regarding information.

The Monthly calendar lists either the contact's first initial and last name or the company name (depending upon whether you selected the Show Contact Name or Show Company Name option in ACT!'s calendar preference settings) for each activity that you've scheduled. The particulars for the selected day's activities are displayed in the Activities List.

The commands and features available in the Weekly and Monthly calendar (including scheduling) are also available in the Daily calendar and are explained earlier in this chapter.

When you have an activity that spans more than one day, its banner extends over those days in the Monthly calendar.

Customizing the Look and Feel of Your Calendars

To change the appearance — font, font size, font style, font color, and background color — of the Daily, Weekly, or Monthly calendars, open the Preferences dialog box (choose Edit⇨Preferences) and select the Colors and Fonts tab. Changing colors and fonts works the same way for every ACT! window and tab. All the information you need is in Chapter 27.

Printing Your Calendar

If you absolutely love the leather-bound daily planning book that you've been using for years, ACT!'s calendar-printing options give you the ability to print your schedule on pages that will fit almost any daily planner. Now you can take your schedule with you whenever you leave the office.

You can access the Print dialog box from a number of different places within ACT!:

✔ Click the Print button in the Daily, Weekly, or Monthly calendars or in the Task List.

✔ Choose File⇨Print.

✔ Press the Ctrl+P key combination.

From the Print dialog box, you can also print your phone number and address book on pages that fit in your favorite daily planner. I discuss this feature in Chapter 20. And you can print your ACT! reports, envelopes, and mailing labels from the Print dialog box, too. I discuss ACT! reports in Chapter 24.

These are the printing options that are available from within the Print dialog box:

- ✔ **Selecting the printout type:** Before you can print your calendar, you need to choose the type of calendar that you want to print: Daily, Weekly, or Monthly. To choose the type of calendar, select Printout Type with your mouse pointer, or use the up- and down-arrow keys to highlight the desired calendar format from within the Printout Type field. (You can also use the Printout Type drop-down menu. Just place your cursor in the Printout Type field and press the Alt+down-arrow key combination.)

- ✔ **Selecting the size and type of your paper:** After you select the type of calendar you want, you must select a paper size on which to print your calendar. Just scroll through the list in the Printout Type box to select a form.

  If you would like to see a preview of your selected printout, select the Show Preview option.

- ✔ **Choosing your calendar options:** After you've selected your calendar format and paper size, you can select the information that you want to have printed on your calendar. To select the information, click the Options button. The Calendar Options dialog box appears.

  From the Calendar Options dialog box, you can select whether you want to print the Company Name, Saturday and Sunday, a column for priorities, and a five-week view on your calendar. You can also select the starting hour when you print the Daily calendar.

- ✔ **Filtering your calendar:** Click the Calendar Options dialog box's Filter button, and the Filter Calendar Printout box appears. From this box, you can decide which user(s) you want to include activities from, which type of activities to include in your printed calendar, and more.

- ✔ **Getting ink on paper:** After you make your selections in the Calendar Options dialog box, click OK to return to the Print dialog box. When you're ready to print your calendar, click the OK button, and the Windows Print dialog box appears.

Click OK to start the printing process. (This may sound confusing because the dialog box in which you make your calendar printing selections and the dialog box in which you make your printing selections are both called Print.)

The first few times you print out your calendar, print it on regular paper (not your expensive calendar paper) so that you can determine the right format and layout for your calendar.

Chapter 16

Using the Task List

1 find the ACT! Task List to be one of the most important productivity improving features in the entire program. I refer to it throughout the day because it provides me with a visual list of all my unfinished activities. In two of my best-selling books, *Time Management For Dummies* and *Success is a Journey* (published by the fine folks at IDG Books Worldwide, Inc., and McGraw-Hill, respectively), I go into great detail about how you can use a list of things to-do — I call it a Master List — to master your day.

But instead of keeping your Master List on a pad of paper or inside a daily planning book, keep your activities inside ACT! and use the Task List to master your day.

With ACT!'s Task List, you can manage all the items that were formerly on your things-to-do list — your calls, meetings, and to-dos — from inside your computer. This eliminates the need to write and rewrite information on a pad of paper. And then by pressing a button (F7) or clicking an icon, you can bring up your electronic Master List, the ACT! Task List.

To view the Task List, shown in Figure 16-1, do any of the following: Choose View➪Task List, or click the Task List icon with your mouse, or press F7.

Items on the Task List are displayed in color. High-priority activities are displayed in red, medium-priority activities in blue, and low-priority items in black.

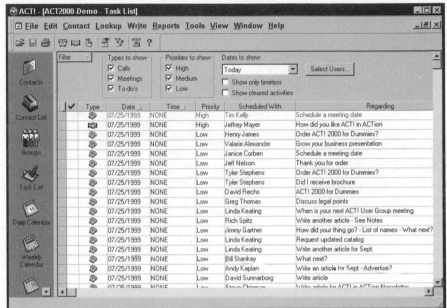

Figure 16-1:
The ACT!
Task List.

Filtering Your Activities

With the Filter command, you can select which activities you want to view, the dates of the activities you want to view, which types of activities you want to view, and which level of priority you want to view.

To open the Filter Activities dialog box, choose View➪Filter Task List from the menu bar, or right-click in the Task List and select the Filter Activities command from the menu that appears.

A Filter button is located at the top of the Task List window. Click the button, and you can make the same selections that are described in the Filter Activities dialog box.

The Filter Activities dialog box offers these options:

✔ **Users:** In the Users area, you can choose to view the activities of selected users or all users.

✔ **Activity Dates:** From within the Task List, you can view your scheduled activities for many different periods of time:

- **Today:** To display a list of today's activities, select Today.

- **All Dates:** To display a list of all your activities — past, present, and future — select All.

The difference between the Task List and the Activities tab

The features of the Task List and Activities tab (which are discussed in Chapter 5) are identical. However, you find one difference between these two ACT! features:

✔ In the Activities tab, you view the calls, meetings, and to-dos that you've scheduled with a single person.

✔ In the Task List, you're looking at all the calls, meetings, and to-dos that you've scheduled with everybody in your database for the selected date.

In this chapter, I explain how to use the Task List, but keep in mind that the functions of the Task List and the Activities tab are identical.

- **Past Dates:** To display a list of your past activities — you know, the things you should have done but didn't get around to — select Past.

- **Today and Future:** To display a list of today's activities and your future activities, select the Today and Future option.

- **Date Range:** If you want to view a list of your activities for a specific date or range of dates, select Date Range, and a drop-down calendar appears. From the calendar, you can view a range of dates by highlighting the dates with your mouse.

✔ **Activity Type:** In the Activity Type area, you can choose which activities you want to view or not view by checking the boxes for calls, meetings, or to-dos.

✔ **Activity Priority:** If you want to see your activities based upon a specific level of priority (high, medium, or low), select the desired priority level in the Activity Priority area. To list all activities, regardless of priority, select all three boxes.

✔ **Show Only Timeless:** If you want to view only your timeless activities — the activities to which you haven't assigned a time to — select the Show Only Timeless option.

✔ **Show Cleared Activities:** If you want to view your cleared activities, select the Show Cleared Activities option.

✔ **Show Outlook Activities:** The Show Outlook Activities option enables you to display Outlook appointments and tasks. To display Outlook appointments, you must select the Meetings option. To display Outlook tasks, you must select the To-do option. (You do, of course, need to have Microsoft Outlook 98/2000 installed on your computer. I cover ACT!'s integration with Microsoft Outlook in Chapter 13.)

Scheduling, Clearing, and Modifying Your Activities

From the Task List, you can schedule new activities, clear completed activities, and modify previously scheduled activities.

Scheduling a new activity

To bring up the Schedule Activity dialog box, do any of the following from the Task List:

- Choose Contact⇨Schedule [Call, Meeting, or To-do] from the menu bar.
- Choose Schedule [Call, Meeting, or To-do] from the right-mouse-button menu.
- Press Ctrl+L, Ctrl+M, or Ctrl+T to schedule a call, meeting, or to-do, respectively.

Scheduling activities is covered in Chapter 13.

Clearing an activity

To clear a completed activity, just click the box below the check mark — the Completed column — that is located to the left of the activity, bringing up the Clear Activity dialog box. Clearing activities is covered in Chapter 13. (If you aren't displaying grid lines, you just see white space. Showing and hiding grid lines are discussed later in this chapter.)

You can also highlight the activity that you want to clear and choose Contact⇨Clear Activity from the menu bar, choose Clear Activity from the right-mouse-button menu, or press Ctrl+D.

To clear several activities at the same time, highlight the activities by clicking the boxes to the left of the activities, and choose the Clear Multiple Activities command from the right-mouse-button menu or press Ctrl+Shift+E. ACT! then asks you whether these activities were Completed or Not Completed, or whether you want to erase them.

Unclearing an activity

If you've cleared an activity and want to unclear it, this is what you do:

1. **Select the Show Cleared Activities option on the Task List Filter, if it isn't already selected.**

   Cleared activities appear as stricken or grayed out, depending upon the selection you made in the Scheduling tab of the Preferences dialog box; a check mark appears in the Completed column of the Task List.

2. **Highlight the activity by clicking the box to the left of the activity.**

3. **Click the check mark in the Completed column.**

   A message box appears asking whether you want to unclear the cleared activity.

4. **Click Yes.**

   ACT! unclears the cleared activity.

Erasing activities

To erase an activity, highlight the activity by clicking the box to the left of the activity and choose the Erase Activity command from the right-mouse-button menu. Release the right mouse button, and ACT! erases the activity. You can also press Ctrl+X.

Modifying activities with the Schedule Activity dialog box

To modify a previously scheduled activity, just double-click the box to the left of the activity. The Schedule Activity dialog box appears, where you can make changes to the activity.

Modifying activities directly from the Task List

In addition to being able to modify the particulars of an activity from the Schedule Activity dialog box, you can modify an activity's particulars directly from the Task List itself.

Because the Task List is laid out like a spreadsheet, I'll use spreadsheet terms. A column is the information at the top of the list: Date, Type, Time, Scheduled With, Regarding, and so on. A row is the list of activities displayed down the side of the table. A cell is where a column and a row come together. Here are some interesting things about those columns:

- ✓ **Type column:** Click an activity in the Type column, and you can change the activity from whatever it is to a call, meeting, or to-do.

- ✓ **Scheduled With column:** To change the person with whom an activity is scheduled, double-click the contact's name in the Scheduled With column, and the Select Contacts dialog box appears.

- ✓ **Priority column:** To change the priority of an activity, highlight the activity's priority in the Priority column and select High, Medium, or Low from the drop-down menu.

- ✓ **Regarding column:** To change the particulars of what an activity is regarding, highlight the information in the Regarding column and choose an option from the drop-down menu if one appears. You can also enter the regarding information with the keyboard.

   To bring up the Regarding Edit List dialog box, press the F2 key.

- ✓ **Duration column:** To change an activity's duration, highlight the duration in the Duration column and select a duration from the drop-down menu.

- ✓ **Date column:** To change an activity's date, highlight the date in the Date column and select a new date from the drop-down calendar.

- ✓ **Time column:** To change an activity's time, highlight the time in the Time column and select a new time from the drop-down Time Selector. To make an activity a timeless activity, select the Timeless bar at the bottom of the drop-down Time Selector.

- ✓ **Group column:** To change the group that an activity is associated with, click the group in the Group column and select a new group from the drop-down menu.

- ✓ **Company column:** The Company column displays the name of the contact's company. It cannot be changed.

- ✓ **Phone column:** The Phone column displays the contact's phone number. It cannot be changed.

Messing Around with Columns

In the preceding section, I discuss the different ways that you can modify an activity directly from the Task List. What I didn't mention was how you can add and remove columns, change their position, and change their size. That's what I'm going to do now.

- ✓ **Adding columns to the Task List:** To display a new column in the Task List, right-click the Task List, and choose the Add Columns command from the menu. The Add Columns dialog box appears. Select the column that you want to add and click OK.

✓ **Changing the position of your columns:** To change the position of a column, click the column's heading (the cursor turns into a hand), drag it left or right to its new position, and drop it there by releasing the mouse button.

✓ **Removing a column from the Task List:** To remove a column, click the column's heading, drag it up (the cursor turns into a garbage can), and release the mouse button.

✓ **Changing the width of a column heading:** To change the width of a column heading, place the cursor on the line between two column headings (it turns into a sizing tool), and move it left or right to make the column wider or smaller.

✓ **Locking your columns:** To lock your columns so that only columns to the right move when you scroll, click the Column Lock bar located at the left edge of the column headings (your cursor turns into a sizing tool) and drag it to the right of the column(s) that you want to lock. When you scroll left or right — by clicking the scroll buttons at the bottom of the window — the columns to the left of the column lock remain in place.

✓ **Showing and hiding grid lines:** To display grid lines between your column headings, you must first open the Preferences dialog box (choose Edit➪Preferences). Next, select the Colors and Fonts tab, and then select the Task List in the Customize box. To show grid lines, select the Show Grid Lines option.

Sorting Your Task List

To change the Task List's sort, just click any of the column headings, such as Date, Time, Priority, and so on, and ACT! re-sorts the Task List. (You can't sort on the Scheduled With, Company, or Phone columns.)

You can also place your cursor on these column headings and click the right mouse button. A menu appears in which you can select Sort Ascending or Sort Descending. Make your selection, and ACT! re-sorts the items. An upward or downward arrow shows the sorting selection.

Creating Lookups from the Task List

You can create a lookup from within the Task List three ways:

✓ **Create a lookup of the entire Task List:** To create a lookup of all the contacts whose activities are displayed on the Task List, just select the Create Lookup command from the right-mouse-button menu, and the contact records appear on the Contact window.

✔ **Create a lookup for a single contact:** To select a specific person's contact record, just highlight the activity in the Task List by clicking the Activity button at the left edge of the Task List window. Then choose the Create Lookup command from the right-mouse-button menu, and that person's contact record appears in the Contact window.

✔ **Create a lookup for several contacts:** To create a lookup of two or more contacts, highlight the desired activities in the Task List window. (To highlight several activities that are next to each other, just hold down the Shift key while you click the first and last activity selection buttons. If the activities are not next to each other, hold down the Ctrl key while clicking the activity buttons.)

After you've highlighted the selected activities, choose the Go to Contact command from the right-mouse-button menu, and the contact records of the people with the selected activities appear in the Contact window.

Printing the Task List

ACT! gives you several ways to print your Task List:

✔ If you want to print the activities of your Task List just as you see them on your computer screen, choose File➪Print Task List from the menu bar.

✔ If you want to print the activities of your Task List on the pages of your favorite daily planner, choose File➪Print from the menu bar, select a form, and click the Print button with your mouse, or press Ctrl+P. The Print dialog box appears. Choose the appropriate options and click OK. (Printing ACT! calendars is covered in Chapter 15.)

✔ You can also print your Task List by choosing Reports➪Task List. (For a detailed discussion on printing ACT! reports, see Chapter 24.)

Part V
Using ACT! as a Sales Tool

The 5th Wave   By Rich Tennant

"I'm just not sure it's appropriate to send a digital resume to a paper stock company looking for a sales rep."

In this part . . .

*A*CT! 2000 has some new features that will help you automate your sales processes.

In Chapter 17 you discover how you to create your sales opportunities. In Chapter 18, I explain how you keep track of those opportunities. And in Chapter 19, I walk you through the process of scheduling a series of activities that remind you to do specific things on specific dates for your contacts.

Chapter 17

Creating Sales Opportunities

· ·

In This Chapter

▶ Using the General tab

▶ Using the Additional Information tab

▶ Completing the sale

▶ Creating sales stages

· ·

*H*ave you ever wanted to know the answers to any of these questions: Which products and/or services are your contacts interested in purchasing? Where are each of your sales opportunities within your sales cycle? How much is each potential sale worth? What is the probability of closing the sale?

With ACT! 2000's Sales/Opportunity feature, you can keep track of each of your individual sales opportunities: the value of the opportunity, the anticipated closing date, and the probability of closing it successfully.

You create your sales opportunities in the Sales/Opportunity dialog box, shown in Figure 17-1.

You have three ways to open the Sales/Opportunity dialog box:

✔ **Menu bar:** Choose Sales⇨New Sales Opportunity from the menu bar in either the Contact window or the Groups window.

✔ **Contact window:** Click the Sales/Opportunities tab in the Contact window and choose New Sales Opportunity from the menu that appears when you right-click within the tab. You can also press Ctrl+F11.

✔ **Group window:** Click the Sales/Opportunities tab in the Groups window and choose New Sales Opportunity from the menu that appears when you right-click within the tab.

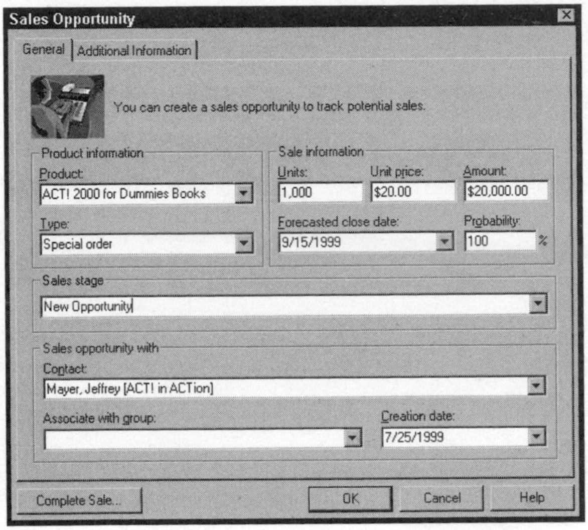

Figure 17-1:
The Sales/
Opportunity
dialog box.

The General Tab

You keep track of each sales opportunity by entering information in the Sales/Opportunity dialog box's General tab. The General tab is composed of four different sections.

Product Information

The Product Information section has two fields in which you enter product information: Product and Type.

✓ **Product:** In the Product field, you enter the name of your product.

✓ **Type:** In the Type field, you enter the type of sale.

Each time you make a new entry in either the Product or Type field, it is automatically added to the list of products. You can edit the list by pressing the F2 key, which brings up the Edit List dialog box.

From the Edit List dialog box, you can import and export list items. So if you have a list of products or types of sales in another program, you can import that list into ACT! or export your ACT! list for use in another program.

From the Edit List dialog box, you can also add, modify, or delete an item.

Sales Information

The Sales Information section lets you enter units, unit price, amount, forecasted close date, and probability.

Enter the number of units in the Units field and the price per unit in the Unit Price field, and ACT! automatically calculates the amount.

Sales Stage

The Sales Stage section lets you keep track of where you are within the sales cycle. Creating and modifying your sales stages is discussed later in this chapter.

Sales Opportunity With

The Sales Opportunity With section lets you record the person and group with whom you have this opportunity. You have these choices:

- ✔ **Contact:** In the Contact field, you select the person who is associated with this sales opportunity. Click on the down arrow (or press the down arrow key), and you can assign this sales opportunity to any contact in your ACT! database.

- ✔ **Associate with Group:** In this field, you can assign the sales opportunity to any of your ACT! groups. If you don't want to assign this sales opportunity to a group, select the No Group option at the bottom of the drop-down list.

- ✔ **Creation Date:** You enter the date on which you created this sales forecast in the Creation Date field.

The Additional Information Tab

In the Additional Information tab (shown in Figure 17-2), you enter information about your main competitor, select the record manager, and record notes about the sales opportunity.

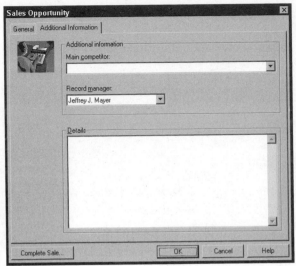

Figure 17-2:
The
Additional
Information
tab.

> ✔ **Main Competitor:** Enter the name of your main competitor in the Main Competitor field, and ACT! automatically adds the name to the drop-down list.
>
> ✔ **Record Manager:** Select the Record Manager of this sales opportunity in the Record Manager field. You can choose from the list of users of the database.
>
> ✔ **Details:** In the Details field, you can enter a specific description, or anything else you would like to record, about this sales opportunity.

In the Main Competitor field, you can also import and export, and add, modify, or delete list items.

Completing the Sale

After you have completed the sale — you have either closed/won or lost the sale — you need to record its ultimate resolution. Click the Complete Sale button on the General tab of the Sales/Opportunity dialog box to record the outcome of the sale. The Complete Sale dialog box, shown in Figure 17-3, opens.

Sales opportunities can also be marked as won or lost from within the Sales/Opportunities tab in the Contact or Groups window. This feature is discussed in Chapter 18.

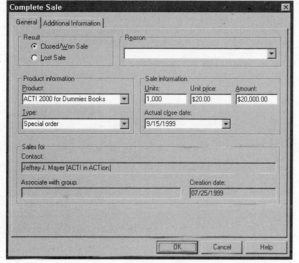

Figure 17-3:
The
Complete
Sale dialog
box.

In the Complete Sale dialog box, you record the result of your sale: You either closed/won the sale or lost the sale, and you record the reason in the Reason field.

Each time you enter a new reason in the Reason field, it is automatically added to the list of reasons. You can edit the list by pressing the F2 key, which brings up the Edit List dialog box.

Creating Your Sales Stages

You use the sales stages to determine where you are within your sales cycle. In every business, a number of steps need to be followed from the moment the new opportunity presents itself to the final close.

You select your sales stage by selecting a stage from the drop-down list in the Sales Stage field of the Sales/Opportunity dialog box. ACT! comes with a predefined list of stages, which are shown in Table 17-1.

Table 17-1	ACT!'s Sales Stages	
Stage	*Name*	*Description*
Sales Stage 1	New Opportunity	Potential sales opportunity
Sales Stage 2	Pre-Approach	Gather information on potential opportunity
Sales Stage 3	Initial Communication	First contact with the prospect (fax, e-mail, letter, brochure, call, and so on)
Sales Stage 4	First Interview	First exchange of dialogue with the prospect
Sales Stage 5	Opportunity Analysis	Gather and analyze information in order to understand the opportunity
Sales Stage 6	Solution Development	Creating focused solution(s) to meet prospect's need(s)
Sales Stage 7	Solution Presentation	Presentation of the proposed solution(s)
Sales Stage 8	Customer Evaluation	Customer evaluation of the proposed solution(s)
Sales Stage 9	Negotiation	Negotiate acceptable terms (price, delivery, quantity, and so on)
Sales Stage 10	Commitment to Buy	Customer has agreed to move the sale to a level of closure
Sales Stage 11	Follow up	Follow up with customer; opportunity to maintain a sales relationship

Modifying Your Sales Stages

Although ACT! comes with a predefined list of sales stages, you will probably want to modify them to fit your specific needs. Follow these easy steps to do so:

1. **Place your cursor in the Sales Stage field.**

2. **Press F2, or click the down arrow and select Edit List from the drop-down list.**

The Edit Sales Stages dialog box, shown in Figure 17-4, opens. (You can also open the Edit Sales Stages dialog box by choosing Sales⇨Modify Sales Stages from the menu bar in the Contact or Groups windows.)

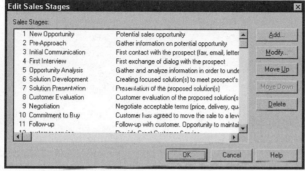

Figure 17-4:
The Edit
Sales
Stages
dialog box.

3. **From within the Edit Sales Stages dialog box, you have the following options:**

   - **Add:** Click the Add button to add a new sales stage and corresponding description. The new sales stage will appear on the sales stage list just below the highlighted sales stage.

   - **Modify:** To modify a sales stage or its description, highlight the sales stage and click the Modify button.

   - **Delete:** To delete a sales stage or its description, highlight the sales stage and click the Delete button. The Delete Sales Stage dialog box, shown in Figure 17-5, appears.

     This dialog box tells you that the selected sales stage is the currently selected sales stage for one or more contacts. You can either replace this stage with another one by selecting from the drop-down list, or you can leave it blank.

   - **Move Up or Move Down:** After you have added new sales stages or modified existing ones, you can change their position by clicking the Move Up or Move Down buttons.

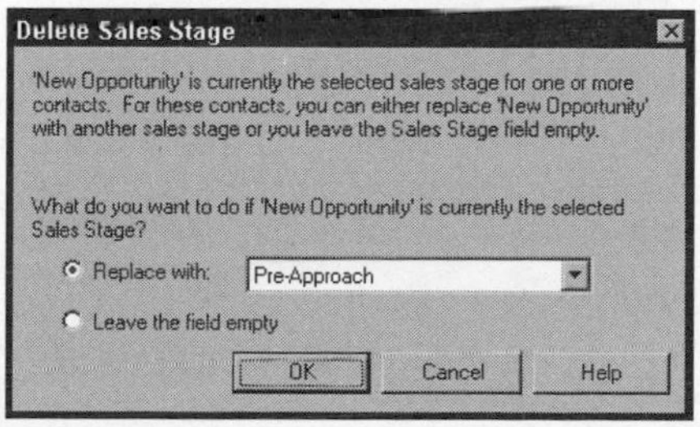

Figure 17-5:
The Delete
Sales Stage
dialog box.

Now that you understand how to create your sales opportunity, read Chapter 18. It describes how to use ACT!'s sales opportunity feature within the Contact and Sales/Opportunities tabs.

Chapter 18

Managing Your Sales Opportunities

In This Chapter

▶ Creating a new sales opportunity

▶ Completing a sale

▶ Finding your sales opportunities

▶ Printing your sales opportunities

▶ Viewing your sales opportunities as a graph or funnel

After you have created your sales opportunity, you can view the particulars of the opportunity from within the Sales/Opportunities tab of the Contact and Groups windows. The Contact window's Sales/Opportunities tab is shown in Figure 18-1.

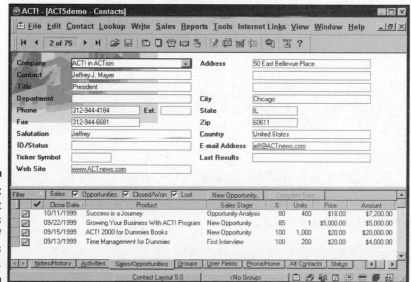

Figure 18-1: The Contact window's Sales/ Opportunities tab.

In the Contact window, you view all your sales opportunities by contact, and in the Groups window, you view all the sales opportunities that are associated with each specific group.

Creating a New Sales Opportunity

You create a new sales opportunity by choosing Sales⇨New Sales Opportunity from the menu bar in the Contact or Groups window. You can also select New Sales Opportunity from the menu that appears when you right-click within the Sales/Opportunities tab. The Sales/Opportunity dialog box is shown in Figure 18-2.

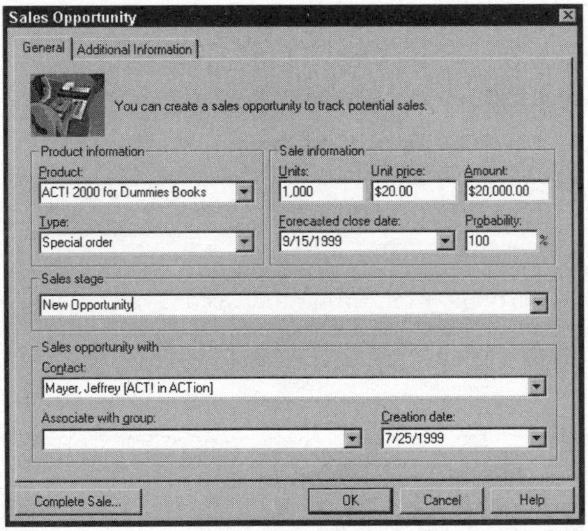

Figure 18-2:
The Sales/
Opportunity
dialog box.

The features of the Sales/Opportunity dialog box are described in Chapter 17. If you haven't read Chapter 17, I suggest that you do so now and then come back to this chapter.

Viewing your Sales/Opportunity columns

From within the Sales/Opportunities tab, you can select which columns you want to view.

The Sales/Opportunities tab can display up to 15 columns: Amount, Close Date, Company, Creation Date, Details, Group, Main Competitor, Price, Probability, Product, Reason, Record Manager, Sales Stage, Type, and Units.

These columns are the same for both the Contact window and the Groups window.

ACT! enables you to change the look and feel of your columns. You can do the following:

- **Add columns:** Select the Add Columns command from the menu that appears when you right-click within the Sales/Opportunities tab, and the Add Columns dialog box appears. Choose the column that you want to add and click OK.

- **Change the position of columns:** Click the column heading (the cursor turns into a hand) and drag it to its new position.

- **Remove columns:** Click the column heading and drag it up (the cursor turns into a garbage can) and off the Sales/Opportunities tab.

- **Show and hide column headings:** Choose the Show/Hide Column Headings command from the menu that appears when you click the right mouse button.

- **Change the width of column headings:** Place the cursor on the line between two column headings (it turns into a sizing tool) and move the column left or right to make the column smaller or wider.

- **Lock columns:** To lock columns in place, click the small bar located at the left edge of the column heading and drag it to the right of the column(s) that you want to lock. The columns to the left of the column lock remain in place when you scroll left or right.

- **Show grid lines:** Select the Show Grid Lines option in the Sales/Opportunities tab settings in the Colors and Fonts tab of the Preferences dialog box. (Did you get all that?) To open ACT!'s preferences, choose Edit⇨Preferences from the menu bar.

Modifying the particulars of a sales opportunity

In the Sales/Opportunities tab, you can modify the particulars of each sales opportunity by either opening the Sales/Opportunity dialog box or editing the information that appears within a column. You can do the following from within the Sales/Opportunities tab on both the Contact and Groups windows:

- **Edit a sales opportunity:** To edit sales-opportunity information, just place your cursor in the particular cell (spreadsheet language for the point at which a column and row come together) and enter the new information.

✔ **Change the sort order:** To change the sort order of your sales opportunities, just click any of the column headings. ACT! re-sorts the items in the Sales/Opportunity. An up arrow or down arrow shows the sorting selection.

✔ **Delete a sales opportunity:** To delete a sales opportunity, highlight the opportunity by clicking the selection button. Choose Sales➪Delete Sale from the menu bar, or choose the Delete Sale command from the menu that appears when you click the right mouse button, or press the Delete key. A message box appears asking: "Are you sure you want to delete the selected item(s)?" To delete the selected sales opportunity, click Yes.

To highlight two or more entries next to each other, hold down the Shift key while you click the first and last entries. To highlight entries that are not next to each other, hold down the Ctrl key while you select each entry individually. A highlighted item can also be deleted by pressing Ctrl+X.

✔ **Move or copy sales opportunities:** From time to time, you may want to move or copy a sales opportunity from one contact to another. You do this by using the Cut (Ctrl+X), Copy (Ctrl+C), and Paste (Ctrl+V) commands. Just highlight the item that you want to cut or copy, and select either the Cut or Copy command. Switch to another contact record, and paste the sales opportunity into the contact's Sales/Opportunities tab.

Filtering your sales opportunities

With the Sales/Opportunity Filter command, you choose what sales opportunity information you want to view for a given range of dates.

A Filter button appears at the top of the Sales/Opportunities tab. (Refer to Figure 18-1.) Click the button, and you can make the same selections in the Filter Sales/Opportunities dialog box as described earlier for the Sales/Opportunities dialog box.

To open the Filter Sales/Opportunities dialog box, choose the View➪ Filter Sales/Opportunities command from the menu bar, or select the command Filter Sales/Opportunities command from the menu that appears when you right-click in the Sales/Opportunities tab.

In the Filter Sales/Opportunities dialog box, shown in Figure 18-3, you have the following options:

✔ **Users:** In the Users section, you apply the filter options to selected users or to all users of the database.

✔ **Sales to Show:** Choose which information to view by selecting or not selecting the Sales/Opportunities, Closed/Won Sales, or Lost Sales options.

✔ **Close Dates:** Your options for viewing dates include All Dates, Today, Past Dates, Future Dates, or a range of dates in the Close Dates section.

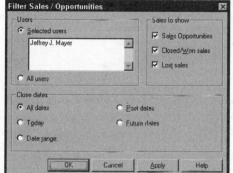

Figure 18-3:
The Filter
Sales/
Opportunities
dialog box.

Completing a Sale

You complete a sale by highlighting a sales opportunity and doing one of the following:

✔ Choosing the Sales⇨Complete Sale command from the menu bar

✔ Choosing the Complete Sale command from the menu that appears when you click the right mouse button

✔ Clicking the Complete Sale check box

The Complete Sale dialog box opens, where you can enter whether you closed/won or lost the sale, and the specifics. (Completing the sale is discussed in Chapter 17.)

If you've marked a sale as complete and want to re-open it, click the check mark in the Complete Sale check box. The sales opportunity is re-opened.

Finding Your Sales Opportunities

You locate your sales opportunity by choosing the Lookup⇨Sales Stage command, which opens the Lookup Sales Stage dialog box. The Lookup Sales Stage dialog box is shown in Figure 18-4.

Figure 18-4:
The Lookup
Sales Stage
dialog box.

Here, you enter the sales stage that you want to look up, and ACT! finds each contact that is in the selected sales stage.

Printing Your Sales Opportunities

ACT! gives you two ways to print your sales opportunities. You can use either of the following:

✓ Instant reports

✓ Detailed reports

Printing an instant sales report

You print an instant report from within the Sales/Opportunities tab by choosing File⇨Print Sales/Opportunities from the menu bar. ACT! prints a custom report. You can also access the Print Sales/Opportunities command from the menu that appears when you right-click inside the Sales/Opportunities tab.

ACT! prints the report exactly as the data appears within the Sales/Opportunities tab.

Printing sales reports

You can print detailed sales reports by choosing Reports⇨Sales Reports and then selecting the desired report from the Sales Reports submenu. ACT! provides you with the following sales reports:

- **Sales Totals by Status:** This report provides a total of all sales opportunities, closed/won sales, and lost sales. The name of this report is SLSTOTA5.REP.

- **Sales Adjusted for Probability:** This report lists all sales opportunities with totals. It is sorted by contact. The name of this report is SLSFRCS5.REP.

- **Sales List:** This report includes complete information for each closed and/or lost sales opportunity. The name of this report is SLSDTAI5.REP.

- **Sales Funnel Report:** This report includes a complete listing of each sales opportunity sorted by sales stage. The name of this report is SLSFUNL5.REP.

- **Sales by Record Manager:** This report displays a complete list of all the open sales opportunities, the closed/won sales, and the lost sales by Record Manager. The name of this report is SLSBYMG5.REP.

- **Sales by Contact:** This report displays sales information for each contact with an open sales opportunity or a closed sale. It is sorted by company. The name of this report is SLSCNTC5.REP.

ACT! doesn't have a Sales/Opportunities window, which would be similar to the Task List window, where you can view a complete list of all your sales opportunities. As a work-around, print out an ACT! sales opportunity report and use it to view a complete list of all your sales opportunities.

After you have selected your sales report, the Run Report dialog box appears. On the General tab, you select your output. You can print, preview, fax, or e-mail the report. Or you can save it to file in the ACT! report format or as editable text. Creating ACT! reports and editing ACT! report templates is covered in Chapter 24.

On the Sales/Opportunities tab, you can modify your report's output. You have the following options:

- **Sales section:** In the Sales section, you can include Sales Opportunities, Closed/Won Sales, and/or Lost Sales in the report. You can also choose a date range from the drop-down list or create a custom date range.

- **Sort Sales By section:** In the Sort Sales By section, you select the sales field on which you want ACT! to sort the report.

- **Include Data for Sales Managed By section:** In the Include Data for Sales Managed By section, you can select All Users or Selected Users.

Viewing Your Sales Opportunities as a Graph or Funnel

In addition to creating reports, you can also view your sales opportunities as either a graph or a funnel.

Graphing your sales opportunities

You have two ways to view your sales opportunities as a graph:

- ✔ Choose Sales⇨Sales Graph
- ✔ Choose Reports⇨Sales Reports⇨Sales Graph

The Graph Options dialog box, shown in Figure 18-5, opens.

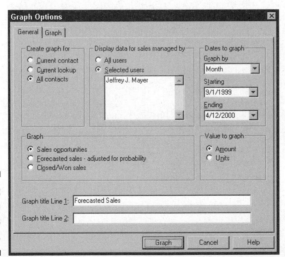

Figure 18-5:
The Graph
Options
dialog box.

On the General tab, you have the following options:

- ✔ **Create Graph For section:** In this section, you select the contacts whose sales opportunities you want included in the graph.

- ✔ **Display Data for Sales Managed By section:** In this section, you choose all users or selected users.

- ✔ **Dates to Graph section:** This section lets you select the time frame (day, week, month, quarter, or year) and the starting and ending dates.

✔ **Graph section:** This section lets you choose Sales Opportunities, Forecasted Sales — Adjusted for Probability, or Closed/Won Sales.

✔ **Value to Graph section:** In this section, you choose either Amount or Units.

✔ **Graph Title Lines section:** This section lets you enter two title lines.

On the Graph tab, you have the following options:

✔ **Type:** You can create a bar or line graph.

✔ **Style:** You can create a 3-D or 2-D graph.

✔ **Graph Size:** You tell ACT! whether you want to print out a full-sized graph or shrink to fit.

✔ **Scale:** You can have ACT! determine the amount of unit labels on the left side of the graph (Auto), or you can select your own minimum and maximum amount of unit labels.

✔ **Show Grid Lines:** You can show or hide the horizontal and/or vertical grid lines.

✔ **Colors:** You can select specific colors for the graph, text, and background.

After the graph has been created, you can print it, save it as a bitmapped image, or copy it to the Windows Clipboard.

Viewing your sales opportunities in the Sales Funnel

You have two ways to view your sales opportunities as a funnel:

✔ Choose Sales⇨Sales Funnel

✔ Choose Reports⇨Sales Reports⇨Sales Funnel

The Sales Funnel Options dialog box opens.

In the Sales Funnel Options dialog box, you have the following options:

✔ **Create Graph For section:** In this section, you select the contacts whose sales opportunities you want included in the graph.

✔ **Display Data for Sales Managed By section:** In this section, you choose all users or selected users.

✔ **Assign Colors section:** In this section, you select a color for each sales stage.

After the sales funnel has been created, you can print it, save it as a bitmapped image, or copy it to the Windows Clipboard.

Chapter 19

Creating Activity Series

· ·

In This Chapter

▶ Creating an activity series

▶ Editing an activity series

▶ Scheduling an activity series

· ·

*A*fter you've found a sales prospect, you may want to set up an automatic schedule for staying in touch with him or her. ACT!'s Activity Series feature enables you to create a series of scheduled activities and then apply that series to one or more contacts.

Creating an Activity Series

Create an activity series by following these steps:

1. **Choose Contact⭢Create/Edit Activity Series from the menu bar.**

   The Introduction Wizard appears.

2. **Select Create a New Activity Series, and click Next.**

   The Series Date Wizard appears.

3. **Select Start Date or Due Date if the series of scheduled activities is to be based upon a start date or a due date.**

4. **Click Next.**

   The First Activity Wizard, shown in Figure 19-1, appears.

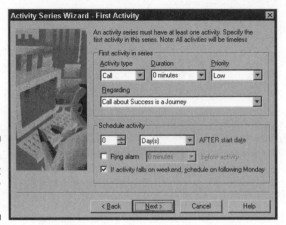

Figure 19-1:
The First
Activity
Wizard.

5. **Schedule the first activity in the series.**

   Enter the activity's type, duration, priority, and regarding information.

6. **In the Schedule Activity section, enter the number of days/weeks/months that this activity will be scheduled after the Start Date or before the Due Date.**

7. **Set the alarm, if desired.**

8. **Select the If Activity Falls on Weekend, Schedule on Following Monday option if you want ACT! to automatically move an activity from a Saturday or Sunday to Monday.**

9. **Click the Next button.**

   The Series Wizard, shown in Figure 19-2, appears listing all activities.

10. **Click the Add, Edit, or Delete buttons to add, edit, or delete an activity.**

11. **Click the Next button.**

    The Finish Wizard appears.

12. **Give the series a name and a brief description.**

13. **Click Finish.**

    Your series is saved.

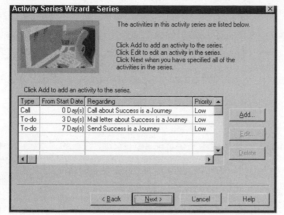

Figure 19-2:
The Series
Wizard.

Editing an Activity Series

After you've created an activity series, you may decide to modify its particulars. This is how you do it:

1. **Choose Contact⇨Create/Edit Activity Series from the menu bar.**

   The Introduction Wizard appears.

2. **Select Edit an Activity Series, and click Next.**

   The Select Series Wizard appears.

3. **Select the series that you want to edit and click Next.**

   The Series Wizard (refer to Figure 19-2) appears, listing all activities.

4. **Click the Add, Edit, or Delete buttons to add, edit, or delete an activity.**

5. **Click the Next button.**

   The Finish Wizard appears.

6. **Change the series name and/or description, if desired, and click Finish to save your changes to the series.**

Scheduling an Activity Series

After you've created your activity series, this is how you apply the series:

1. **Choose Contact⇨Schedule Activity Series from the menu bar.**

   The Schedule Activity Series dialog box, shown in Figure 19-3, appears.

2. Select the contact(s) with which you want to schedule this series.

You can select All Contacts, Current Contact, or Current Lookup.

3. Select the activity series that you want to apply to this contact.

4. Select a series Start Date or Due Date.

5. Click Schedule.

ACT! schedules the activities in the series for the selected contacts.

Figure 19-3:
The
Schedule
Activity
Series
dialog box.

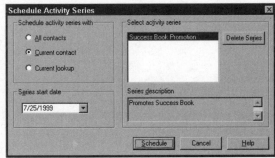

Part VI
Communicating with the Outside World

The 5th Wave   By Rich Tennant

"Now, when someone rings my doorbell, the current goes to a scanner that digitizes the audio impulses and sends the image to the PC where it's converted to a Pict file. The image is then animated, compressed, and sent via high-speed modem to an automated phone service that sends an e-mail message back to tell me someone was at my door 40 minutes ago."

In this part . . .

In addition to being a scheduling tool and contact manager, ACT! is filled with features that can help you stay in touch with your contacts.

In Chapter 20, I present ACT! phone features. In Chapter 21, I show you how to create letters and other documents within ACT!. In Chapter 22, I detail ACT!'s fax-related features. Chapter 23's focus is ACT! e-mail features. Chapter 24 is all about creating and working with reports.

I know that it seems like I'm trying to cover an awful lot of material in this part; that's because I am. Just take it one chapter at a time, let the material sink in, maybe play with your newly-learned ACT! features, and then move on to the next chapter. There's no rush. You didn't rent this book; you bought it, didn't you?

Chapter 20

Using ACT!'s Telephone Features

● ●

In This Chapter

▶ Making ACT! calls the easy way

▶ Keeping track of your calls with the Record History dialog box

▶ Using ACT! with Caller ID

▶ Setting your dialing preferences

▶ Creating phone formats for foreign telephone numbers

▶ Adding phone fields

● ●

ACT! makes it easy to store all the different phone numbers that you may have for your contacts — including their numbers at work, at home, and the cell phones they carry in their pockets, as well as their fax numbers and the phone numbers of their assistants.

The Easy Way to Make an ACT! Call

The easiest way to make a call in ACT! is to click the Dial Phone icon, which brings up the Dialer dialog box. The Dialer dialog box is shown in Figure 20-1. (You can also bring up the Dialer dialog box by choosing Contact⇨Phone Contact from the menu bar or by choosing the Phone Contact command from the right-mouse-button menu.)

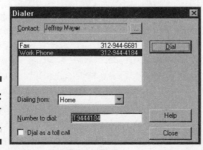

Figure 20-1:
The Dialer
dialog box.

If you have a modem and your telephone shares a voice line with your computer, ACT! can dial the phone for you. If you don't have a modem, or if you do but it doesn't share a line with your telephone, you can still use ACT! to find the telephone numbers that you want to dial, but you'll have to dial them manually.

This is how you use ACT! to dial the telephone:

1. **Find the contact that you want to call by using ACT!'s powerful Lookup feature.**

   (ACT! lookups are covered in Chapter 10.)

2. **Click the Dial Phone icon.**

   The Dialer dialog box opens.

3. **From the displayed list, select the phone number that you want to dial.**

4. **Click the Dial button.**

   ACT! dials the phone number, and the Call Status message box appears and instructs you to "Lift the receiver and click Talk."

5. **Pick up the telephone receiver and click Talk to disconnect the modem from the telephone call.**

   The Record History dialog box, where you can record a summary of the conversation, opens. (The Record History dialog box is discussed in the next section.)

Now wasn't that easy? I do this all day long; it saves me a great deal of wear and tear on my fingers, and I don't dial many wrong numbers.

Here is a brief summary of the Dialer dialog box's features:

- **Choosing whom to call:** If you want to call a person, other than the person whose name appears in the Dialer dialog box, click the Browse button to the right of the contact's name. The Select Contact dialog box appears, from which you can select a different person to call.

- **Deciding where you are calling from:** In the Dialing From field, you tell ACT! where you're dialing from. ACT! needs to know the area code you're dialing from so that it can distinguish between a local and long-distance call. If you travel with your laptop, this feature is important because you could be making a call from your office, your home, a regional office, or an out-of-town hotel. If you're working from your desktop computer, you enter this information once and then forget about it.

  ACT! also needs to know what numbers it must dial in order to access a local or long-distance line. (These settings are created in ACT!'s Dialer Preferences dialog box, which is discussed later in this chapter.)

✔ **Dialing as a toll call:** If you are dialing a number within your area code that requires dialing a "1" before the number, select the Dial as a Toll Call option.

Here are a couple of dialing tips:

✔ Always enter a person's extension in the Extension field so that you don't have to go through a phone system's menu when you dial the main number.

✔ To speed up your calling, always record the number(s) of the phone system's menu items. This way, you don't have to waste your time listening to a description of each menu item. (You can store this information in a blank user field.)

Keeping Track of Your Calls with the Record History Dialog Box

ACT!'s Record History dialog box, shown in Figure 20-2, opens automatically for your outgoing calls after you click the Talk or Hang Up button in the Call Status dialog box. From the Record History dialog, you can enter a note to yourself about the results of a call. You can view these notes in the contact's Notes/History tab.

Managing your calls from inside ACT!

If you are using a telephone equipped with TAPI (Telephone Application Programming Interface) hardware and software, or if you are using a modem that supports call-management features, you can use ACT! to manage your telephone calls.

TAPI functions as a link between your computer and your modem or telephone. This enables you to place and manage calls by using your computer. (ACT!'s dialer uses the TAPI technology that comes with the Windows 95/98 or Windows NT operating systems.) ACT! supports the following call-management features: hold, call

forwarding, call transfer, and three-way conference calling.

Unless you have TAPI hardware and the appropriate telephone driver software installed on your computer, you do *not* have access to these features.

If you have questions about which features your modem supports, refer to the documentation that came with your modem or contact your modem vendor. If you have questions about using your telephone with your ACT! dialer, contact your company's telephone administrator or your telephone system vendor.

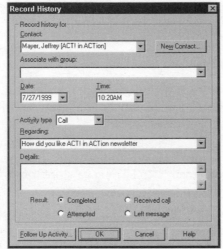

Figure 20-2:
The Record
History
dialog box.

You can also open the Record History dialog box by pressing Ctrl+H, choosing Contact⇨Record History from the menu bar, or choosing the Record History command from the right-mouse-button menu.

The features of ACT!'s Record History dialog box are discussed in Chapter 5.

Using ACT!'s Timer

ACT! has a timer option in the Dialer tab of the Preferences dialog box (which is discussed later in this chapter) named Start Timer Automatically on Outgoing Calls. Select this option, and ACT!'s timer starts automatically when you dial the phone. When the call ends, just click the timer's Stop button, and the Record History dialog box opens.

After you've entered your history notation and clicked OK, ACT! enters the duration of the timed call in the note's Regarding field, along with your notation.

To start the timer manually — when you're receiving a call, for example — choose Tools⇨Timer or press Shift+F4, and the timer appears. Click the Start button to start the timer. Click the Stop button, and the Record History dialog box appears.

Improve your productivity by using a telephone headset

Does your neck ever get stiff from cradling the telephone handset between your ear, chin, and shoulder? Do you find it difficult to take notes while you're on the phone because you can't find an easy way to hold the phone to your left ear, use your left elbow to keep the pad of paper from moving while writing with your right hand, and remain comfortable, all at the same time?

If you answered yes to any of these questions, you should be using a telephone headset, instead of the traditional handset. In fact, if you spend any time at all on the phone, you should be using a telephone headset. I've been using

one for years and have found that not only is it comfortable, but it has greatly improved my productivity and efficiency as well.

Plantronics makes a full line of headsets for people who work in offices — corporate or SOHO offices — and for those on the go. For a catalog and a current price list, contact Plantronics at 345 Encinal St., Santa Cruz, CA 95060. You can call the company at 800-544-4660, 831-458-7700, or 831-426-5858. You can also visit its Web site at www.plantronics.com.

Using ACT! with Caller ID

Caller ID tells you who is calling before you answer a telephone call. (Contact your local phone company to see whether Caller ID is available in your area.) If Caller ID is available, you can set the Lookup Contact Using Caller ID option in the Dialer Preferences dialog box, which is discussed later in this chapter, to display the contact record on a caller.

As you probably know, in order for you to use ACT!'s Caller ID features, your local telephone company must provide the Caller ID service, Caller ID must be enabled on your telephone line, and your telephone equipment must support Caller ID.

When the telephone rings, ACT! looks at the number of the incoming caller and searches the database for a contact record with a matching number. If ACT! finds a matching number, ACT! displays the first contact record of a lookup based on that telephone number. If ACT! finds more than one contact record containing that telephone number, it displays all the contact records containing that number in the lookup.

Don't forget to schedule an activity

One of ACT!'s greatest strengths is that it associates tasks with contact records. And almost every time you speak with someone on the phone, you'll need to generate some kind of follow-up activity.

You can schedule a new activity from within the Record History dialog box by clicking the Follow Up Activity button.

Let me give you some examples:

✔ You have an appointment scheduled with someone, and that person's assistant calls to tell you that he or she won't be able to keep it. At the conclusion of the call, add a call item to the person's contact record so

that you won't forget to reschedule the appointment. At the same time, remove the appoinyment from your calendar.

✔ When the person you're talking to says, "I want to think it over," schedule a call for seven to ten days in the future so that you won't forget to call again. Or better yet, ask whether you can schedule a telephone call for sometime during the following week, and pick a specific date and time for the call before the conversation ends.

✔ When you're asked to do or send something, schedule a to-do as soon as you get off the phone.

Setting Your Dialer Preferences

To set your dialing preferences, you first open ACT!'s Preference dialog box and then select the Dialer tab. To open ACT!'s Preferences dialog box, choose Edit⇨Preferences from the menu bar or select the Preferences command from the right-mouse-button menu.

Here are the Dialer tab's options:

✔ **Using the dialer:** If you want to use the dialer (the feature that dials the phone for you if your hardware is properly set up), select the Use Dialer option.

✔ **Setting up your modem:** In the Modem or Line field, select your modem from the list of modems that are installed on your computer. After you select your modem, click the Setup button, and in the subsequent dialog box, tell ACT! where to find your modem, as well as a few other things.

✔ **Specifying your address:** From the drop-down list in the Address field, choose the telephone extension or modem address that you want to use. (This feature is applicable only if you're dialing from a corporate telephone system.) Confused? A telephone or modem "address" is actually a telephone number. Some telephone lines can support multiple addresses. For example, the telephone line in your office may have two extensions, and each of those extensions is considered a separate address.

✔ **Setting other dialing options:** In the Dialer tab of the Preferences dialog box, you have some additional options:

- **Hide Dialer after Dialing:** This one's pretty self-explanatory.

- **Lookup Contact Using Caller ID:** If you have Caller ID, you can have ACT! look up the caller when you receive a call.

- **Start Timer Automatically on Outgoing Calls:** ACT! can start the timer on your calls if you so desire.

- **Modem Has Speaker Phone Capabilities:** If your modem has speaker phone capabilities, select this option.

✔ **Indicating your location:** In the Location field, you tell ACT! where you are dialing from. Click the Properties button, and the Dialing Properties dialog box appears. In the Dialing Properties dialog box, you enter the particulars of each location from which you'll be dialing.

In the Where I Am section of the My Locations tab, you enter the following information:

✔ In the **I Am Dialing From** field, select a location (for example, office, home, regional office, summer home, and so on). To add a new location, click the New button and enter the name of the new location in the Create New Location dialog box. To remove an unused location, select the location from the drop-down menu and click the Remove button.

✔ In the **Area Code Is** field, you enter the area code of the location that you're calling. The information in this field lets ACT! know whether you're making a local or long-distance call.

✔ In the **I Am In** field, you enter the country you are dialing from. The number in parentheses is the country's country code.

In the How I Dial from This Location section of the My Locations tab, you enter the following information:

✔ **To access an outside local line,** enter a number in the Local box. (This number is often 9.)

✔ **To access an outside long-distance line,** enter a number(s) in the Long Distance box. (The numbers are often 9,1.)

✔ **To insert pauses, because your computer may be dialing a set of numbers faster than the phone company's computer can recognize them,** insert one or more commas between sets of numbers.

✔ **To use a calling card,** select the Dial Using Calling Card option. The Change Calling Card dialog box appears. In the Change Calling Card dialog box, select the calling card you are using and its access number. (AT&T, for example, is 1-800-321-0288.) In the Calling Card Number field, you enter (what else?) your calling card number.

After you've selected the Calling Card option, ACT! displays the access number in the Dialer's Number to Dial field.

✔ **To disable call waiting,** select the This Location Has Call Waiting option.

✔ **To choose tone or pulse dialing,** select Tone or Pulse by clicking the appropriate button at the bottom of the Dialing Properties dialog box.

Creating Phone Formats for Foreign Telephone Numbers

If you would like to change a phone field's format from the standard 123-456-7890 format to some other format, this is what you do:

1. **Open the Contact window if it's not open already.**

2. **Place your cursor in the phone field whose format you want to change.**

3. **Click the phone field's Browse button or press F2.**

   The Country Codes dialog box appears, as shown in Figure 20-3.

Figure 20-3:
The Country Codes dialog box.

4. **Select a country code and phone format.**

   If you select the Free Form option, you can create a phone format that applies only to that specific contact's phone field. If you select the Apply This Format for Country Code option, you can create your own format that applies to every contact in the database.

What about the country code?

You can find the command for displaying or not displaying the country code in phone fields in the General tab of the Preferences dialog box. (Don't ask me why it's there!) If you want ACT! to display the country code in the phone fields, select the Always Display Country Code in Phone Fields option.

Adding New Phone Fields

ACT! comes with a number of fields that are already designated as phone fields, but if you want to include more telephone numbers, ACT! offers you lots of flexibility. In ACT!, you can designate any field as a phone field. To make a field a phone field, open the Define Fields dialog box by choosing Edit⇨Define Fields from the menu bar. From the subsequent dialog box, follow these steps:

1. **Select the field that you want to make a phone field from in the List of Fields box.**

2. **Select Phone as the Attribute Type in the Type field.**

3. **Change the field name to a name that's appropriate.**

4. **Click OK to save your changes.**

With the flexibility to make any field a phone field, you can include a person's car phone, cell phone, home phone, vacation-home phone, fax machine, home fax machine, beeper, and every other phone number that person may have. Defining ACT! fields is discussed in detail in Chapter 6.

The name that you select as the field name appears in the Dialer when you select the Phone Contact command.

Chapter 21

Writing Letters

● ●

In This Chapter

▶ Selecting your word processor

▶ Writing a letter

▶ Printing, faxing, and e-mailing

▶ Creating form letters

▶ Using the Mail Merge feature

▶ Using ACT!'s word processor

▶ Using third-party products

● ●

ACT!'s creators realized that ACT! users can be more productive if they have the capability to merge the names and addresses in their database with form letter templates. To fill this need, they give you two choices. You can use the word processor included as part of ACT!, or you can use Microsoft Word as your word processor. (WordPerfect is no longer supported by ACT!.)

Selecting Your Word Processor

In the General tab in the Preferences dialog box, you tell ACT! which word processor you'd like to use. To open the Preferences dialog box, select Edit⇨Preferences from the menu bar or select the Preferences command from the right mouse button menu.

In the Default Applications section of the General tab, select your word processor from the Word Processor drop-down list. You can choose Word or ACT!'s word processor.

I run my publicity campaigns from ACT!

I do all my own promotion and publicity — for my books, for my business of working with people who want to grow their businesses, and for my work with individuals who want to expand their careers. ACT! has helped me to improve my efficiency four- or five-fold.

Over the years, I've spoken with several hundred newspaper reporters, magazine writers, and radio and television broadcasters. Before I got ACT!, I stored all their names in a WordPerfect merge file. When I needed to send someone a press release, a copy of a new book, or some other material, I used WordPerfect to merge the recipient's name and address into a letter, and then I had to run the merge a second time to print the envelope or mailing label.

I've since imported all these people into ACT!, and my media database has grown to more than 3,000 people.

I get the same results — quicker, faster, and better — using ACT!, and I've greatly improved my productivity. When someone tells me that he or she is interested in reviewing one of my books, I just select the publicity letter from the Write menu, and ACT! automatically merges the contact's name and address into my form letter. All I have to do is click the Print button.

I now do in seconds what used to take me several minutes — the letter and mailing label are often printed before the telephone conversation has ended — and I do it over and over, day after day. This ACT! feature alone saves me two hours of work each week. It enables me to be both efficient and effective.

Writing a Letter

One of the neat things about the letter-writing capabilities of ACT! is that contact information (the Contact Name, Company Name, and Address, for example) automatically merges into a form letter when you select Letter, Memorandum, Fax Cover Page, or Other Document from the Write menu to create a new document. This feature — which works the same way in Word or in ACT!'s word processor — makes you much more productive and efficient because you don't have to waste your valuable time retyping your contact's name and address into your correspondence.

When you select Write⇨Letter or click the Letter icon, ACT! automatically inserts specific contact information — the contact's name, address, and a salutation, as well as the date — into the letter. (In case you're interested, the name of the ACT! letter template is LETTER.TPL; if you're using Word, the template is called LETTER.ADT. These templates are stored in ACT!'s template directory.)

ACT! also automatically inserts your name and title on the letter's signature line. ACT! takes this from the My Record information of the current database user — presumably you. This feature is another way in which ACT! is so intuitive. Because each ACT! user on a multi-user database has his or her own My Record contact record, ACT! always knows who is using the program and is able to insert that person's name on the signature line in a letter.

Figure 21-1 shows a letter I'm sending to Linda Keating. (Linda is an ACT! Certified Consultant in Palo Alto, California, who specializes in database marketing. She's a very good friend and also happens to help run the San Francisco Bay Area ACT! Users Group.)

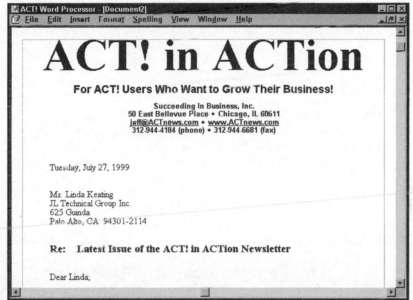

Figure 21-1:
A letter from
me to Linda
Keating.

For more information about the ACT! Users Group, call 650-323-9141, or send Linda an e-mail message at `lkeating@jltechnical.com`. You can also visit her Web site at `www.jltechnical.com`.

As you can see, ACT! inserted Linda's name and address into the letter. (What you can't see is the closing and my signature line, because the word processor viewing area isn't large enough.) Now, I just type the text of the letter and print it. Doesn't that sound easy? (If you're wondering why my letterhead is in the template, it's because I created my own letterhead inside my ACT! Letter template. This way, I don't have to have letterhead printed anymore.)

If you choose to use Word as your word processor, you can utilize all its high-powered word processing features, including graphics, tables, and more.

When you add a new contact to your ACT! database, you can have ACT! automatically insert the person's first or last name in the Salutation field. (The default is first name only.) This is a nice feature if you send lots of letters, memos, and other correspondence. To make your selection, open ACT!'s Preferences dialog box by selecting Edit⊃Preferences, and select the Names tab.

Printing, Faxing, and E-Mailing

After you've created your document, you can print it, fax it, e-mail it, or just save it to a file. I discuss these options in this section.

Printing your letter

When you print your letter, ACT! does some very interesting things. To print an ACT! letter, select File⊃Print from the menu bar (the Print command is the same for Word and for the ACT! word processor). The Print dialog box appears; where you can change your printing options if you wish.

Then click OK, and ACT! prints the document and opens the Create History dialog box, shown in Figure 21-2, even when you're in Word.

Add frequently used envelopes and labels to the Reports menu

If you have some envelopes or mailing labels that you use frequently, you can add them to the Reports pull-down menu. This makes printing them a breeze. This is how you do it:

1. **Select Reports⊃Modify Menu.**

   The Modify Menu dialog box opens.

2. **Click the Add Item button.**

   The Add Custom Menu Item dialog box opens in which you select a file and write a description.

3. **Click the Browse button.**

   The Report dialog box opens with a list of reports displayed.

4. **Select Envelopes (*.env) from the drop-down list in the Files of Type section.**

   The list of available envelopes is now displayed. (For a list of available labels, select Labels (*.lbl) from the drop-down.)

5. **Select the envelope that you want to add to the menu, and click OK.**

   You return to the Modify Menu dialog box.

6. **Click OK.**

   Your envelope is added to the Reports menu.

Whenever you need to print an envelope, just select your envelope from the Reports pull-down menu and put an envelope in the printer.

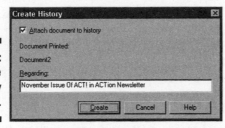

Figure 21-2:
The Create
History
dialog box.

The Create History dialog box appears when you print, fax, or e-mail a document. From the Create History dialog box, you have the following options:

✔ **Attach Document to History:** This option enables you to attach the document to the contact. Click the Attachment icon in the contact's Notes/History tab, and ACT! opens the document.

If you have selected the Attach Document to History option but haven't saved the document, the Save As dialog box appears when you click the Create button. Give the document a name, click the Save button, and you're done.

✔ **Document Printed:** The Document Printed section of the Create History dialog box displays the name of the document that was printed, faxed, or e-mailed.

✔ **Regarding:** In the Regarding field, you can enter a description of the document that will appear in the Regarding field in the Notes/History tab.

After you've made your selections, click the Create button, and the information appears in the contact's Notes/History tab, and the letter's date is automatically inserted in the Letter Date field located on the contact's Status tab.

Always spell-check your letters, memos, and faxes before you print them. ACT!'s word processor comes with an 80,000-word dictionary. To activate the spell checker, select Spelling⌐Check Document from the word processor's menu bar.

All ACT! documents created in the ACT! word processor have the *.AWP extension and are saved to the ACT!'s Document directory.

Printing envelopes and labels

ACT! comes with a rather elaborate label and envelope printing program, but for myself, I think a program called DAZzle is much easier to use. (I talk about DAZzle in the last section of this chapter.) You can do these things with labels and envelopes:

✔ **Printing a label or envelope:** To print an envelope or label, select File⇨Print or press Ctrl+P, and the Print dialog box appears. This is the same dialog box that you use to print your address book, and Daily, Weekly, and Monthly calendars.

Select Labels or Envelopes as your Printout Type. Then select the label or envelope that you want to print from the list of available labels or envelopes, and click OK.

✔ **Editing a label or envelope:** From the Print dialog box, you can also edit a label or envelope by clicking the Edit Template button, which opens ACT!'s Report Designer. For information on the features of the Report Designer, read Chapter 24.

✔ **Creating a new label or envelope:** To create a new label or envelope, select File⇨New, and the New dialog box appears. Select Envelope Template or Label Template, click OK, and the label or envelope creation process begins.

Sending your document as a fax from WinFax PRO

You select your faxing software from the Fax Software drop-down list in the Default Applications section of the General tab of the Preferences dialog box.

This is how you send your document as a fax:

1. **Select File⇨Send⇨Fax.**

   In Word, you select File⇨Send Fax Using ACT!. ACT!'s Send Fax dialog box appears (shown in Figure 21-3.)

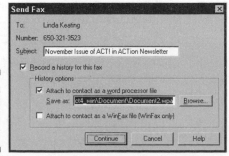

Figure 21-3:
The Send Fax dialog box.

2. **Make your Create History choices.**

   ACT!'s Send Fax dialog box gives you the following options:

- **Subject:** Enter the subject of the fax in the Subject field.

- **Record History for This Fax:** To make a record of the fax in the contact's Notes/History tab, select this check box.

- **History Options:** ACT! gives you two history options. You can attach the fax to the contact as a document, and/or you can attach the fax to the contact as a WinFax file. If you want to save the file, this is where you give it a name.

Make your selection and click the Continue button. ACT! launches WinFax Pro and the WinFax Pro Send dialog box appears.

3. **Choose from the additional faxing options that are available in the WinFax PRO Send dialog box.**

4. **Click the Send Button.**

The WinFax PRO Preview window opens so you can view your fax.

5. **Click the Send Fax button.**

WinFax PRO sends your fax.

ACT! and WinFax PRO now have complete integration. I discuss using WinFax PRO and ACT! in Chapter 22.

If you send lots of faxes, launch your faxing software prior to faxing a document. This will save you time because ACT! doesn't have to launch WinFax PRO.

Sending your document as e-mail

This is how you send your document as an e-mail message:

1. **Select File⇨Send⇨E-mail from the menu bar in your word processor.**

   The Send E-mail dialog box appears (see Figure 21-4). In Word, you select File⇨Send E-mail Using ACT!.

Figure 21-4:
The Send
E-mail
dialog box.

2. **Make your sending selection.**

   Your choices are as follows:

   - **Entire Document as File Attachment:** Choosing this option attaches your entire document to an e-mail message.

   - **Entire Document in Message Body:** Selecting this option sends your entire document in the body of an e-mail message.

   - **Selected Text in Message Body:** This option lets you send selected text (highlighted text) in the body of an e-mail message.

3. **Click OK.**

   ACT! opens the E-mail window and creates an e-mail message. (If you've chosen the Entire Document as File Attachment option, ACT! first asks you to save the document, if it hasn't been saved. ACT! then opens the E-mail window and attaches the document to the e-mail message.)

4. **Enter your description of the e-mail message in the subject line.**

5. **Click the Send button.**

   ACT! sends your e-mail message, creates an E-mail Sent Notes/History attachment, and enters the subject line in the Regarding field. To open your e-mail message, just double-click on the attachment icon.

Using ACT! to send e-mail is covered in more detail in Chapter 20.

Saving your document

After you write a letter, memo, fax, or other document, you'll probably want to save it.

To save a document, just select the Save (or Save As) command from the File Menu. The Save As dialog box appears, and you give the document a name. In Word, you save an ACT! document with the .DOC file extension. Using ACT!'s word processor, you can save the document as an ACT! word processing document, with the .WPA extension.

With the File➪Save As command, you can save an ACT! word processing document in Rich Text Format (with an .RTF extension), which is a file that retains basic formatting codes and can be read by other word processors. You can also save your file as an ACT! form letter template or a report template.

Other word processing programs may not be able to read documents created in ACT!'s word processor. To get around this problem, save your document in Rich Text Format.

Deleting, renaming, or doing other things to your document

From within the Save As dialog box, you can delete, rename, or do other things to your document by highlighting the file and selecting the desired option from the menu that appears when you click the right mouse button. This is a basic Windows file management feature.

Creating Form Letters

The strength of ACT!'s word processing functionality comes from its ability to merge contact information into form letter templates. Earlier in this chapter, I describe how you can use ACT! to merge a contact's name and address into a Letter, Memo, or Fax template. Now it's time to think this through a bit further. Instead of writing all your letters from scratch, why not create some boilerplate form letters that you can use to send to your customers, clients, prospects, or anyone else?

That's the beauty of ACT!'s mail merge functions: You create a form letter template and then merge that letter with one contact, a dozen contacts, or several hundred contacts, all at once. Now you're working smarter and saving lots of time by automating the entire process of creating letters.

You can create a form letter template from scratch (by selecting File⇨New and then choosing your word processing template from the New dialog box), but you'll find that it's much easier to modify an existing form letter template than it is to create a new template from scratch.

Before you start editing an existing template, save the template file with a new name (using the File⇨Save As command) because you don't want to make changes to the original template. This way, if you make a mistake or if you don't like the way the modified template turned out, you can delete the modified template and start over. If you do mess up your original ACT! templates, you can perform a custom installation from your original ACT! CD-ROM and reinstall your letter and report templates. The people at ACT! Technical Support (phone them at 541-465-8645) can help you reinstall these files.

Saving your form letter template

When you are satisfied with your new template, you'll probably want to save it. Do this by selecting File⇨Save or pressing Ctrl+S. If the file already has a name — you should always be working with a copy of a form letter template, not the original — ACT! saves the updated version of the file, replacing the previous version.

If the file doesn't have a name, the Save As dialog box appears. Give the file a name, and click Save. (The .TPL extension is automatically attached to the template, and the file is saved in the ACT! Template directory.)

If you're modifying an ACT! template in Word, you must remember to add the .ADT extension to the template and save these templates in ACT!'s Template directory.

Using form letter templates

ACT! stores all form letter templates in the Template directory. ACT! templates carry the .TPL extension. All Word form letter templates have the .ADT extension. LETTER.TPL is the ACT! template for the standard letter. The following is a list of ACT! templates:

- **LETTER.TPL:** This is the template that ACT! uses when you select Letter from the Write menu.

- **FAXCOVER.TPL:** This is the template that ACT! uses when you select Fax Cover Page from the Write menu.

- **MEMO.TPL:** This is the template that ACT! uses when you select Memorandum from the Write menu.

Inserting ACT! merge codes into a form letter template

In this section, I explain how the LETTER.TPL Letter template was created. (For this example, I've modified the LETTER.TPL template to include my letterhead.) After you understand this process, creating any ACT! form letter template is easy.

The process of creating a word processing template is the same if you're using Word, but you must remember to save your template in ACT!'s Template directory with either the file extensions .TPL (for templates created in ACT!'s word processor) or .ADT (for templates created in Word).

To open LETTER.TPL, select Write➪Edit Document Template, and the Open dialog box appears. Scroll through the list of files until you find the LETTER.TPL file. Highlight the file, and click Open. The LETTER.TPL file opens in the ACT! word processor.

To create a new document or form letter template from scratch, select File⇨New, and the New dialog box appears. Highlight the word processing document or template for your word processor (ACT! or Word), and click OK.

The strange-looking codes that you may see in a document are ACT!'s merge codes. (The < > marks are called delimiters.) These codes tell the word processor which fields of information to extract from the contact record and where to place them on the form letter template. In this letter template, ACT! extracts the Contact, Company, Address 1, Address 2, Address 3, City, State, and ZIP fields from the contact's record and inserts them in the new letter.

You have two ways of inserting merge codes into an ACT! template. You can type them in, which is a big waste of time, or you can open ACT!'s Mail Merge Fields dialog box, and let ACT! enter them for you.

To access the Mail Merge Fields dialog box, select InsertÍMail Merge Fields from the menu bar in the word processor.

Here are some tips for using the mail merge fields and the Letter template:

✔ The Mail Merge Fields dialog box is active only while you're working in a Letter template.

✔ The basic LETTER.TPL template uses the contact address displayed in the Contact window. To create a Letter template that sends correspondence to the contact's home address, insert the following codes in place of the present codes in the LETTER.TPL template:

```
<Contact.:26>
<Home Address 1>
<Home Address 2>
<Home City>, <Home State> <Home Zip>
```

Then give this file a new name, such as HOMEADDRESS.TPL.

Testing your letter template

After you create your new Letter template, you'll probably want to test it to see how it really looks. (If you like the way it looks, save it. If you don't, go back to work.)

To preview your template, select the File⇨Mail Merge command, and the Mail Merge dialog box appears. The Mail Merge dialog box gives you the opportunity to select which contacts you want to include in this letter merge and where you want to send the output: Printer, E-mail, Fax, or Word processor. (I discuss performing ACT! mail merges next.)

Here are some additional ACT! template tips:

- ✔ When you're experimenting with a new template design, select the active contact (the contact record presently displayed on the ACT! contact screen) and send the output to the document screen in which you can view your creation.

- ✔ If you have standard, boilerplate phrases that you frequently use in your letters or documents, create separate document files for each one of these phrases and then choose File⇨Insert from the menu bar to insert the phrases into your document.

- ✔ Use form letter templates to create order forms, quotation or bid forms, and invoice forms.

- ✔ If you're using Word you can use the table features — with formulas — to create invoices or purchase orders, and the word processor will perform the mathematical calculations.

Adding form letter templates to the Write menu

ACT! makes it easy for you to use any form letter templates that you've created by enabling you to add them as additional commands on the Write menu. To add your form letter template to the Write menu, select Write⇨Modify Menu. The Modify Menu dialog box appears, in which you can add custom form letters that appear on the Write menu.

If you're a touch typist and like to use the keyboard instead of the mouse, you can assign underlined letters to your ACT! custom menu items so that you can initiate ACT! commands by pressing the ALT key plus an underlined letter. When you're adding a new item to an ACT! menu, such as your Write Modify Menu, place an ampersand (&) before the letter that you want ACT! to underline. If you number your documents, use &1 as 1 and &2 as 2. To open document number 1, you press Alt+W+1.

Using ACT!'s Mail Merge Feature

After you've created a form letter template, I'm sure you'll find situations in which you want to send the same form letter to several, or maybe hundreds, of people. Well, this is easy to do from ACT!, and here's how you do it:

1. **Select Write⇨Mail Merge.**

   The Mail Merge dialog box, opens. From the Mail Merge dialog box, you make the following selections:

   - **Merge With:** Select the contacts to whom you're sending this letter — Current Contact, Current Lookup, All Contacts, or a Selected Group.

   - **Send Output To:** Select where you want to send the finished documents. You can choose Printer, Fax, E-mail, or the Word Processor.

   - **Template:** Choose your form letter template from the displayed list. You can also create a new template or edit an existing one.

   - **Regarding:** If you selected the Printer, Fax, or E-mail option, you can enter information about the document in the Regarding field.

2. **Make your selections.**

3. **Click the OK button.**

   ACT! merges the selected ACT! contacts with the selected form letter template.

To record a History Notation for your document, select the Create History When Sent option. You can also enter information in the Regarding field.

When sending a form letter to a group of people, make sure that the text of the form letter is appropriate for everyone to whom you're sending the letter. You don't want to have to customize each and every letter.

ACT! doesn't give you the flexibility of changing the mail merge defaults when you open the Mail Merge dialog box, but here's a work-around if you're so inclined: Record a macro that opens the Mail Merge dialog box and selects the settings that you want. Then add the macro to the Write menu in place of the Mail Merge command. Writing macros and customizing your menus are covered in Chapter 27.

Using ACT!'s Word Processor

In this section of this chapter, I cover how to format your text by using ACT!'s word processor.

Before I begin, I should mention that I don't want you to think that ACT!'s word processor is the greatest word processor that's ever been created, because it isn't. However, ACT!'s word processor can play a very big part in helping you save time and become more efficient because it integrates seamlessly with your ACT! database and it's fast.

When you know how to take advantage of its major strengths, ACT!'s word processor is a huge time-saver.

And you may find that ACT!'s word processor is more convenient to use than Word for sending routine correspondence, writing form letters, and creating fax cover sheets.

Opening ACT!'s word processor

To open an existing word processing document or template from within ACT!, just select File⇔Open and then select ACT! Word Processor Document from the Files of Type menu. The list of files in ACT!'s Document folder appears, and you select your file. (To open an ACT! word processing template, select ACT! Word Processing Template from the Files of Type menu.)

When you want to create a new document or a form letter template from scratch, select File⇔New, and the New dialog box appears. Highlight either ACT! Word Processor Document or ACT! Word Processor Template, and click OK.

Formatting your documents

This is how you format your ACT! word processing documents.

✔ **Setting your word processing preferences:** To set ACT!'s word processing preferences, open the Preferences dialog box by selecting Edit⇔Preferences from the menu bar.

In the Preferences dialog box, you can specify the measurement units that you want ACT! to use. You can also enable or disable the Tool Tips option (when you pass your cursor over a button, a description appears). In the Spelling tab, you specify which dictionaries you want to use when spell-checking documents.

✔ **Setting up your page size:** Select File⇔Page Setup, and the Page Setup dialog box appears. Here, you can change the page orientation, paper size, default margins, and paper source for both new documents or previously created documents.

✔ **Setting your default page margins:** To set your page margins for the whole document, select Format⇔Page Margins, and the Page Margins dialog box appears.

✔ **Changing a paragraph's margins:** To change a paragraph's margins, place your cursor within a paragraph or highlight a block of text (if you want to change the justification of several paragraphs). Then reposition the margin markers on the ruler bar that's displayed at the top of the word processor screen.

From the ruler bar, you can change the position of the left and right margins for a highlighted block of text, or for the entire document, by dragging the margin marker to the left or right with your mouse pointer. When you release your mouse button, the highlighted text lines up with the margin marker. You can also change how far the first line in the paragraph is indented from the left margin by moving the inverted-T marker.

✔ **Viewing and hiding page margins:** If you want to see or hide your page margins (top, bottom, left, right, headers, and footers) on the word processing screen, select View⇨Page Guides.

✔ **Justifying your text:** When you justify text, you determine its alignment within a paragraph. In ACT!'s word processor, you have four justification choices: left, center, right, and full.

To justify a paragraph or block of text, position your cursor within the paragraph whose text you want to justify, or highlight a block of text if you want to change the justification of several paragraphs, and click one of the paragraph justification buttons located on the ruler bar.

✔ **Changing the spacing of your text:** In ACT!, you have a number of line spacing choices. You can have single spacing, one-and-a-half-line spacing, double spacing, and spacing at a user-defined measure.

To change line spacing, just position your cursor within the paragraph whose text you want to change the spacing of, or highlight a block of text if you want to change the spacing for several paragraphs, and click the line spacing buttons on the ruler bar.

✔ **Keeping your paragraphs together:** Many times, when you're writing a letter or creating a document, you want to keep specific lines of text or paragraphs together on the same page, thus preventing the automatic insertion of a page break between the lines of text or paragraphs.

To keep a paragraph or block of text together, just highlight the text, select the Format⇨Paragraph command, and check the Paragraph dialog box's Keep With Next option.

✔ **Setting your tabs:** In ACT!, you can add, move, and remove tab markers from the ruler bar or from the Tabs dialog box, which you open by selecting Format⇨Tabs from the menu bar. You can also access the Tabs command by right clicking within a word processor document.

✔ **Applying your tab and margin settings to another paragraph:** If you want to copy a specific paragraph's setting (margins, tabs, and so on) from one paragraph to another paragraph within the same document without having to redefine the paragraph's settings, use the Copy Ruler command.

To copy your ruler settings, place your mouse pointer anywhere within a paragraph that contains the margin or tab settings that you want to copy. Choose the Copy Ruler command from the Edit menu or the right mouse button menu to copy the ruler settings.

To apply the settings to another paragraph, position your mouse pointer within the paragraph, or highlight a block of text, and choose the Apply Ruler command from the Edit menu or the right mouse button menu.

Inserting headers, footers, and more into your document

In ACT!, you can insert headers, footers, page breaks, dates, time, and special characters into a document. This list shows you how.

✔ **Inserting headers and footers:** If you would like to insert a header or a footer in a document, choose the Header and Footer command from the Format menu, and the Header and Footer dialog box appears.

To enter header or footer information in your document, move to the top or bottom of the first page of your document, place the cursor in the header or footer box with your mouse, and enter the text. When you've finished, use your mouse to move the cursor to the main body of the document.

✔ **Exclude header or footer from first page:** If you're placing a header or footer in your document and don't want the header or footer to appear on the document's first page, select the Exclude Header and Footer From First Page option.

✔ **Inserting a page break:** When you want to insert a page break in your document, position the cursor where you want the pages to break and choose Page Break from the Insert menu or press Shift+Enter. A gray bar indicates the start of the new page.

To remove a page break, move your cursor to the top of the new page and press the Backspace key.

✔ **Inserting the current date into your document:** To insert the current date into an ACT! document, place your cursor where you want the date inserted, select Insert⇨Date, and the Insert Date dialog box appears.

Choose the Short Format if you want your date to appear as 12/31/99, or the Long Format if you want your date to appear as Friday, December 31, 1999.

Choose the Always Update in Document option if you want ACT! to show the current date whenever you open the document. If you want the document's date to remain unchanged whenever you open the document, select the Never Update in Document (Insert as Text Only) option.

✔ **Inserting the current time into your document:** To insert the time into an ACT! document, select Time from the Insert menu, and the Insert Time dialog box appears.

Choose the Always Update in Document option if you want ACT! to show the current time whenever you open the document. If you want the document's time to remain unchanged whenever you open the document, select the Never Update in Document (Insert as Text Only) option.

✔ **Inserting page numbers within your document:** When you write a letter, the automatic insertion of page numbers gives your letter a very polished look. To insert a page number in your document, place your cursor where you want the page number positioned and select the Page Number command from the Insert menu. ACT! automatically inserts the page number in your document. Remember, though, that ACT! doesn't offer page numbering options such as Roman numerals.

To remove a page number from your document, highlight the number and delete it.

To number the pages in your document, place the Page Number command in a header or a footer. If you don't want the page number to appear on the first page of your letter or document, place the page number in a header or a footer and then select the Exclude Header and Footer From First Page option in the Header and Footer dialog box.

Some Useful Third-Party Products

ACT! has many powerful features for doing merges with template documents. The products I discuss in this section either make ACT! better or do things better than ACT!.

DAZzle

When you want to print an envelope or a label, let DAZzle do it. DAZzle is an envelope and label printing program that makes it easy for you to design and print envelopes, labels, and flyers on any paper size. With just a click of your mouse, you select where you want the return and main addresses to appear. Then you can import graphic images, include messages, and add POSTNET bar codes.

POSTNET bar codes are the ZIP+4 bar codes that identify the destination of the mailing piece: the zip code, delivery point, and carrier route. The presence of the POSTNET bar code is important because your letter will be handled with electronic sorting equipment, which means that it should be processed faster and more efficiently.

DAZzle can import information directly from ACT!, so you don't even have to play the paste-and-cut game. And if you have the contact's ZIP+4 zip code, DAZzle prints POSTNET bar codes.

Oh, you don't have the ZIP+4 zip codes? Not to worry! DAZzle has a great feature called Dial-A-Zip. After you've imported an ACT! address (or any other kind of address) into DAZzle, Dial-A-Zip dials into a Zip-Station — a remote CD-ROM directory of addresses in the United States. When it makes a connection, DAZzle gets the ZIP+4 zip code, adds it to the address on your envelope, and updates the zip code on your contact's contact record. The whole process takes about 20 seconds.

I've been using DAZzle to print my envelopes and labels (you can even print single labels) for both individual contacts and lookups. It's just a great product. DAZzle is made by Envelope Manager Software, and you can contact the company at 247 High St., Palo Alto, CA 94301; phone 800-576-3279; Web site www.envelopemanager.com.

Label printers

If you've ever printed labels from your laser printer, you know it's easy to print a whole page of them. But what do you do when you need to print just one label? I hope you're not still using a typewriter or, worse yet, writing them by hand. If you are, I've got a better idea. Use a label printer.

Seiko's Smart Label Printer Pro prints laser-quality labels on a variety of label sizes, incorporating text, photo-like graphics, special messages, and bar codes. So get rid of your typewriter, and use your computer to type all your labels. You'll save yourself hours of time.

For more information, contact Seiko Instruments USA, Inc., 1130 Ringwood Court, San Jose, CA 95131; phone 800-888-0817; Web site www.seikosmart.com.

FedEx Ship

I find filling out FedEx shipping forms to be very time-consuming. Then I learned about Federal Express's *free* shipping software — FedEx Ship.

FedEx Ship enables you to create and print your FedEx shipping forms with your computer. And best of all, FedEx Ship reads your ACT! database.

To get a copy of FedEx Ship, call 1-800-Go-FedEx. It's free.

Chapter 22

Faxing from ACT!

● ●

In This Chapter

▶ Setting your faxing preferences

▶ Sending faxes

▶ Using other sending options

▶ Working with your ACT! database from within WinFax PRO

● ●

ACT! and WinFax PRO (version 8.03 or higher) have complete integration. You can launch and operate WinFax PRO from within ACT!'s Contact window and Contact List window.

You can read and edit your WinFax PRO directory from within ACT!, and you can read your ACT! database from within WinFax PRO.

If you do much faxing from your computer, you should use WinFax PRO — it makes faxing a breeze. A trial copy of WinFax PRO is included on your ACT! CD-ROM. For more information, you can call Symantec Customer Service at 800-441-7234. Or visit Symantec's Web site at www.symantec.com.

Setting Your Faxing Preferences

To make ACT! and WinFax PRO work properly, you need to do two things:

1. **Select WinFax PRO as your faxing software.**

   You do this by selecting Edit⇨Preferences from the menu bar, which opens the Preferences dialog box. On the General tab, you make your faxing selection.

2. **Select your WinFax options.**

   You do this by selecting the WinFax Options tab from within the Preferences dialog box, which is shown in Figure 22-1.

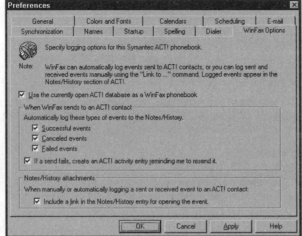

Figure 22-1:
ACT!'s
WinFax PRO
Preferences
settings.

From the WinFax Options tab, you have a number of faxing options. You select faxing options by placing a check mark in the check box. You deselect options by removing the check marks from checked boxes. Here are your options:

- Do you want to use the currently open ACT! database as a WinFax phone book?

- What information do you want WinFax to log in the contact's Notes/History tab when a fax is sent to an ACT! contact? You can select from the following:

    - **Successful Events:** The fax was sent and received.

    - **Canceled Events:** The fax transmission was canceled.

    - **Failed Events:** The fax wasn't received.

- If a send fails, do you want ACT! to automatically schedule a reminder to resend it?

- Do you want ACT! to automatically attach a fax — either sent or received — to the contact's Notes/History?

Sending Faxes

ACT! enables you to send faxes in a variety of ways. The following sections show you how.

Sending Quick Faxes from the Contact window

ACT!'s Quick Fax command enables you to send a fax to someone directly from the Contact window. This is what you do:

1. **Click the Quick Fax icon.**

   ACT! launches WinFax PRO. The WinFax PRO Send dialog box, which is shown in Figure 22-2, opens.

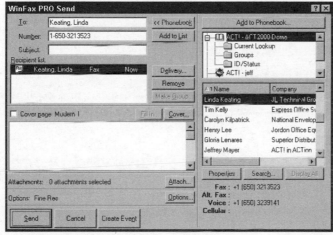

Figure 22-2:
WinFax PRO
Send dialog
box with
phone-
book open.

2. **Click the Phonebook button.**

   The list of contacts in your ACT! database appears.

3. **Select the person to whom you want to send, and click the Add To List button.**

   The person's name is inserted in the Recipient List field.

4. **Enter the fax regarding information in the Subject line.**

5. **Type your message in the Quick Cover Page box, and click the Send button.**

   ACT! opens the WinFax PRO Preview window.

6. **Click the Send Fax button from within WinFax PRO.**

   WinFax PRO sends your fax, makes an entry in the contact's Notes/History tab, and logs the fax in WinFax PRO's Send Log folder.

If you want to send the fax to additional recipients, you can choose them from the current lookup, the selected ACT! groups, or the categories listed in the ID/Status field. You make your selection by highlighting the contact(s) and clicking the Add to List buttons.

Sending Quick Faxes from the Contact List window

ACT! also gives you the ability to send the same fax to several people. This is how you do it:

1. **Open the Contact List window.**

2. **Highlight or tag the people to whom you want to send a fax.**

3. **Click the Quick Fax icon.**

   ACT! launches WinFax PRO.

4. **Follow the steps outlined in the preceding section on sending Quick Faxes from the Contact window.**

Sending faxes from your word processor

ACT! also enables you to send faxes from your word processor, which I discuss in Chapter 21.

Working with ACT! and WinFax PRO

From within WinFax PRO, you can send faxes to people who are in your ACT! database, and you can add people to your ACT! database from within WinFax PRO.

From within WinFax PRO, you can send faxes to people who are in your ACT! database. This is how you do it:

1. **Select Send⇨New Fax from the menu bar.**

   The WinFax PRO Send dialog box opens (refer to Figure 22-2).

2. **Select the person to whom you want to send a fax from the list of ACT! databases.**

   The person's name appears in the To field, and his or her fax number appears in the Number field.

3. **Enter the fax regarding information in the Subject line.**

4. **Click the Add to List button.**

   The person's name is added to the Recipient List.

5. **Type the fax message in the Quick Cover Page field, or select an attachment.**

6. **Click the Send button.**

   The WinFax PRO Preview window opens.

7. **Click the Send Fax button.**

   WinFax PRO sends your fax.

From within WinFax PRO, you can add people to your ACT! database by using the WinFax PRO Send dialog box. This is how you do it:

1. **Enter the person's name in the To field and his or her fax number in the Number field.**

2. **Select the ACT! database to which you want to add this person.**

3. **Click the Add to Phonebook button.**

   The Symantec ACT! 4.0 Contact Properties dialog box opens with the person's name and fax number displayed.

4. **Enter the person's other information, such as Company, Phone Number, and Address information.**

5. **Click OK.**

   WinFax PRO adds the person to your ACT! database.

Chapter 23

ACT! and E-Mail

· ·

In This Chapter

▶ Setting your e-mail preferences

▶ Adding an e-mail address to an ACT! contact's record

▶ Creating an e-mail message

▶ Using the e-mail Drafts folder, Inbox, and Briefcase

· ·

*W*ith ACT!'s e-mail features, you can perform numerous tasks that will help you to grow your business and expand your career because you'll be saving time and increasing your productivity. Here are some of the other things you can do:

- ✔ Attach one or more files of any type to an e-mail message.

- ✔ Attach a single Contact Record, a Lookup, or a Group to an e-mail message. And, you can include the contact's or group's notes, history, and activities.

- ✔ Attach contact records using the Internet Standard format (vCard), making them compatible with Microsoft Outlook.

- ✔ Send confirmations of scheduled calls, meetings, and to-dos from the Schedule Activity dialog box.

- ✔ Send documents directly from your word processor.

- ✔ Create reports and send them as e-mail attachments.

- ✔ Set your preferences such that when you send an e-mail message, ACT! automatically makes a history record.

And you can do all of this with just a few clicks of your mouse.

By the way, ACT! supports the following e-mail systems:

- ✔ Any standard Internet e-mail client

- ✔ Microsoft Outlook

- ✔ Microsoft Exchange

✔ Lotus Notes

✔ Eudora

✔ cc:Mail

✔ CompuServe

Setting Your E-Mail Preferences

Before you begin using ACT! to send and receive e-mail, you need to choose your e-mail system and set up the e-mail default settings. You can access ACT!'s e-mail setup by doing one of the following:

✔ Select Help➪QuickStart Wizard.

✔ Click the E-mail System Setup button on the E-mail tab inside the Preferences dialog box.

✔ Click the E-mail System Setup button on the E-mail Addresses dialog box. You open this dialog box by selecting Contact➪E-mail Addresses from the menu bar within the Contact window.

You setup your default e-mail preferences from within the Preferences dialog box, which you open by selecting Edit➪Preferences and then clicking the E-mail tab. ACT!'s E-mail Preferences options are shown in Figure 23-1.

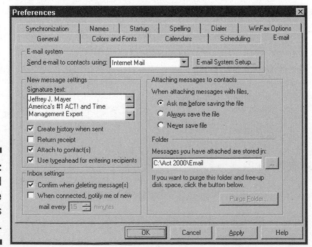

Figure 23-1:
The E-mail
tab of the
Preferences
dialog box.

Why can't I use America Online as my e-mail system?

ACT! users have been asking the question: "Why can't I use AOL as my e-mail system?" for several years. The answer is quite simple. AOL's e-mail system is proprietary. To date, they have not allowed Symantec's ACT! programmers to have access to their e-mail code. Maybe someday they'll lighten up!

New message settings

In the New Message Settings section of the E-mail Preferences, you can do the following:

- ✔ **Signature Text:** Here, you create default text to appear as the signature for all your e-mail messages.

- ✔ **Create History When Sent:** If you want ACT! to automatically create a history item for each e-mail message you send, select this option.

- ✔ **Return Receipt:** To request a return receipt for each e-mail message you send, select this option.

- ✔ **Attach to Contact:** To automatically attach this e-mail message to the recipient's contact record, choose this option. If the recipient is not in your ACT! database, the message attaches to the My Record contact record.

- ✔ **Use Typeahead for Entering Recipients:** To select e-mail recipients from an address book by typing the first few letters of their names, select this option. (Typeahead also works in the Type In Recipient Name field, located at the top of the E-mail message window.) Otherwise, you need to enter the recipient's full name or select the recipient from a list.

Inbox settings

ACT! gives you the option of setting the following in-box default settings:

- ✔ **Confirm When Deleting Message:** To have ACT! ask you if you really want to delete this message, select the Confirm When Deleting Message(s) box.

✔ **Notify Me of New Mail:** Checking the When Connected, Notify Me of New Mail Every __ Minutes check box lets you can set the frequency with which ACT! checks your e-mail system for incoming messages. (This option works only if you are logged on and permanently connected to your e-mail server.)

Attaching messages to contacts

When attaching files to e-mail messages, you have the following choices:

✔ **Ask Me:** ACT! always asks before saving the file.

✔ **Always Save:** ACT! always saves the file.

✔ **Never Save:** ACT! never saves the file.

E-mail messages are stored in ACT!'s Email folder by default. Click the Browse button to select a different folder.

To purge all e-mail messages that are attached to contact records, click the Purge Folder button.

Selecting and setting up your e-mail system

You select your primary e-mail system, the default system for sending all e-mail messages from ACT!, from the Send E-mail to Contacts Using drop-down menu.

You set up your e-mail system by clicking the E-mail System Setup button. ACT!'s E-mail Setup Wizard appears.

The Wizard walks you through the setup process for whichever e-mail system(s) you choose. Your choices are: cc:Mail, CompuServe, Eudora, Internet Mail (Any standard Internet e-mail client), Lotus Notes, MS Exchange, and MS Outlook.

If you're using Eudora, Internet Mail, MS Exchange, or MS Outlook, you need to know such information as your user name, outgoing SMTP server, and incoming POP3 server. You can find this information inside each program's default settings. Or you may need to contact your Internet service provider.

Selecting a format for attaching ACT! contacts

ACT! gives you the option of attaching ACT! contact records to e-mail messages in both the ACT! format and the Internet Standard Format (vCard/vCal), which is compatible with Microsoft Outlook. With this enhancement, you can share ACT! contact information with people using ACT! and/or people using Microsoft Outlook. And people who are using Microsoft Outlook can share their contact information with you.

You make the default selection in the Attaching Contacts/Activities to Messages section of the General tab of the Preferences dialog box.

You can also make this selection when you're attaching the contact to the e-mail message.

Adding an E-Mail Address to a Contact's Record

To add an e-mail address to an ACT! contact record, just place your cursor in the E-mail Address field in the Contact window and type the address.

You can also open the E-mail Addresses dialog box by placing your cursor in the E-mail Address field and pressing F2, or clicking the down-arrow and selecting Edit E-mail Address from the drop-down menu.

To edit an existing e-mail address, or add additional addresses to the contact's record, just place your cursor in the E-mail Address field, click the down-arrow, and select Edit E-mail Address from the drop-down menu (or press F2). The E-mail Addresses dialog box appears. (You can also select Contact⇨E-mail Addresses from the Contact window menu bar.)

From the E-mail Addresses dialog box, you can do the following:

- ✔ Add a new address.
- ✔ Edit an existing address.
- ✔ Delete an old e-mail address.
- ✔ Access the E-mail Preferences dialog box.

Creating an E-Mail Message

You can open the E-mail Message window, which is shown in Figure 23-2, in any of the following ways:

- ✔ Select Write⇨E-mail Message from the menu bar in the Contact, Contact List, Group, Calendar, or Task List windows.

- ✔ Click the View E-mail button to open the E-mail window, and select the E-mail⇨Create Message command.

- ✔ Press Ctrl+E in the E-mail window.

- ✔ Select the Send E-mail Message to Activity Participants option in the Advanced Options tab of the Schedule Activity dialog box; then click OK.

- ✔ Select Write⇨E-mail Message from the right mouse button menu in the Contact, Contact List, or Groups windows.

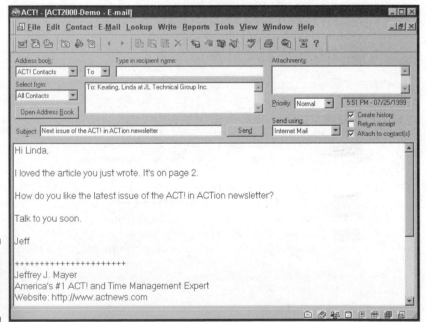

Figure 23-2:
The E-mail
Message
window.

Addressing your e-mail message

The first thing you have to do when you want to send an e-mail message is select the person to whom it will go. This is the easy way to do it:

1. **Find the person in your ACT! database by using ACT!'s Lookup feature.**

2. **Select Write⇨E-mail Message.**

   ACT! opens the E-mail Message window and selects this person as the e-mail recipient.

Here are some e-mail addressing tips:

✔ Click on the person's e-mail address in the Contact window, and ACT! opens the e-mail message window and selects this person as the e-mail recipient.

✔ Open the Contact List window, and highlight (or tag) several contacts. Then select Write⇨E-mail Message. ACT! opens the E-mail Message window and selects these people as the e-mail recipients.

✔ Drag and drop a contact from the Contact window, or several contacts from the Contact List window, onto the e-mail message's Recipient section. ACT! inserts the name(s) as e-mail recipients.

✔ Begin typing the person's last name and then first name in the E-mail Message window's Type in Recipient Name, and ACT! locates the person in the database and makes the person the e-mail recipient. For you to use this ACT! feature, you must select the Use Typeahead For Entering Recipients option in ACT!'s E-mail Preferences settings, which were discussed earlier in this chapter.

Using your e-mail address books

In the E-mail Message window, click the Open Address Book button, and ACT!'s address book, as shown in Figure 23-3, opens. When you select your ACT! database as your e-mail address list, you can search for e-mail addresses from within the entire database, the current lookup, or every member of an ACT! group.

When you select your CompuServe, Eudora, MS Exchange, MS Outlook, Lotus Notes, or cc:Mail address book as your e-mail address list, you can search for e-mail addresses from your address book(s) for that particular service provider or e-mail program.

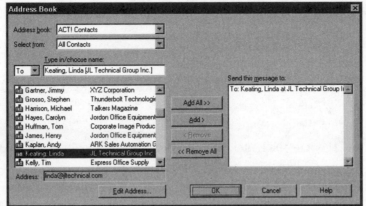

Figure 23-3:
The Address
Book dialog
box.

Select Internet Directory as your Address Book, and you can search the Yahoo!, BigFoot, or WhoWhere Internet directories for e-mail addresses. Searching for e-mail addresses over the Internet is covered in Chapter 10.

Here's how you select an e-mail recipient:

1. **Select an address book from the e-mail system(s) listed in the Address Book drop-down list.**

   The address book opens.

2. **Select To, cc, or bcc from the drop-down list.**

   You follow the same steps when creating cc (carbon copy) and bcc (blind carbon copy) e-mail addresses. If you send a carbon copy of an e-mail message, the e-mail message includes the list of the people who received a copy. In a blind carbon copy, the e-mail message does not include a list of the people who received a copy.

3. **Highlight a name, or several names, in the Address Book Entries field.**

4. **Click the Add button.**

   ACT! inserts that name in the Send This Message To box.

To edit the person's e-mail address, highlight the name and click the Edit Address button.

Entering the subject line

The subject line is one of the most important parts of an e-mail message. You use this line to summarize the content of your message in a very brief but descriptive manner.

If you make your subject line so descriptive that it grabs your readers' attention, they'll probably read your message first.

Typing your e-mail message

You enter your e-mail message in the Message Body field of the E-mail Message window.

When writing your e-mail message, write short, easy-to-read sentences and paragraphs. Put the most important information in the first few sentences of the first paragraph.

Here are some other e-mail writing tips:

- ✔ Try to keep your e-mail message short.

- ✔ If you're including a list of items, use a numbered or bulleted list (like this one). It's easier to read.

- ✔ If you must send a long message, attach the file as an enclosure. (See the next section to find out how to attach a file to your e-mail message.) Write a brief description of the message in the subject line. The e-mail message itself should contain a description of the enclosed file.

- ✔ If you attach a document to an e-mail message, write a brief but thorough description of the document. Don't forget to include the purpose of the document, detailed instructions regarding what the recipient is supposed to do with the document, and the date you need a response. This item of business should then be added as an ACT! activity.

Attaching stuff to your e-mail messages

This is how you attach files, contacts, groups, and activities to your e-mail messages:

✔ **Attaching files:** The easiest way to attach a file — a word processing document, spreadsheet, or report, for example — to an e-mail message is to open Windows Explorer, and drag and drop the file onto the e-mail message. The file's name and path are inserted in the Attachments field in the E-mail Message window.

You can also use ACT!'s attach file command by pressing Ctrl+I or selecting the E-mail⇨Attach to Message⇨File command.

✔ **Attaching a contact record to your e-mail message:** The easiest way to attach a contact record to an e-mail message is to open the Contact window, and drag and drop the contact record onto the Attachments section of the e-mail message.

If you want to attach multiple contacts to your e-mail message, the easiest way is from within the Contact List window. Just highlight, or tag, the contacts, and drag and drop them onto the Attachments section of the e-mail message.

✔ **Attaching contacts with the Attach to Message command:** ACT!'s Attach to Message command offers you more e-mail attachment options than you have by dragging and dropping. Select E-mail⇨Attach to Message⇨Contact from the menu bar, and the Attach Contact(s) dialog box appears. From the Attach Contact(s) dialog box, you have the following options:

  • You can select from All Contacts, Current Lookup, or the members of any group.

  • You can send the contact record in the ACT! format, the Internet Standard format, or both.

  • You can include Notes/History, Activities, and/or Sales Opportunities with the contact record attachment.

✔ **Attaching groups to your e-mail messages:** When you want to attach a group to an e-mail message, select E-mail⇨Attach to Message⇨Contact from the menu bar. The Attach Group(s) dialog box appears. From the Attach Groups dialog box, you can select from all your groups, or from the current lookup; and you can include group Notes/History and/or Activities with the group record attachment.

✔ **Attaching activities:** When you want to attach an activity to an e-mail message, just highlight the activity in the Activities tab, or highlight several activities in the Task List window, and drag and drop the activity onto the Attachments section of the e-mail message.

✔ **Deleting attachments:** If you change your mind and decide that you don't want to include a specific contact record, group record, or file as an attachment, just select the attachment in the E-mail Message window and press Delete.

Additional e-mail options

ACT! gives you some additional e-mail options:

- ✔ **Setting the priority:** In the E-mail Message window, you can designate your e-mail message as Low, Normal (which is the default), or High priority by selecting one of these three choices on the right side of the dialog box.

- ✔ **Creating a history:** To create a history for this e-mail message, select the Create History check box.

- ✔ **Attach to contact(s):** To attach this e-mail message to selected contact(s), select the Attach to Contact(s) check box.

- ✔ **Getting a receipt:** To receive an acknowledgment that your message was received and opened, select the Receipt check box.

Sending your e-mail message now or later

After you've written your e-mail message, ACT! gives you a choice. You can send your message now or later. To send your e-mail message now, click the Send button, select E-mail⇨Send Mail Now, or press Ctrl+Enter. If you want ACT! to store your e-mail message in the Drafts folder, to send at a later time, select E-mail⇨Send Mail Later or press Ctrl+Shift+Enter. (ACT!'s Drafts folder is discussed later in this chapter.)

More Ways to Create an E-Mail Message

You can also create an e-mail message from your word processor, when you're scheduling an activity, and when you're creating a report. This section tells you how.

Creating an e-mail message with your word processor

You can send e-mail from within your word processor. Here's how:

1. **Create your document.**

2. **Select File⇨Send⇨E-mail from the menu bar.**

   The Send E-mail dialog box appears.

When sending an e-mail message from your word processor, you choose which parts of the word processing document you want to include in your e-mail message and how you want to include them. You have the following options:

- Include the entire document as a file attachment.

- Include the entire document in the message's body.

- Include selected text in the message's body. (This option is available only if text has been selected.)

3. **Make your choice, and click OK.**

   ACT! sends your e-mail message.

Sending a mail merge as e-mail

When you want to send a custom e-mail message to many people, use ACT!'s Mail Merge feature by selecting the Write⇨Mail Merge command. From the Mail Merge dialog box, you select the contacts to whom to send the letter; the output, which will be e-mail; and the form letter template that you want to use.

ACT! performs the mail merge and creates separate letters for each e-mail recipient, just as if you were performing a mail merge and sending the output to your printer. Performing mail merges is covered in Chapter 21.

Confirming a scheduled activity

When you schedule a new activity or modify a previously scheduled activity, you can send an e-mail message from the Schedule Activity dialog box.

Select the Advanced Options tab, and choose the Send E-mail Message to the Activity Participants option. Click OK, and ACT! opens the E-mail Message window, inserts the contents of the Regarding field into the E-mail Subject field, and enters the activity information in the Message Body area.

Sending a report as an e-mail message

When you create a report, you can send it as an attachment to an e-mail message without ever printing it out or viewing it on-screen. First, select the type of report to create from the Reports menu or the Open Report dialog box (choose Reports⇨Other Report). The Run Report dialog box appears.

From the Run Report dialog box, select the report's particulars (which Contacts, Notes/History items, Activities, and Sales/Opportunities you want included in the report). In the Send Output To section, select E-mail and click OK. ACT! compiles the report, opens the E-mail Message window, and adds the report as an attachment.

To attach a report that's already been created and saved, attach it to your e-mail message as a file. Preparing ACT! reports is discussed in Chapter 27.

Using the Drafts Folder

Use ACT!'s Drafts folder to store your outgoing e-mail messages so that you can send them at a later time. For example, you may create an e-mail message and then decide that you want to put it aside for a little while so you can think about it and edit it further before sending it out.

Or you may want to create several e-mail messages before you log onto your e-mail system, and send them all at once, instead of sending each message one at a time. This is a nice feature when you're traveling or working from home. When you're ready to send your messages, select the ones that you want to send and then select E-mail⇨Send Mail Now from the menu bar.

ACT! uses icons to indicate whether a message has an attachment and to designate an e-mail message's priority. These icons are positioned to the left of an e-mail message in ACT!'s E-mail window.

 ✔ A paper clip appears next to the icon if the message has attachments.

 ✔ A plain envelope icon appears next to a low-priority message.

 ✔ A shaded envelope icon appears next to a normal-priority message.

 ✔ An exclamation point appears next to a high-priority message.

From within the Drafts folder, you can read, print, save, or delete the e-mail messages that you have written but have not yet sent.

 ✔ **Reading your e-mail messages:** To read an e-mail message stored in your Drafts folder, select the message and choose the Read Message command from the E-mail menu, or double-click on the message itself, and the E-mail Message window appears. Here, you can edit your message or add attachments. The E-mail Message window is shown back in Figure 23-2.

 ✔ **Printing your e-mail messages:** Select the message that you want to print, and choose File⇨Print from the menu bar. The Print dialog box appears. Click OK to print your e-mail message.

✔ **Saving your e-mail messages:** Select the message that you want to save, and choose File⇨Save. The Save dialog box appears. Give the file a name, specify a storage location, and click the Save button.

✔ **Deleting your e-mail messages:** Select the message that you want to delete, and press the delete key.

✔ **Attach the e-mail message to a contact:** Select the E-mail⇨ Attach E-mail to⇨Contact command, and the Attach E-mail to Contact dialog box opens opens so you can attach the message to one or more contacts.

✔ **Attach the e-mail message to a group:** Select the E-mail⇨ Attach E-mail to⇨Group command, and the Attach E-mail to Group dialog box opens so you can attach the message to one or more groups.

E-mail etiquette

You should be aware of the many informal rules, regulations, and other requirements for writing proper e-mail messages. Here are some of them:

✔ Don't send carbon copies (cc) of messages to people who don't have to see the message.

✔ Don't send out blind copies (bcc) casually; they can imply that you're going behind someone's back.

✔ Don't ask for a receipt unless it's really necessary. You may be insulting the recipients by implying that they don't read their mail.

✔ Beware of crying wolf. Use the "urgent message" notation sparingly. If you use it too often, your future messages may be ignored.

✔ Don't use all capital letters. WHEN YOU TYPE YOUR MESSAGE IN ALL CAPITALS, IT'S KNOWN AS SHOUTING IN THE E-MAIL WORLD, and people don't like to be shouted at. Use upper- and lowercase letters just as you do when you type an old-fashioned letter.

✔ Put addresses in the To, Copy (cc), and Blind Copy (bcc) lines in alphabetical order by the recipients' last names. Doing so keeps you from accidentally insulting people — such as your boss, supervisor, or manager — because you listed them in the wrong place. (If you're going to go out of your way to insult someone, do it on purpose!)

✔ Don't overuse your mailing list. Send your messages only to people who need to receive them. By limiting your list of recipients, you'll build your credibility as an e-mail sender. The fewer messages you send, the greater the attention they receive.

✔ Send only work-related messages when you're at work. Messages such as jokes or invitations to non-work-related events are best handled outside of e-mail.

✔ Type positive messages that your readers look forward to receiving. Even when you must communicate a negative message, try your best to say it in a positive way.

✔ If your message is very important, controversial, confidential, or could easily be misunderstood, use the telephone or set up a face-to-face meeting.

Using Your E-Mail Inbox

When you receive e-mail messages, they appear in your Inbox when you're online. The Folders section of the E-mail window lists inboxes for the e-mail services you're using.

If you have multiple supported e-mail systems listed in your My Record contact record, a Combined Inbox is available in the E-mail window. The Combined Inbox contains messages from all the supported e-mail systems.

To open an e-mail system Inbox, just double-click the Inbox, or select E-mail⇨Get/Send Mail. (If you're using CompuServe, you select E-mail⇨ Open Inbox.)

You print, save, and delete messages from the Inbox the same way you do from the Drafts folder (ACT!'s Outbox), which is described earlier in this chapter.

Connecting to an e-mail system

You can create a new e-mail message without logging on to your e-mail system, but, as you probably know, you eventually need to log on to the system to send and receive your e-mail messages. You use the E-mail window to log on because it contains the E-mail menu, which offers all the commands you need to send and receive e-mail messages.

Follow this procedure to log on to an e-mail system:

1. **Select View⇨E-mail when you are in the Contact window, or click the E-mail icon at the bottom of the Contact window.**

   The E-mail window appears.

2. **Select your e-mail service, and choose the Get/Send Mail command from the E-mail menu.**

   With some e-mail systems, a dialog box appears prompting you to log on to the e-mail system.

3. **If some sort of Logon dialog box appears, enter your name and password and then click OK.**

   You are now logged on to your e-mail service, and the Inbox for that e-mail system appears.

After you receive an e-mail message, you can do the following:

✔ Read, reply, forward, or delete the message.

✔ Attach the message to a contact by selecting E-mail⇨ Attach E-mail to Contact.

✔ Attach the message to a group by selecting E-mail⇨ Attach E-mail to Group.

✔ Add the contact to your ACT! database by choosing E-mail⇨ Create Contact From Sender.

Merging or saving e-mail attachments

This is how you merge, or save, an ACT! e-mail attachment:

✔ **Merging contact or group record attachments:** If a contact record or group record is attached to the e-mail message, highlight the attachment and select Open Attachment from the right mouse button menu. (You can also double-click on the attachment.) The Merge Options dialog box opens in which you decide how you want the contact or group merged into your ACT! database.

✔ **Merging activity attachments:** If you receive an e-mail reminder for a scheduled activity — the activity is attached to the e-mail message — you can merge the activity into your database (by following the above steps), and it appears on your calendar.

✔ **Saving an attached file:** If a file is attached to the e-mail message, highlight the attachment and select Save Attachment from the right mouse button menu. The Save As dialog box opens. Here, you give the attachment a name and save it.

Using ACT!'s Briefcase

ACT!'s Briefcase gives you a place to store your downloaded messages and serves as your Inbox when you are not connected to your e-mail system. Your ACT! Briefcase provides all the options available to you when you're connected to your host system from the Inbox and allows for e-mail message management when you're not connected to your host system.

To access the Briefcase, which is identical to the Inbox, click the Briefcase icon in the Folders section of the E-mail window. (Note that the Briefcase does not have password protection.)

Chapter 24

Working with Reports

● ●

In This Chapter

▶ Generating and accessing ACT! reports

▶ Creating custom reports

▶ Inserting graphics and merge fields into a report template

▶ Selecting default report settings

▶ Testing your report

▶ Adding your new report to the Reports menu

● ●

*A*CT! comes with a set of standard reports that you can use to analyze the results of your daily activities. I explain how to use these reports in this chapter. I also explain how to create custom reports.

But first, I want to talk about reports in general. Your ACT! reports are only as good or as useful as the information you put into your ACT! database. This list details what you can do to make your ACT! database a much more powerful reporting tool (because you can then review the information in the contact's Notes/History tab):

✔ Always enter activity information in the Regarding field so that when you clear an activity, ACT! can properly record the purpose or nature of that activity as a History item.

✔ If you want to record additional information about the activity, click the Schedule Activity dialog box's Details tab. Here you can enter notes of up to 30,000 characters.

✔ Always clear your scheduled activities after you complete them so you have a record of what you've done.

✔ Always record the results of your phone calls — Completed, Attempted, Left Message, or Received Call — in the Record History dialog box so that you know what happened with every phone call.

✔ If you want to keep track of how much time you spent on a call or activity, use ACT!'s timer.

- ✔ When you send out correspondence — letters, memos, faxes, and e-mail messages — always create a History notation so that the correspondence is logged as a History item or Attachment item.

- ✔ Use the Record History dialog box to record what happened during impromptu meetings.

- ✔ Use the Record History dialog box to record the completion of to-dos that weren't on your things-to-do list.

- ✔ Use the Last Results field to summarize the results of your last meeting, phone call, or other contact activity.

- ✔ Use the Insert Notes command to open the Notes/History tab, in which you can write detailed notes about what took place at a meeting or what was discussed during a phone conversation. I find the habit of keeping notes of meetings and phone conversations to be an enormous timesaving, productivity-improving tool.

Generating ACT!'s Instant Reports

ACT!'s instant reports enable you to print out a report identical to the information that you see on your computer screen.

The following reports can be printed by clicking on their tabs from within the Contact window:

- ✔ **Notes/History report:** Select File⇨Print Notes/History to print the selected contact's notes, history, and attachments.

- ✔ **Activities report:** Select File⇨Print Activities to print the selected contact's scheduled activities.

- ✔ **Sales/Opportunities report:** Select File⇨Print Sales/Opportunities to print the selected contact's sales opportunities.

- ✔ **Printing the Group report:** Select File⇨Print Groups to print the list of groups of which the selected contact is a member.

To print a report of all the information — contact information, scheduled activities, sales/opportunities, groups, and notes/history information — in the Contact Record, select Reports⇨Contact Report.

The Contact List and Task List reports print from their respective windows:

- ✔ **Contact List report:** From within the Contact List window, select File⇨Print Contact List.

- ✔ **Task List report:** From within the Task List window, select File⇨ Print Task List.

The following instant reports can be printed from within the Group window:

- ✔ **Notes/History report:** Select File⇨Print Notes/History to print the selected group's notes, history, and attachments.

- ✔ **Activities report:** Select File⇨Print Activities to print the activities scheduled for a selected group.

- ✔ **Sales/Opportunities report:** Select File⇨Print Sales/Opportunities to print the selected group's sales opportunities.

- ✔ **Contact Members report:** Select File⇨Print Group Members to print the list of the members of the selected group.

Generating a Standard ACT! Report

The process of generating an ACT! report is the same for each ACT! report. Here's how you do it:

1. **Select a report from the Reports menu.**

   The General tab of the Run Report dialog box appears, as shown in Figure 24-1.

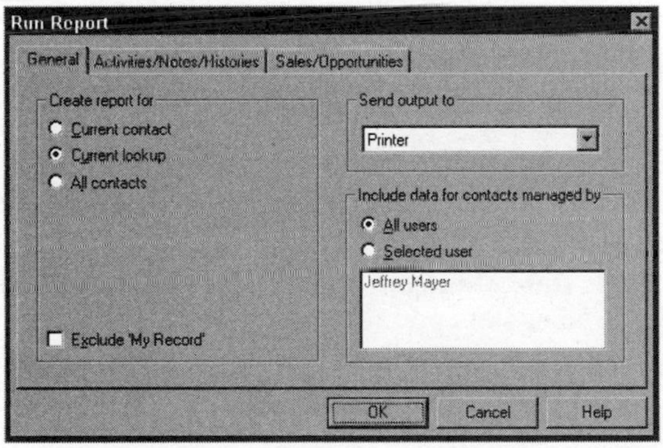

Figure 24-1:
The General tab of the Run Report dialog box.

ACT! offers many standard reports from which to choose. (If you want to create a report that isn't on the list of available reports, select the Reports⇨Other Report command, and select from the list of available reports in the Report directory.)

2. **In the General tab of the Run Report dialog box, make selections from each of the following options:**

   - **Contacts:** Select the group of contacts — Current Contact, Current Contact Lookup, or All Contacts — that you want to appear in the report.

- **My Record:** Include or exclude the My Record information from the report.

- **Output:** Select where you want the report to go: Printer, Preview, Fax, E-mail, or File.

- **Users:** Select the users whose records you want to include in the report.

3. **In the Activities/Notes/Histories tab of the Run Report dialog box, you specify what data you want to include in the report.**

   You have the following choices:

   - **Notes/History:** From the Notes/History section, you include or exclude notes, history, attachments, or e-mail from your report. Then you select the date or range of dates to span.

   - **Activities:** From the Activities section, you include or exclude calls, meetings, to-dos, cleared activities, or Outlook activities from your report. Then you select the date or range of dates to include.

   - **Include Data From:** In this section, you select the users whose data you want to include in the report.

4. **In the Sales/Opportunities tab of the Run Report dialog box, you specify what Sales/Opportunities data you want to include in the report.**

   You have the following choices:

   - **Sales:** From the Sales section, you can include or exclude Sales/Opportunities, Closed/Won sales, and Lost sales. Then you select the date or range of dates to include.

   - **Sort Sales By:** From the Sort Sales By section, you select how you want your sales opportunities to be sorted.

   - **Include Sales Data Managed By:** In this section, you select the users whose sales data you want to include in the report.

5. **After you've made your selections, click OK.**

   ACT! compiles your report and sends it to the printer, sends it as a fax, sends it as an e-mail message, or saves it to a file. You can also preview the report before printing it.

Here are some ACT! reporting tips:

- ✔ Depending upon the type of report you are running, some of the options in the Activities/Notes/Histories or Sales/Opportunities tabs may or may not be available.

- ✔ You can create ACT! reports by selecting File⇨Print or by pressing Ctrl+P to bring up the Print dialog box. Choose Reports as your Printout Type, and select from the list of files. Scroll through the list of available reports, and highlight the report you want. Click OK, and the report generation process begins. From the Print dialog box, you can also print your address book, Daily calendar, Weekly calendar, Monthly calendar, envelopes, and labels.

✔ For reports that you run frequently, record a macro to run your report. This speeds up the report-compiling time. (I cover macros in Chapter 27.)

✔ If you run certain reports frequently, add them to your Report menu. This feature is discussed later in this chapter.

✔ You can speed up the report-compiling time by compressing and re-indexing your ACT! database. (I discuss database maintenance in Chapter 28.)

✔ Creating an ACT! report can be a tedious and time-consuming process, especially if you haven't done it before. You may want to hire an ACT! Certified Consultant to help you design your reports.

Accessing ACT! Standard Report Templates

ACT! comes with a number of standard report templates that you can use to view and print information about your contacts. You can also modify these report templates to create your own custom reports. All these reports — except the Group List and Group Report — appear in the Reports menu. To choose the Group List or Group Report, choose Other Report from the Reports menu and then select the report you want to use. A summary description of ACT!'s standard reports appears in Table 24-1.

There are also several Sales reports, including the following:

✔ Sales by Record Manager (SLBSBYMG5.REP)

✔ Sales by Contact (SLBCNTC5.REP)

✔ Sales Detail (SLSDTAI5.REP)

✔ Sales Totals by Status (SLSTOTA5.REP)

Sales reporting is such an important ACT! feature that I've devoted an entire part to it, so if you want to learn all about ACT!'s Sales/Opportunities management features, read Part V.

Table 24-1	ACT!'s Standard Reports
Report Title	**Description**
Contact Report (CONTACT5.REP)	This report displays all contact information, including the history, activities, and notes, for the selected contacts.
Contact Directory Report (DIRECT5.REP)	This report displays the primary address and home address for each contact.
Phone List Report (PHONELS5.REP)	This report lists the company, contact, and primary phone number (including extensions) of a selected group of contacts in a spreadsheet format.
Task List Report (TASKLIS5.REP)	This report displays the calls, meetings, and to-dos scheduled with all the contacts in your ACT! database for the specified range of dates.
Notes/History Report (NOTEHIS5.REP)	This report displays the contact's notes and history items for a specified date range.
History Summary Report (HISTOR5.REP)	This report displays the number of attempted calls, completed calls, meetings held, and letters sent for an individual contact or group of contacts over a selected range of dates.
History Summary Classic (HISTCLA5.REP)	This report shows the total number of attempted calls, completed calls, meetings held, and letters sent for each contact during a specified date range.
Activities/Time Spent Report (ACTIVIT5.REP)	This report displays a list of the activities scheduled and time spent with each contact during a specified date range.
Contact Status Report (STATUS5.REP)	This report displays the information in the ID/Status field and the Last Results field, as well as to-do information for the selected group of contacts.
Source of Referral Report (REFERRA5.REP)	This report displays Referred By information for each contact.
Group Membership Report (GRPMEMB5.REP)	This report displays a list of all ACT! groups and all contacts in each group.

Creating Custom Reports

Earlier in this chapter, I discussed how to create ACT! reports using the standard report templates that came with ACT!. However, you can do a lot more with ACT!'s reporting capabilities by creating your own custom reports, and that's what I cover here.

You can create an ACT! custom report in two ways: You can create a report from scratch, or you can modify an existing ACT! report template.

✔ To create an ACT! report from scratch, select File➪New or press Ctrl+N. The New dialog box appears. Choose Report Template, and ACT! opens a blank report template in the Report Designer.

✔ To modify an existing ACT! report template, select Reports➪Edit Report Template, and the Open dialog box appears. Highlight the report that you want to modify, click Open, and the report appears in ACT!'s Report Designer. For illustrative purposes, the Task List report template is shown in Figure 24-2.

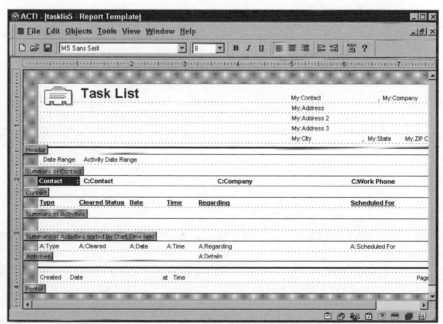

Figure 24-2:
The Task List report template.

Here are some ACT! reporting tips:

✔ When you create a new ACT! report template by modifying an existing ACT! report template, always save the template with a new name (use the File⇨Save As command) before you start making changes to it. Doing so ensures that should you make a mistake, you can always start over with the original template.

✔ If you accidentally make changes to an original ACT! report, you can reinstall it by performing a custom ACT! installation from your original ACT! CD-ROM.

✔ To learn more about how ACT! reports work, print all the standard ACT! reports for the active contact and study the corresponding report templates on your computer's monitor. Put them side-by-side to study the layout of the merge codes in the template. In the upcoming section, you see how the contact information is merged into the actual report.

Setting up the Report Designer

Before you start designing your report, you need to consider several options:

✔ To choose the paper size on which you want your report printed, select File⇨Page Setup from the menu bar. The Page dialog box appears and lets you select the paper size, the orientation (portrait or landscape), the margin sizes, and your printer.

✔ To configure your ruler settings (the rulers display on the top and left sides of the Report Designer screen), open the Ruler Settings dialog box by selecting View⇨Ruler Settings from the menu bar. In the Ruler Settings dialog box, select the units of measurement and the number of division markers you want displayed. (The default is 16 division markers.)

✔ To show or hide the Tool Palette, select View⇨Show/Hide Tool Palette from the menu bar.

✔ To show or hide your rulers, select View⇨Show/Hide Ruler from the menu bar.

✔ To show or hide the grid lines, select View⇨Show/Hide Grid from the menu bar. The number of dots on the grid line corresponds to the number of division markers that you selected for the ruler settings.

✔ If you want your objects to snap (stick to) to the grid, select the Snap to Grid option from the View menu.

✔ To show or hide the report's section titles, select the Show/Hide Section Titles command from the View menu.

For more reporting power, try Crystal Reports

If ACT!'s report-generating capabilities aren't powerful enough for you, or if you're spending too much time trying to create custom ACT! reports, get a copy of Crystal Reports. Crystal Reports is a powerful yet easy-to-use program designed to create custom reports with graphs, lists, and labels, using data from your ACT! database.

Crystal Reports is made by Crystal Services, 1050 West Pender St., Suite 2200, Vancouver, B.C., Canada V6E 3S7; phone 800-877-2340 (U.S.); Web site `www.seagatesoftware.com/crystalinfo`.

Understanding the sections of an ACT! report

The most important concept to understand when you're working with report templates is that ACT! report templates contain different sections of information, and every report must have at least one section. The various report sections are labeled on-screen.

For example, a very simple report may have just three sections: header, contact, and footer. You add, modify, or delete ACT! report sections from the Define Sections dialog box. Defining the sections of an ACT! report is covered in the next section, but here I give you a brief explanation of each of the sections you can include in an ACT! report template:

- ✔ **Header:** A header appears at the top of every page, unless you add a separate title header, which is placed above the header on the first page of the report. Use a header for any information or graphic object that you want to appear on every page, such as the current date, column headings, or a company logo.

- ✔ **Footer:** A footer appears at the bottom of every page. Use a footer for information that you want on every page, such as the page number, date, or time.

- ✔ **Title header:** The title header appears only on the first page of a report, above the header.

- ✔ **Title footer:** The title footer appears only on the first page of a report, just above the footer.

✔ **Contact section:** The Contact section contains information from the fields in a contact's record. The information in the Contact section appears for each contact that you include when you run the report. The Contact section of the Phone List report, for example, contains information from the Company Name, Contact Name, Phone, Phone Extension, and Car Phone fields.

A report can contain only one Contact section or one Group section. It cannot contain both. A Contact section can, however, contain a Group subsection, and vice versa.

• **Group subsection of Contact section:** The Group subsection of the Contact section contains information from fields in the Groups tab of a Contact record. For this reason, you can only include a Group subsection if you have a Contact section in the report template.

• **Group section:** Here you find information from fields in your Group records. The information in the Group section appears for each group that you include when you run the report. The Group section of the Group report, for example, contains the group name and address, the group's description, the name of the primary contact, his or her phone number, and much more.

• **Contact subsection of Group section:** The Contact subsection of the Group section contains information from fields in the Contact's tab of a group record. For this reason, you can only include a Contact subsection if you have a Group section in the report template.

✔ **Notes/History section:** This section contains information from fields in the Notes/History tab of a Contact or Group record. Therefore, you can include a Notes/History section below either a Contact section or a Group section, as long as you have a Contact or Group section in your report template.

✔ **Activities section:** The Activities section contains information from fields in the Activities tab of a Contact or Group record. So you can include an Activities section below either a Contact section or a Group section if you have the corresponding section in your report template.

✔ **Sales section:** The Sales section contains information from fields in the Sales/Opportunities tab of a Contact or Group record. You can include such fields as Amount, Close Date, Creation Date, Price, Probability, and more.

✔ **Summary section:** Summaries can be totals, averages, counts, or minimum and maximum values. A Summary section can contain one or more summary fields. You can place the Summary section above or below the section it summarizes.

✔ **Summary Sorted By section:** The Summary Sorted By section contains a summary of the values sorted by a specific field. For example, the History Summary report includes a Summary Sorted By section that displays total counts of the notes and histories sorted by type. You can also use a Summary Sorted By section just to sort a section without putting in any summary fields.

Adding, changing, and deleting sections

You add, change, and delete sections of an ACT! report by opening the Define Sections dialog box, which you access by choosing Edit⇨Define Sections from the menu bar. The Define Sections dialog box for a Task List report is shown in Figure 24-3. The Define Sections dialog box always displays the sections currently included in the report template.

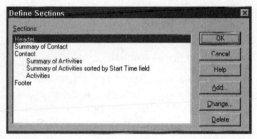

Figure 24-3: The Define Sections dialog box for a Task List report.

By default, every report template has a header, Contact section, and footer.

You add a section to an ACT! report template from the Define Sections dialog box. Here's how:

1. **Click the Add button.**

   The Add Section dialog box appears, as shown in Figure 24-4.

   The available sections appear in the Sections box. If a section name is dimmed, you cannot add it to the currently selected section. (For example, if you select the Contact section, the Group section is dimmed because you cannot add a Group section to a Contact section. You can, however, add a Group subsection to a Contact section.)

   The Add Section dialog box and Change Section dialog box do the same things; they just have different names.

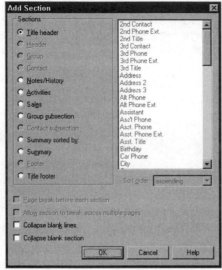

Figure 24-4:
The Add
Section
dialog box.

2. **Select the section(s) that you want to add.**

   A basic report contains a header, a footer, and a Contact, Group, or Sales section. Under the Contact or Group section, you can add Notes/History and Activities sections and Contact or Group subsections. Under the subsection, you can add notes/history items and activities.

   You can place a Summary and Summary Sorted By section above or below a selected Contact, Group, Notes/History, or Activities section, or above or below a Sales section.

   When you select the Summary Sorted By section, the Field list on the right side of the dialog box and the Sort Order drop-down list become available. Select the field by which you want to sort the data, and select Ascending or Descending Order from the Sort Order drop-down list. Click OK, and place the section either above or below the selected section.

3. **Specify how you want the information in the selected section to display and print.**

   You have the following options:

   - **Page break before each section:** This option starts a new page at the beginning of the selected section.

   - **Allow section to break across multiple pages:** This option displays and prints all the information in a section, even if it doesn't fit on a single page. If you turn this option off, a page break inserts before the section if the section can't fit in the remaining space on the current page.

- **Collapse blank lines:** This option eliminates lines in the selected section that contain fields with no data or fields that are duplicated. Any graphic objects whose upper-left corners fall within the line are also eliminated.

- **Collapse blank section:** This option eliminates sections in the report that contain no data. Any graphic objects whose upper-left corners fall within the section are also eliminated.

4. **Click OK to add your section settings to the ACT! report.**

   ACT! closes the Add Section dialog box and returns you to the Define Sections dialog box, where you can add, change, or delete another section or subsection.

5. **When you finish editing sections, click OK.**

   The new sections appear in the report template.

Now that you've created the sections of your ACT! report, you probably want to add fields to your report. Adding fields is covered in the "Inserting Merge Fields into a Report Template" section of this chapter.

Here are some additional things that you can do with the sections of an ACT! report:

✔ **Changing sections of an ACT! report:** To change a section in an ACT! report, highlight the section in the Sections box of the Define Sections dialog box, click the Change button, and the Change Section dialog box appears (which is identical to the Add Section dialog box). Make your changes, click OK, and you return to the Define Settings dialog box.

✔ **Deleting sections from an ACT! report:** To delete a section from an ACT! report, highlight the section in the Sections box of the Define Sections dialog box and click the Delete button. If the section contains any fields, graphic objects, text objects, or subsections, a message appears asking, "Are you certain that you want to delete the report section, the objects it contains, and related sections?" If you are sure, click Yes, and the section, along with its objects, is deleted from the report template.

✔ **Changing the size of a report's section:** To change the size of a report's section within the Report Designer, click on the section's title and move it up to enlarge the report section or down to reduce the section. If the section titles aren't displayed, select View⇨Show Section Titles from the menu bar to display them.

Working with Graphic Objects

Items you place on an ACT! report template — fields, field labels, text, rectangles, ellipses, and lines — are referred to as *graphic objects*. You place graphic objects on a report template from the Tool Palette.

You use the tools on the Tool Palette, shown in Figure 24-5, to design and edit your report templates.

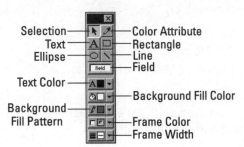

Selection — Color Attribute
Text — Rectangle
Ellipse — Line
— Field
Text Color —
Background Fill Pattern — Background Fill Color
Frame Color
Frame Width

Figure 24-5:
The Tool
Palette.

From the Tool Palette, you can do the following:

- ✔ Insert graphic objects (a graphic object includes ACT! fields and field labels, text, rectangles, ellipses, and lines)
- ✔ Change the object's background color
- ✔ Change the object's fill pattern
- ✔ Change the object's frame style
- ✔ Change the object's frame color
- ✔ Change the object's frame width
- ✔ Change the color of the object's font

After you have created a graphic object, you can do the following:

- ✔ Move graphic objects
- ✔ Move objects from front to back and vice versa
- ✔ Make objects the same size
- ✔ Get objects to line up
- ✔ Align your objects to the grid

The way you insert and manipulate graphic objects is exactly the same for both the Report Designer and the Layout Designer. Because most ACT! users spend more time designing and modifying their layouts than editing their reports, I cover the features of ACT!'s Layout Designer and Tool Palette in Chapter 26. Please read that section now, and then come back and finish reading this chapter.

Inserting Merge Fields into a Report Template

A Merge Field command instructs ACT! to pull information from a specific ACT! field and insert it into an ACT! report. You insert merge fields into an ACT! report from the Field List dialog box, which is shown in Figure 24-6.

Figure 24-6: The Field List dialog box.

This is how you open the Field List dialog box:

1. **Click the Tool Palette's Field tool, and the cursor becomes a large cross-hair.**

   If the Tool Palette is hidden, select the Show Tool Palette command from the View menu.

2. **Place the cursor in the section of the report in which you want to insert the field, hold down the mouse button, drag the cursor right or left until the field is the desired width, and then release the mouse button.**

   The Field List dialog box appears.

The Field List dialog box has six tabs: Contact, Group, Notes/History, Activities, Sales, and System. ACT! automatically selects the tab that corresponds to the section of the report into which you want to insert a field.

ACT! has two types of merge fields: Detail fields and Summary fields.

> ✔ A Detail field is any ACT! field that contains contact information. This includes any field in the Contact or Group layouts and any column available for viewing in the Notes/History tab or the Activities tab.

> ✔ A Summary field contains information from any field designated as a numeric, currency, date, or time field.

Both of these types of fields are discussed on the following pages.

Inserting Detail fields into an ACT! report template

The following options are available to you when you select Detail as the field type:

> ✔ **Selecting the Contact tab** displays every Contact field in the database in the Available Fields box.

> ✔ **Selecting the Group tab** displays all the Group fields in the database in the Available Fields box.

> ✔ **Selecting the Notes/History tab** shows every available column from the Notes/History tab in the Contact window.

> ✔ **Selecting the Activities tab** shows you every column available in the Activities tab in the Contact window.

> ✔ **Selecting the Sales tab** shows you every column available in the Sales tab in the Contact window.

> ✔ **Selecting the System tab** enables you to insert the page number, date, time, activity date range, or notes/history date range into your report template.

Place the page number, date, or time in the report's header or footer.

To insert a Detail field into an ACT! report template from the Field List dialog box, follow these steps:

1. **Select one of the six tabs — Contact, Group, Notes/History, Activities, Sales, or System — if one is not already selected.**

2. **Select Detail Field in the Field Type section if it's not already selected.**

3. **Select the field that you want to insert from the list of available fields in the Available Fields box.**

4. **Select the Add Field Label option if you want a label to appear with the field that you are adding.**

5. **Select the Use My Record option if you want to insert a merge command that pulls contact information from the My Record contact record.**

   The Use My Record option is only available on the Contact tab.

   The information from the My Record contact record is usually placed in the header of a report. It includes such information as your name, company name, address, and so on.

6. **Click the Add button to insert the selected field into the ACT! report template.**

7. **When you've added the fields that you want in your report template, click Close to close the Field List dialog box.**

   You can then position the fields in the appropriate places on the template.

Inserting a Summary field into your ACT! report template

A Summary field is one containing information from more than one contact record. For example, if you want ACT! to count the number of records with information in a selected field, you select Count as the summary type for that field.

To give you another example, suppose that you made the User 1 field an Amount of Last Sale field and made it a Numeric or Currency field, in which you can insert only numbers. When you select Total as the field's summary type, ACT! gives you a total of all your last sales. If you select Average as the field's summary type, ACT! gives you the average size of all your last sales.

If you make a field a Numeric, Currency, Date, or Time field and select Minimum or Maximum as the summary type, ACT! can find the lowest or highest number and the earliest or latest date or time.

Only fields you designate as Numeric, Currency, Date, or Time fields in the Define Fields dialog box appear in the Available Fields list when you select Total, Average, Minimum, or Maximum as the summary type.

You insert a Summary field into an ACT! report template by taking the following steps:

1. **Select Summary Field in the Field Type section of the Field List dialog box.**

2. **Select a summary type — Count, Total, Average, Minimum, or Maximum — in the Summary Type section.**

3. **Select a field from the list of fields in the Available Fields box.**

4. **Enter a field label name for the Summary Type field that you're creating in the Summary Field Label field.**

5. **Click the Add button to insert the selected field into the ACT! report template.**

6. **After you've added the fields that you want in your report template, click Close to close the Field List dialog box.**

   You can then position the fields in the appropriate places on the template.

Making Your Reports Look Nice

After you've placed all your merge fields (*objects* in ACT!-speak) onto a report template, you'll certainly want to make your reports look nice. You do this by changing each field's, or object's, properties — the field's style, font, field type, and format. You do this from the Object Properties dialog box.

You access the Object Properties dialog box by double-clicking the selected object or by selecting the Properties command from the menu that appears when you right-click an object.

To change the properties of several Merge fields or field labels at the same time, hold down the Shift key and click the desired Merge fields or field labels.

Changing a Merge field's style

From the Style tab, which is shown in Figure 24-7, you can make the following changes to the selected Merge field:

- ✔ Change the background fill color
- ✔ Change the background fill pattern
- ✔ Change the frame style
- ✔ Change the frame color
- ✔ Change the frame width

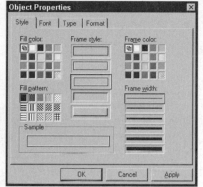

Figure 24-7:
The Style
tab of the
Object
Properties
dialog box.

Changing a Merge field's font

From the Font tab, you can change the font's appearance within the Merge field. You have the following options:

- ✓ Change the font
- ✓ Change the font style (italic, bold, bold italic, and so on)
- ✓ Change the font size
- ✓ Choose strikeout
- ✓ Choose underline
- ✓ Choose a color

Confirming a field's type

In the Type tab, ACT! displays the basic information about the field, which includes the following:

- ✓ The field name
- ✓ The field type (Detail, Summary, or System)
- ✓ Summary options, if the field is a Summary Type field
- ✓ Use My Record info

If the Merge field is a My Record field, the Use My Record box is checked. (The Use My Record check box only appears if a My Record field has been selected.)

Selecting a field's format

From the Format tab, ACT! enables you to set the Merge field's format. You have these options:

- ✔ **Don't Print If Duplicated:** Choose this option if you don't want ACT! to print the selected field if more than one of them is in the template. If you are creating a report that includes a company's name, for example, choose this option if you don't want the name inserted with each contact.

- ✔ **Wrap Text:** If you want text in the selected field to wrap at the end of a line, choose this option.

- ✔ **Close Up Blank Space:** Select this option if you do not want any blank space between the text and the right edge of the field.

- ✔ **Field Name:** This field displays the Merge field's name.

- ✔ **Data Type:** The Data Type field displays the Merge field's data type: Detail, Summary, Date, Time, Numeric, and so on.

- ✔ **Appearance:** In the Appearance box, you can select how a Numeric, Date, or Time field appears. For a Numeric field, you can also select how negative numbers display and how many decimal places appear. (The Appearance box only appears if you have selected a Numeric, Date, or Time field.)

Only the options that apply to the specific field type appear in the Format tab.

Changing a merge field's appearance from the toolbar

You can also change a selected Merge field's appearance by clicking buttons on the toolbar. From left to right, you can access these options: font, font size, bold, italic, underline, left justification, centered, right justification, align left, and align right. The toolbar is shown back in Figure 24-2.

You customize your toolbar by right-clicking on a blank portion of the toolbar and selecting the Customize Window command. The Customize ACT! Report Template Window dialog box opens, and lets you choose options to customize the toolbar, the menus, and the keyboard.

Enhancing the appearance of your report by adding rectangles, ellipses, lines, and text

To improve the appearance of your report, you may want to create fancy and elaborate report titles or section headings by adding rectangles, ellipses, lines, and text to your report. You can then position these objects in front of or behind each other to create the look you want.

To add a rectangle, ellipse, or line to your ACT! report, select the appropriate tool from the Tool Palette, place the cross-hair pointer where you want the object to start, and drag it up, down, left, or right until your graphic is the desired size.

To make a square, circle, or straight line, hold down the Shift key while you create the object with the Rectangle, Ellipse, or Line tool.

To change a rectangle, ellipse, or line's style, select the rectangle, ellipse, or line with the Selection tool, and double-click the object. The Style tab of the Object Properties dialog box appears. The Object Properties box is discussed earlier in this chapter. You can also change the rectangle, ellipse, or line's style using the Tool Palette's appearance tools.

To add text to your ACT! report, select the Text tool from the Tool Palette. Place the cross-hair pointer where you want the text box to start, and drag the pointer left or right until the box is the desired size. Release the mouse button, ACT! creates a text box, and begin typing your text.

To change the text's style, select the text object with the Selection tool and double-click. The Object Properties dialog box appears. You can select from the features of the Style, Font, and Format tabs, which were discussed earlier in this chapter. You can also change the text's style by using the Tool Palette's appearance tools or the text appearance icons on the toolbar, both of which were discussed earlier in this chapter.

Selecting Default Settings for Reports

After you've laid out the Merge fields of your report, ACT! gives you the capability to select the *default* settings that you want to have applied to this report. You create these default settings for the General, Activities/Notes/Histories, and the Sales/Opportunities tabs from the Define Filters dialog box. The Define Filters dialog box is identical to the Run Report dialog box (refer to Figure 24-1). It just has a different name. You open the Define Filters dialog box from within the Layout Designer by selecting Edit⇨Define Filters from the menu bar.

Here are a few examples of how you can use your filtering defaults:

✔ To create a report giving you information about your activities, including any notes or history entries during the last quarter, set the filtering options to display this information for the last quarter only.

✔ You can create a report that displays your scheduled activities for the next week, month, or quarter, making it easy to answer your boss's question: "What do you have lined up for the next month?"

You use the General tab to specify which contacts to make the report for, where to output the report, and whether to include the My Record contact record.

Testing Your Report

After you've created your report, you'll probably want to test it to see whether it comes out the way you want it to. Here's how you run a report directly from the Report Designer:

1. **Select File⇨Run from the menu bar, or press Ctrl+R.**

   The Filters dialog box appears.

2. **Make your filtering choices in the General and Filter tabs, and click OK.**

   ACT! runs the report.

Adding Your New Report to the Reports Menu

After you've created a custom report, ACT! makes it easy for you to use it. You can add the report template as an additional option that's available from the Report menu. To add your report template to the Reports menu, select Reports⇨Modify Menu, and the Modify Menu dialog box appears. Here, you can add items to the Report menu. In Chapter 21, I discuss how to add envelopes and labels to the Reports menu in the "Printing envelopes and labels" section. The process for adding reports to the Reports menu is identical.

Part VII

More ACT! Features

The 5th Wave By Rich Tennant

"Can someone please tell me how long 'Larry's Lunch Truck' has had his own page on the intranet?"

In this part . . .

ACT! has some more great features, and I cover them here. In Chapter 25 I tell you how you can use ACT! and the Internet. In Chapter 26 I'll show you how to design your own custom ACT! layouts. In Chapter 27, I explain how you can customize ACT!'s toolbar and menu, assign commands to shortcut keys, and create your own custom ACT! commands. And in Chapter 28, I talk about how to manage and protect your ACT! database.

Chapter 25

ACT! and the Internet

● ●

In This Chapter

▶ Logging onto a contact's Web site

▶ Getting directions to your next meeting

▶ Getting information about the company

▶ Finding people over the Internet

▶ Forging additional Internet links

▶ Linking to Symantec's ACT! Web site

▶ Adding new sites to your list

● ●

*T*he use of the Internet has exploded, and ACT! has correspondingly
expanded its Internet functionality. With the click of a button, you can log
on to selected Web sites, find people using Internet searches and add them to
your ACT! database, and log on to selected Web sites directly from the ACT!
menu bar.

Logging On to a Contact's Web Site

Let's say that you had an appointment scheduled with one of your clients or
prospects and wanted to get the latest information about company as you
planned for the meeting. The first thing you would probably want to do is
visit the company's Web site and review or download the latest corporate or
financial information.

So just click on the Web site address in the contact's Web Site field — which
is on the Alt Contacts tab — and ACT! launches your browser, logs on to the
Internet, and goes to the selected site. Neat!

If you want to add additional Web site (URL) fields — URL is the abbreviation
for Uniform Resource Locator, which is a fancy name for a Web site — to your
layout all you've got to do is open the ACT!'s Define Fields dialog box, (select
Edit⇨Define Fields), select the field you want to become a Web site field, and
select URL Address from the drop-down list in the Types box.

Getting Directions to Your Next Meeting

Before you walk out the door you may want driving directions from where you are to where your client is located. This is how you get them:

1. **Select Internet Links⇨Yahoo! Driving Directions.**

   The Yahoo! Driving Directions dialog box appears, as shown in Figure 25-1.

2. **Select the Origin location from the drop-down list of contacts.**

3. **Select the Destination location from the drop-down list of contacts.**

4. **Click the Drive It! button.**

   ACT! logs onto Yahoo! Maps and displays both a map and detailed driving instructions.

You can then print out the directions or save them to your computer and attach them to the contact's Notes/History tab.

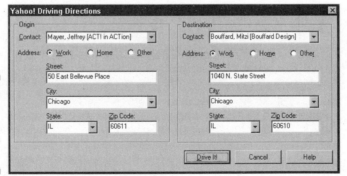

Figure 25-1: The Yahoo! Driving Directions dialog box.

Getting Information about a Company

If you would like detailed business and financial information about a company, you can select from any of the following Internet links. Once you're connected to Yahoo!, just enter the company's stock symbol in the Get Quotes field.

- ✔ **Yahoo! Corporate News:** You can view recent articles about the selected company or use any of the available search engines, including Alta Vista, WebCrawler, HotBot, Lycos, Infoseek, Excite, and more.

- ✔ **Yahoo! Stock Quote:** You can view the price of the last trade, the change in price from the previous day in both a dollar amount and a percentage, the day's volume, and lots more.

✔ **Yahoo! Ticker Symbol Lookup:** You can view the price of the last trade, the day's range, its 52-week range, and lots more.

Finding People on the Net

To find people over the Internet, you can use Yahoo! Person search. With this search, Yahoo! searches for everybody who has the first and last name of the currently displayed contact.

To perform a lookup from one of the Internet directories — Bigfoot, WhoWhere, or Yahoo! — select Lookup⇨Internet Directories from the menu bar, and the Internet Lookup dialog box opens. In this dialog box, you enter a person's name, select which directory you want to use, and click the Search button.

A list of people who match your search criteria comes up. You can then add the person to your ACT! database, send an e-mail message, or both.

Using the Internet Directory is discussed in Chapter 10, where I cover ACT! Lookups.

Forging Additional Internet Links

Here are some additional Internet links:

✔ **Yahoo! Weather:** To find out the weather, just select Yahoo! Weather, and Yahoo! displays the weather forecast for the city of the currently displayed contact.

✔ **Bigfoot E-mail Services:** To subscribe to Bigfoot's E-mail Service — and have your e-mail address for life — select this Internet link.

✔ **HotData:** With the Free HotData Area Code Updater you can automatically update your contact's area codes. HotData also provides downloadable plug-ins that integrate seamlessly with ACT! to enhance your existing customer and prospect data with updated addresses, phone numbers, fax numbers, Web addresses, business profiles, and more. HotData delivers customer intelligence from the world's best data providers directly into ACT! instantly via the Internet. Pricing is based upon the number of records in your ACT! database.

✔ **MyProspects:** With MyProspects.com's Get New Sales Leads, you have access to lists of highly targeted prospective customers. Simply select from pre-defined profiles and characteristics that best describe your target customer, and MyProspects.com delivers the names, addresses and phone numbers of only those prospects that match your criteria. You are charged for each contact record you download.

Linking to Symantec's Web Site

When you need ACT! information, one of the quickest ways to get it is to go directly to Symantec's ACT! Web site. ACT! gives you six direct links. You access them by selecting Tools⇨Internet Links⇨Symantec.

- ✔ **ACT!:** The ACT! site gives you direct links to ACT! Product Information, News Releases, ACT! Certified Consultants, Symantec Authorized Training Centers, Publications and Training Materials, ACT! Add-On Catalog, Free Downloads, Technical Support, and lots, lots more.

- ✔ **Small Business Resource Center:** This site has information and tips on how to run your business more efficiently. The center lists some of the best places on the Internet to get "inside information" and cutting-edge technology.

- ✔ **Mobile Resources:** At this Symantec site, you find useful information about cities you may visit for trade shows, conferences, or other business resources. For each city, you find links to several modem-friendly hotels, local access numbers for AOL and CompuServe, names of restaurants for quiet business meetings, links to Visitor Information Centers, and links to street maps.

- ✔ **Technical Support:** At Symantec's Online Technical Support page you can download files, search Symantec's knowledge base, ask questions of ACT! technical support, join ACT! online discussion groups, and more.

- ✔ **Try It Before You Buy It:** From this site, you can try any of Symantec's products before you decide to make a purchase. Just select the product you want to try and download a trial version.

- ✔ **Symantec's Web site:** This site gives you links to all of Symantec's products, including ACT!, Norton AntiVirus, CrashGuard Deluxe, Uninstall Deluxe, Norton Utilities, pcANYWHERE, Visual CafÈ for Java, WinFax, and other products. You also have links to Symantec technical support.

Adding New Sites to Your List

Now I know you'll certainly like the sites that are pre-installed for you, but I'm sure you'll want to add your own sites to the list.

Unfortunately, this can't be done from inside ACT!, but it can be done from the Windows Explorer. This is how you do it:

1. **Open Explorer.**

2. **Go to your ACT! 2000 directory.**

If you don't know where this is, open the Preferences dialog box by selecting Edit⇨Preferences and look for the directory displayed in the Default Location section of the General Tab.

3. Click the ACT! 2000 subdirectory named NetLinks.

The list of files appears in the right-hand pane. The NetLinks folder is shown in Figure 25-2.

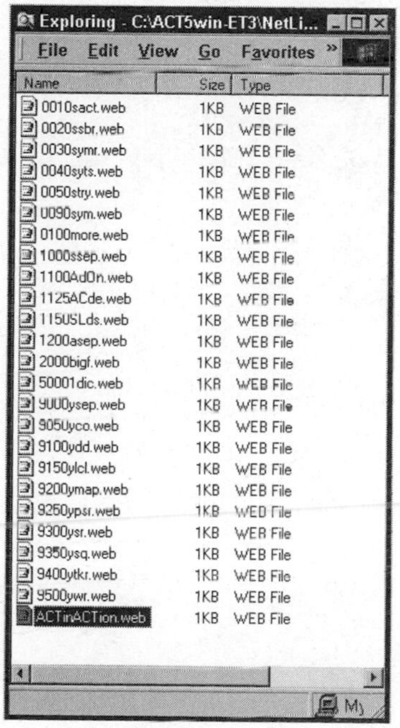

Figure 25-2:
The files of
the NetLinks
folder.

4. Open the first file named 0010SACT.web.

This is the link to the Symantec ACT! Web page. The code looks like this:
[&Symantec|&ACT!]http://www.symantec.com/act/index.html.

- The text inside the brackets, [&Symantec|&ACT!] is the information displayed on the menu bar under Tools, Internet Links.

- The ampersand (&) in front of the "S" in Symantec and the "A" in ACT! places the underline under the "S" and the "A" and makes them appear as Symantec and ACT! on the menu. This turns those letters into hot keys. Press the Alt+T+I+S+A keys and you log on to the ACT! Web page.

- The Symantec submenu is created by placing the bar (|) between the "c" in Symantec and the ampersand "&A".

5. **Save this file with a new name by using File⇨Save As.**

   The file must have the .web extension.

6. **Make the changes to the Web site's description within the brackets, and enter the new Web address.**

7. **Save your file by selecting File⇨Save or by selecting File⇨Exit.**

   If a message box appears asking if you want to save this file as a Word Document, Rich Text Document, or Text Document, select Text Document.

Put a direct link to my ACTnews.com Web site onto your menu bar. On this site, you have access to articles from the *ACT! in ACTion* newsletter, links to products and services that will save you time and help you make more money, and more. The address is www.actnews.com.

Chapter 26

Designing Layouts

ACT! comes with a number of contact and group layouts. But as you use more of ACT!'s features, you'll find that you want to reposition fields, change the size of fields, and even place new fields on your layouts. Then you may want to change their appearance, shape, and color, and add graphics.

With ACT!'s Layout Designer, you can create new layouts or modify existing layouts. You can add or remove fields from layouts, and you can change the appearance of the layouts by using colors and graphic elements.

Using the Layout Designer can become a huge time waster. Unless you're familiar with working with graphic objects, you may find it much more time- and cost-effective to hire an ACT! Certified Consultant to come in and design your layout for you. Chapter 30 tells you about some of the things ACT! Certified Consultants do.

When you're modifying a layout, always work from a copy of the layout by saving it with the File⇨Save As command. This way, if you make a mistake, you can just delete the layout and start over again with the original.

The Layout Designer's Basic Features

To open ACT!'s Layout Designer, choose Tools⇨Design Layouts from the menu bar. Figure 26-1 shows the contact layout in the Layout Designer.

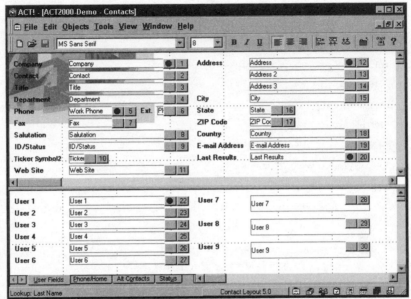

Figure 26-1:
The contact layout in the Layout Design.

The following is a list of the Layout Designer's basic commands:

- ✔ **Opening an ACT! layout:** To open a layout, first open either the Contacts or Groups window and then choose Tools⇨Design Layouts from the menu bar, and the Layout Designer opens the Contact or Group layout.

- ✔ **Changing layouts:** To change from one ACT! layout to another, click the Layout button at the bottom of the Layout Designer window and select a layout from the available list.

  To change an ACT! layout from the menu bar, choose File⇨Open, and the Open dialog box appears. Select your layout and click Open.

  If you're editing a contact layout, only contact layouts are listed in the Open dialog box, and if you're editing a group layout, only group layouts are listed. (Contact layouts have the .CLY extension, and group layouts have the .GLY extension.)

- ✔ **Creating a new layout:** To create a new layout, choose File⇨New. ACT! responds with a blank layout for you to work with. Here, you can design a layout that fills up the entire window.

✔ **Closing the Layout Designer:** To close the Layout Designer, click the Close button on the toolbar or choose View⇨Records from the menu bar.

✔ **Adding the layout to the Layout drop-down menu:** After creating a new contact or group layout, you will certainly want the new layout to be available in the layout drop-down menu at the bottom of the Contacts or Groups window. (That sure makes sense. Why go to the trouble of creating a custom layout if you can't use it?)

In order to have your layout appear in this menu, you need to save the layout and assign a file description to it. To save your layout, choose File⇨Save or File⇨Save As.

To give your layout a description that appears on the drop-down menu, right-click a blank area in the layout and choose the File Description command from the menu that appears. Give the layout a new description, and your description appears on the Layout button.

✔ **Showing or hiding the rulers:** To show or hide your rulers, which appear on the top and left sides of the Layout Designer, choose View⇨ Show/Hide Ruler from the menu bar.

✔ **Changing your ruler settings:** To change your ruler settings, open the Ruler Settings dialog box by choosing View⇨Ruler Settings from the menu bar. In the Ruler Settings dialog box, you can select the unit of measurement (inches, centimeters, or points) and the number of division markers that you want displayed. (The default is 16 division markers.)

✔ **Showing or hiding the grid lines:** To show or hide the grid lines, choose View⇨Show/Hide Grid from the menu bar. The number of dots on the grid line corresponds to the number of division markers that are selected in the Ruler Settings dialog box.

✔ **Snapping to the grid:** If you want your objects to snap to the grid, choose the Snap to Grid command from the View menu.

✔ **Showing or hiding the Tool Palette:** Select Hide Tool Palette or Show Tool Palette to hide or show the Tool Palette.

Using the Tool Palette

The Tool Palette, shown in Figure 26-2, is the tool you use to make any changes to the items that appear on an ACT! layout — fields, field labels, text, rectangles, ellipses, and lines — which are referred to as graphic objects.

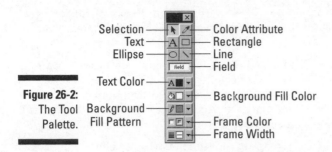

Selection — Color Attribute
Text — Rectangle
Ellipse — Line
— Field
Text Color —

Figure 26-2:
The Tool — Background Fill Color
Palette. Background — Fill Pattern
Fill Pattern — Frame Color
— Frame Width

With the tools on the Tool Palette, you can perform the following tasks:

✔ Insert graphic objects. (A graphic object includes ACT! fields and field labels, text, rectangles, ellipses, and lines.)

✔ Change an object's fill pattern, frame style, frame color, frame width, background color, and the color of an object's text.

From the Object Properties dialog box, you can also edit an object's fill pattern, frame style, frame color, frame width, background color, and font attributes. You do this by double-clicking the object. The features of the Object Properties dialog box are discussed later in this chapter.

Customizing Your ACT! Layout

You can do a lot of things to customize your layout. You can move your fields and field names around, add new fields, remove the ones you don't want to view, and insert additional graphic objects — such as text, rectangles, ellipses, and lines.

Moving fields and field names

The first thing you'll want to do when you begin modifying your fields is to move a field and the corresponding field name from one position on the contact layout or tab to another. This is how you do it:

1. **Click the Tool Palette's Selection tool, which is shown in Figure 26-2.**

2. **Click a field or field name and drag it to another position.**

3. **Release your mouse button.**

Now wasn't that easy. Aligning your fields, field names, and graphic objects is discussed later in the chapter.

If you want to move one or more fields or field names, press and hold the Shift key while clicking the fields or field names. Release the Shift key, drag the objects to another position, and release your mouse button.

Inserting new fields and field names

You insert fields and field names onto a layout from the Fields dialog box. This is how you do it:

1. **Click the Tool Palette's Field tool, which is shown in Figure 26-2. The cursor becomes a large cross-hair.**

   (If the Tool Palette is hidden, choose the Show Tool Palette command from the View menu.)

2. **Place the cursor in the section of the layout in which you want to insert the field, click and hold down the mouse button, drag it until it is the desired size, and release the mouse button.**

   The Fields dialog box appears, as shown in Figure 26-3.

   The only fields that appear in the Fields dialog box are fields that have not been placed on the ACT! layout.

3. **Highlight the field you want to insert from the list of available fields in the Fields dialog box.**

4. **Select the Add Label option if you want a label to appear with the field you are adding.**

5. **Click the Add button.**

Figure 26-3:
The Fields
dialog box.

After you add the fields that you want in your layout, click Close to close the Fields dialog box. You can then position the fields in the appropriate places on the layout.

Removing fields and field names

To remove a field from your layout, highlight the field with the Selection tool and press the Delete key. (If you're deleting a field, you probably want to delete the field's label also.)

If you change your mind and want to restore a just-removed field, choose Edit➪Undo or press Ctrl+Z.

Adding, Moving, and Removing Your Layout's Tabs

In addition to moving, adding, or removing fields on your ACT! layout, you'll probably want to add new tabs to your layout and change the order in which the tabs appear on the layout itself.

You add, move, or remove your tabs from the Define Tabs Layout dialog box, which you open by choosing the Edit➪Tabs command.

From this dialog box, you can do the following:

- ✔ **Add a tab:** To add a tab, click the Add button, and the Add Tab Layout dialog box appears, where you can give the tab a name.

- ✔ **Rename a tab:** To rename a tab, click the Rename button, and the Rename Tab Layout dialog box appears, where you can change the tab's name.

- ✔ **Delete a tab:** To delete a tab, click the Delete button.

- ✔ **Position a tab:** To change a tab's position, highlight the tab and click the Move Up or Move Down button. Moving a tab's name up or down on the list moves it left or right when it appears in the layout.

Assigning a shortcut key to your tabs

A shortcut key enables you to open a contact's tab by pressing Alt+[the shortcut key].

The following is a list of default shortcut keys for tabs.

Tab	Default Shortcut Keys
Activities Tab	Alt+A
Notes/History Tab	Alt+N
Sales/Opportunity	Alt+A
Groups Tab	Alt+G
User Fields Tab	Alt+U
Phone/Home Tab	Alt+P
Alt Contacts Tab	Alt+O
Status Tab	Alt+U

This is how you assign a shortcut key to a tab:

1. **Choose Edit⇨Tabs.**

   The Define Tab Layout dialog box opens.

2. **Select either the Add or Rename button.**

   The Add Tab Layout or Edit Tab dialog box appears. (Both boxes are the same.)

3. **Give the tab a name, if it doesn't already have one.**

4. **Select a letter from the drop-down menu in the Shortcut Key field.**

   You can select a letter from the list of letters in the tab's name.

5. **Click OK.**

   Your shortcut key is assigned.

Changing the Order of the Tab and Group Stops

After you've positioned your fields on the layout, you will probably want to change the order in which your cursor moves between fields when you press the Tab or Enter keys. These are called Tab Stops and Group Stops.

This is how you change the order of your Tab Stops:

1. **Choose Edit⇨Field Entry Order⇨Show from the menu bar to display the Tab and Group Stops within the layout.**

Within each field on the layout, two little gray boxes appear at the field's right-hand edge. The Tab Stop box has a number that designates its position in the Tab Stop sequence. If a field is set as a Group Stop, a red dot appears in the gray box just to the left of the numbered Tab Stop.

2. **Click the number on the fields whose tab order you want to change, and the number disappears.**

If you double-click either the Tab Stop number or the Group Stop sign, the Object Properties dialog box appears. Click Cancel to make it go away.

3. **Click the fields in the new order in which you want the cursor to move when you press the Tab key. ACT! inserts a new number.**

Adding and removing Group Stops is just as simple. To add a Group Stop, just click the Group Stop button, and the red dot appears. To remove a Group Stop, just click the Group Stop button, and the red dot disappears.

Here are some additional things you can do with Tab and Group Stops:

✔ **Clear your Tab and Group Stops:** Choose Edit⇨Field Entry Order⇨Clear. Then click the fields in the order in which you want the cursor to move when you press the Tab or Enter keys.

✔ **Reset your Tab and Group Stops:** Choose Edit⇨Field Entry Order⇨Reset.

✔ **Hide your Tab and Group Stops:** After you set your Tab and Group Stops, you can make them disappear by selecting choosing Edit⇨ Field Entry Order⇨Hide.

Making Your Layout Look Better

To improve the appearance of your layout, you may want to create fancy and elaborate layout titles or section headings by adding boxes, circles, and lines to your layout. You can then position these objects in front of or behind each other to create the look you want. (Moving objects forward and backward is discussed later in this chapter.)

These are the things you can do from the Tool Palette and the Object Properties dialog box:

✔ **Adding text:** To add text to your ACT! layout, select the Text tool from the Tool Palette, place the cross-hair pointer where you want the line of text to start. Then click and drag the pointer left or right until the line is the desired size, release the mouse button, and begin typing your text.

To change the text's style, select the text object with the Selection tool and then double-click, and the Object Properties dialog box appears. You can select from the features of the Style, Font, and Format tabs, which are discussed later in this chapter.

✔ **Adding boxes, circles, and lines:** To add a box, circle, or line to your ACT! layout, select the appropriate tool from the Tool Palette (the features of the Tool Palette are discussed earlier in the chapter), place the cross-hair pointer where you want the object to start, and drag the object up, down, left, or right until it's the desired size.

To make a square, circle, or straight line, hold down the Shift key while you create the object with the Rectangle, Ellipse, or Line tools.

To change the style of a box, circle, or line, select the box, circle, or line with the Selection tool and double-click the object; and the Style tab of the Object Properties dialog box appears, which is discussed earlier in this chapter. You can also change the style of rectangle, ellipse, or line by using the Tool Palette's appearance tools.

Changing the appearance of your fields, field names, lines, text, and other objects

After you've placed all of your objects (fields and field labels) onto a layout, you will probably want to change the way they look on the layout. You do this by double-clicking the selected object, and the Object Properties dialog box appears.

If you'll be making changes to more than one field or field name, hold down the Shift key and then click each of the objects. Then double-click one of the selected objects, and the Object Properties dialog box opens. Make your style or font changes and click OK, and the changes will be applied to each of the selected objects.

These are the things you can do from within the Object Properties dialog box:

✔ **Change a field's style:** From the Style tab of the Object Properties dialog box, you can make the following changes to the selected field: Change the background fill color, change the background fill pattern, change the frame style, change the frame color, or change the frame width.

✔ **Change a field's font:** From the Font tab of the Object Properties dialog box, you can change the font's appearance within a field. You have the following options: change the font, change the font style (regular, italic, bold, or bold italic), change the font size, choose strikeout, choose underline, or choose a color.

✔ **Confirm a field's format:** In the Format tab of the Object Properties dialog box, ACT! displays the basic information about a field:

- • The field's name (Company, Contact, Phone, and so on).

- • The data type (Character, Phone, Date, and so on).

- • In the Appearance box (this box only appears for the Numeric, Date, and Time fields), you can select how you want a Numeric, Date, or Time field to appear. For example, in a Numeric field, you can indicate how you want negative numbers to appear and how many decimal places fields can contain.

You can also change a selected field's appearance by clicking icons on the toolbar, which is shown way back in Figure 26-1. From left to right, here are the buttons on the toolbar: Font List, Font Size, Bold, Italics, Underline, Left Justification, Center Justification, and Right Justification.

Changing your background

After you've designed your layout (you've positioned your fields and field labels; you've changed their fonts, font styles, and colors; and you've added circles, squares, lines, and text), it's time to change your background. Just follow these steps:

1. **Place your pointer over a blank area of the layout.**

2. **Double-click with your left mouse button.**

   The Background Properties dialog box appears. You have the following options: Change the background fill color; change the background fill pattern; choose a bitmap to use as the background; or choose the Tile option to display the bitmap repeatedly until it covers the entire background area.

3. **Make your selections in the Background Properties dialog box and click OK.**

Adding your logo or photo

After you've customized your layout, you may want to do one more thing: Put your corporate logo, another graphic image, or even a photograph of yourself on the layout. This gives you the feeling of ownership.

This is how you add your corporate logo, another graphic image, or even a photograph of yourself to your ACT! layout:

1. **Open Windows Paint (from the Start menu, choose Programs⇨ Accessories⇨Paint) or your favorite graphics program.**

2. **Open your graphic image.**

3. **Choose Edit⇨Copy or press Ctrl+C to copy the image to the Clipboard.**

4. **Press Alt+Tab to toggle over to ACT!'s Layout Designer.**

5. **Choose Edit⇨Paste (Ctrl+V) to paste your graphic into your ACT! layout.**

6. **Click the graphic image to resize and position it on the layout.**

Choose Objects⇨Move to Back to place the graphic behind the fields and field labels.

Positioning Fields, Field Names, and Other Graphic Objects

After you have all of your fields on your layout, you may want to move them around, and you'll certainly want to line them up. This is how you do it:

- **Moving graphic objects:** To move a field, field name, or other graphic object from one position in a layout to another, click the object with the Selection tool and drag it to another position in the layout.

  To move two or more graphic objects at once — a field and its field label, for example — hold down the Shift key while you select each object.

- **Changing an object's size:** To change the size of an object, place the Selection tool on one of the object's handles. The Selection tool changes into a Sizing tool. Move the Sizing tool to make the object larger or smaller.

- **Moving objects from front to back and vice versa:** If you place one object on top of another object, also called layering, you need to be able to move a selected object forward or backward in relation to another object. (For example, you have a black box and want to place white type over it.)

  Use the Selection tool to select the object that you want to move and then choose the Move to Front or Move to Back commands that are available from the Objects menu and the right-mouse-button menu. If you have three or more objects that are layered on top of each another, to rearrange the objects, use the Move Forward or Move Backward commands that are also available from the Objects menu and the right-mouse-button menu.

To access the Move to Front, Move to Back, Move Forward, and Move Backward commands from the right-mouse-button menu, you must place the cursor on the object that you want to move when you click the right mouse button.

✔ **Making objects the same size:** When you're designing your layout, you may want selected fields to be the same size. Instead of trying to make them the same size one at a time, you can use the Make Same Height and Make Same Width commands from the Objects menu. This is how you do it:

    1. **Click the object that is the correct size.**

    2. **Hold down the Shift key and use the Selection tool to select the object that you want to be the same size as the first object.**

    3. **Choose either the Make Same Height or Make Same Width option from the Objects menu. The objects are now the same height or width.**

✔ **Getting objects to line up:** When you're laying out the fields in an ACT! layout, you certainly want your fields to line up properly — both left to right and top to bottom.

To line up objects, you must first select the object that is in the correct position, and then hold down the Shift key and select the objects you want to align with the first object by using the Selection tool. You then align your objects by choosing the Align command from the Objects menu, which opens the Align dialog box.

From the Align dialog box you have the following commands:

    • Left and right alignment selections: None, Align Left Edges, Align Centers, and Align Right Edges.

    • Up and down alignment selections: None, Align Top Edges, Align Centers, and Align Bottom Edges.

✔ **Aligning your objects to the grid:** If you want your objects aligned to the grid, the grid must first be displayed. (To display the grid, choose View⇨ Show Grid from the menu bar.) Select the objects you want to align to the grid and choose the Align to Grid command from the Objects menu.

Chapter 27

Customizing ACT!

· ·

In This Chapter

▶ Automating repetitive tasks with macros

▶ Creating commands to run macros or launch other applications

▶ Customizing the toolbar

▶ Adding commands to the menus

▶ Customizing keyboard shortcuts

▶ Customizing ACT!'s windows and tabs

· ·

*O*ne of the features that makes ACT! such a powerful tool is its macro feature. With ACT! macros, you can automate your repetitive tasks. This enables you to eliminate a lot of unnecessary keystrokes and mouse clicks, thus saving you a tremendous amount of time.

After you have created a macro, you can create a custom command and assign that command to the toolbar, a pull-down menu, or a shortcut key.

Automating Repetitive Tasks with Macros

ACT! macros can save you time and make you much more productive. So if you find yourself repeating the same series of keystrokes over and over again, record them in a macro and let ACT! execute those commands for you.

What is a macro? It's sort of like the redial feature on your phone. A macro enables you to record a series of commands (keystrokes or mouse clicks) so that you can replay those commands without having to enter those same keystrokes or mouse clicks over and over again.

Here is a list of some of the ACT! tasks that many ACT! users have automated with macros:

- Dialing the phone

- Clearing completed calls

- Opening a new database

- Transferring contacts from one database to another

- Scheduling a call, meeting, or to-do

- Sending out a letter to the current contact or lookup

- Sending an e-mail message to the current contact or lookup

- Running a query

- Creating lookups

- Creating fax cover pages

- Inserting new area codes for contacts whose area codes have changed

- Inserting the area code and prefix for the fax number after the contact's phone number has been entered

- Producing custom reports that include specific filtering rules and then sending the report out as an e-mail message

- Printing envelopes for the contact or lookup

- Printing mailing labels for the contact or lookup

- Producing text that is then imported into Excel by an Excel macro

- Performing mail merges

- Starting the timer

Needless to say, almost anything you do from within ACT! can be automated with a macro.

Customizing ACT! commands is a key concept from Jeffrey Mayer's *Growing Your Business with ACT!* program. Jeff's programs are ideal for entrepreneurs, corporate executives, sales professionals and anyone else who wants to grow their business. Call 312-944-4184 for more information.

Recording a macro

This is how you record an ACT! macro:

1. **Choose Tools⇨Record Macro or press Alt+F5.**

   The Record Macro dialog box appears.

2. **Give the macro a name.**

   Enter the name you want to give the macro in the Name Macro to Record field.

3. **Write a description.**

   In the Description field, write a brief description about what this macro does so that you remember what this macro is supposed to do.

4. **Pick a recording option.**

   In the Recording Events field, ACT! gives you three options for recording your keystrokes or mouse actions:

   - **Record Clicks and Drags (mouse events):** This option records all of your mouse actions and ignores any keystrokes and commands you execute from the keyboard.

   - **Record Everything:** This selection records both the ACT! commands you execute with your mouse and the keystrokes you execute from the keyboard.

   - **Record Everything Except Mouse Events:** This option tells ACT! to record any keystrokes you execute from the keyboard and to ignore any commands you execute with the mouse.

   My suggestion is that you execute all of your ACT! commands from the keyboard and ignore the mouse. When you execute your commands from the keyboard, you are forced to be precise as to which commands you want ACT! to perform. You can use the mouse to execute commands that you don't want recorded in your ACT! macro (the actual compiling of a report, for example) or to stop the macro itself.

5. **Click the Record button.**

   The Record Macro dialog box disappears, and you return to the ACT! window.

6. **Record your macro.**

   Execute the series of keystrokes and/or mouse actions you want to record in the precise order you want ACT! to play them back.

   Some ACT! commands are only available from the menu that appears when you right-click. If you need to use one of those commands in your macro, add the command to either the menu bar or a keyboard shortcut. Then record your macro. (Adding commands to the menu bar and keyboard is discussed later in this chapter.)

7. **Stop the recording of your macro.**

   After completing all the keystrokes or mouse actions of your macro, press Alt+F5 to stop the recording of your macro. You can also choose Tools⇔Stop Recording Macro.

To stop the recording of an ACT! macro from almost anywhere within ACT!, press Alt+F5. For example, you can activate a pull-down menu and stop the macro while the menu is displayed. And you can bring up an ACT! dialog box and stop the macro so that you can make your selection manually from the dialog box. (You cannot pause an ACT! macro and then continue recording the macro.)

After you start recording an ACT! macro, ACT! does not have any sort of indicator to remind you that you are in the process of recording a macro. (I hope that Symantec adds such a feature in the future.) The only way you can be sure that the macro recorder is off is to press Alt+F5. If the Record Macro dialog box appears, then you aren't recording a macro.

Practice your keystrokes. ACT! macros can't be edited, so think through exactly what you want your macro to do. Before you record your macro, walk yourself through each step of the macro so that you can identify every command you want the macro to execute. You may even want to write these steps down.

After you begin recording a macro, every keystroke or mouse click you make is recorded, including the mistakes you make — and their corrections — until you stop recording the macro.

Running your macros

The easiest way to run an ACT! macro is to assign the macro to a toolbar icon, a menu item, or a keyboard shortcut.

In the following sections of this chapter, I explain how to turn your macro into an ACT! command, and then add that command to the toolbar or pull-down menu or assign it to a shortcut key.

The secret of the Tab key, the space bar, and the OK button

In many of the ACT! dialog boxes, you must click an OK button to tell ACT! that you've made your selections and you want ACT! to continue doing something. An example would be the Run Report dialog box, where you need to click OK before ACT! can create a report.

The following steps show you how to record a macro involving an ACT! dialog box:

1. **Make your dialog box selections by pressing the Alt and the underlined letter keys.**

2. **After you've made your selections, use the Tab key to move the cursor to the OK button.**

   You know the OK button is highlighted when the letters OK are surrounded by a dotted box.

3. **Press the space bar (not the Enter key).**

   This, in effect, selects the OK button and ACT! continues doing whatever it's supposed to do.

If you press Enter instead of using the Tab key to tab over to the OK button, the macro may stop. (I don't know why this happens, so I can't explain it to you.)

When you run your macro, ACT! opens the dialog box, makes the selections that you chose with the Alt+underlined letter keys, tabs over to the OK button, and continues along to the next macro command.

You can also assign macros to field triggers so that when you enter or exit an ACT! field, ACT! runs the specific macro. Turning a field into a Trigger field is discussed in Chapter 6.

Troubleshooting macros

If your macro isn't running properly, you can run it at the recorded speed, not the playback speed, to troubleshoot it. The following steps show you how:

1. **Choose Tools⇨Run Macro.**

   The Run Macro dialog box appears.

2. **Scroll through the list of macros displayed in the Macros field.**

   Each macro's description is shown in the Description field.

3. **Select the macro you want to run.**

4. **Select the Run at Recorded Speed option to play your macro at the same speed you used to record it.**

   If your macro isn't working properly, this selection enables you to see exactly what went wrong.

5. **Click OK.**

Creating Commands to Run Macros or Launch Other Applications

After you've created your macro, you need to create a custom command so that you can assign it to the toolbar or pull-down menu, or to a shortcut key.

You can also use custom commands to launch other programs or to open files in other applications.

To create a custom command, choose Tools➪Customize [name of window] Window from the menu bar. The Customize ACT! [name of window] Window dialog box opens. Then click the Custom Commands tab, which is shown in Figure 27-1.

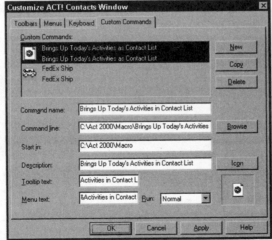

Figure 27-1: The Commands tab of the Customize ACT! Contacts Window dialog box.

After you create a custom command, it's added to the list of commands displayed in the Command drop-down menu in the Toolbars, Menus, and Keyboard tabs. You can then add your new custom command to any toolbar, to any menu, or to your keyboard.

To create a custom ACT! command, do the following:

1. Click the New button.

The Command Name, Command Line, and other fields on the Custom Commands tab are enabled.

2. Click the Browse button.

The Select a Command dialog box opens. Find your ACT! macro (ACT! macros are stored in ACT! 2000's Macro directory and have the .MPR extension) or your specific program's executable file on your hard drive and click Open. ACT! inserts the files path into the Command Line field.

If you want to assign a document or file to an ACT! command, such as a word processing document or spreadsheet, locate that file on your hard drive and insert its path in the Command Line field. And if you're into programming, you can run Visual Basic scripts from the Custom Commands dialog box.

3. **Enter a name in the Command Name field, enter a description in the Description field, enter Tool Tip text, and enter Menu text.**

4. **Click the Icon button to select an icon.**

5. **Click Apply to save your command.**

To delete a custom command, double-click the command to bring up all the information that is entered in the Command Name, Command Line, and other fields, and click Delete.

To copy the custom command, double-click the command to bring up all the information that is entered in the Command Name, Command Line, and other fields, and click the Copy button. Make your changes and click Apply to add the new command to the list of Custom Commands.

Customizing the Toolbar

You can customize the toolbars in each of ACT!'s 14 different windows. The 14 windows are: the Startup window, Contacts window, Groups window, Calendar window, Task List window, Contact List window, Query window, Replace Fields window, Layout Design window, E-Mail window, Report window, Envelope window, Label window, and Browser window.

The look and feel of the ACT! toolbar can be customized and modified. The following are some of the options you can adjust from within an ACT! window:

✔ **Changing the toolbar position:** To change the position of the toolbar, click a blank portion of the toolbar (don't click an icon) and drag the entire toolbar to another position on the window. If you want the toolbar to float as a palette, just leave it positioned anywhere within the window.

✔ **Changing icon size:** To change the size of the icons — make them larger or smaller— right-click a blank portion of the toolbar and make your selection from the menu that appears.

✔ **Showing/hiding the standard toolbar:** To show or hide the standard toolbar, right-click a blank portion of the toolbar and check or uncheck the Standard Toolbar option.

✔ **Deleting a toolbar:** To delete a new toolbar, right-click a blank portion of the toolbar and choose the Delete Toolbar command. The Delete Custom Toolbar dialog box opens, where you select the custom toolbar you want to delete. Adding custom toolbars is discussed later in this chapter.

Customizing commands on the toolbar

To customize toolbar commands, as well as menus, shortcut keys, and custom commands, choose Tools⇨Customize [name of window] Window from the menu bar. The Customize ACT! [name of window] Window dialog box opens. The Toolbars tab for the Customize ACT! Contacts Window dialog box is shown in Figure 27-2.

Another way to open the Customize ACT! [name of window] Window dialog box is to right-click the toolbar and choose Customize Window from the menu that appears.

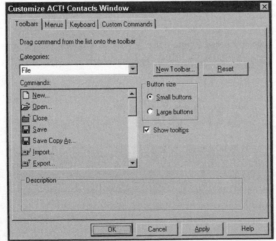

Figure 27-2:
The Toolbars tab for the Customize ACT! Contacts Window dialog box.

From within the Toolbars tab, you can do the following:

✔ **Change an icon's position:** To change an icon's position on the toolbar, click the icon and drag it left or right.

✔ **Add space between icons:** To add a space between icons, select the icon and click the Insert Space button.

✔ **Delete an icon:** To delete an icon, select it and drag it off the toolbar.

✔ **Add an icon:** To add a new icon to the toolbar, follow these steps:

    1. **Select the category of commands — File, Edit, Contact, and so on — from the category drop-down list.**

    2. **Click the command and drag it onto the toolbar.**

✔ **Add a custom command:** If you have created a custom command (creating custom commands was discussed earlier in this chapter), select Custom Commands from the Categories drop-down list.

✔ **Reset your icons:** To reset the icons on your toolbar to their default settings, click the Reset button.

✔ **Show Tool Tips:** If you don't remember what an icon does, just place and rest your cursor over it, and a brief description of what the icon does appears. The description is called a Tool Tip. To enable the Tool Tips option, right-click an empty spot on the toolbar and choose the Customize Window command. The Customize ACT! [name of window] Window dialog box opens. Select the Show Tool Tips option.

Creating a new toolbar

ACT! now enables you to have multiple toolbars for each window. So you can put different commands on different toolbars, which you can then show, hide, or reposition within your ACT! window.

You create a new toolbar by clicking the New Toolbar button and giving it a name. After you've created your new toolbar, you have the same features that were just described.

Adding Commands to Menus

To customize the commands on an ACT! window's menu, click the Menus tab of the Customize ACT! [name of window] Window dialog box. From the Menus tab, you can add, delete, and reorganize the commands on your ACT! menus.

Scroll through the list of commands — File, Edit, Contact, and so on — that are displayed in the Menu field. To expand the list and see all of the commands that are included in a particular menu item, just click the Plus (+) sign with your mouse or press the Right Arrow key.

After locating the command you want, you can make any (or all) of the following changes:

✔ **Change a command's position:** To change the position of a command, select it and drag it to a new position with your mouse.

✔ **Change a command's description:** To change the description of a command as it appears on the menu, highlight the command and click the Rename button. The Rename Menu dialog box opens where you change the menu item's name. Note the position of the ampersand in the description.

An ampersand (&) placed in front of a letter indicates that the letter is underlined when the command appears on the menu. This enables you to execute shortcut commands by pressing the Alt key plus the underlined letter. To open ACT!'s Preferences dialog box, for example, all you have to do is press Alt+E+E (the command is Edit⇨Preferences).

Some ACT! command that appear on the right-click menu do not appear on the drop-down menus. If you're recording a macro that needs to execute one of these commands, you have a problem. With the Menu Customization feature, you can add such commands to the menu bar and then record your macro.

✔ **Add a new command:** To add a new command, you select the position where you want the new command inserted, select the command you want to insert from the list in the Commands box, and drag the command onto the menu.

✔ **Add a menu or submenu heading:** To add a menu or submenu heading to an ACT! menu, you select the command under which you want this new menu or submenu to be inserted and click the New Submenu Menu button.

✔ **Insert a between menu items line:** To add a line between menu commands, select the <Separator> command and drag it onto the command under which you want the line inserted.

✔ **Delete a command:** To delete a menu command or a separator line, highlight the command and click the Delete button.

✔ **Reset your menus:** To reset your menus to their default settings, click the Reset button.

Customizing Keyboard Shortcuts

To customize ACT!'s keyboard shortcuts, click the Keyboard tab of the Customize ACT! [name of window] Window dialog box. From the Keyboard tab, you can add, delete, and modify the shortcut keys that activate ACT! commands.

This is how you add a shortcut key:

1. **Select the category of commands — File, Edit, Contact, and so on — from the category drop-down list.**

2. **Select the command from the list of commands that appear within the Commands box.**

3. **Click the Assign Shortcut button. The Assign Shortcut dialog box opens.**

4. **Press your key combination.**

   You can use the Alt, Ctrl, and Shift keys (including all three keys at once) in combination with any of the keys on the keyboard or the function keys.

To change a keystroke combination, just select the command, click the Assign Shortcut button, and press your new key combination.

To delete a shortcut key combination, just select the command and click the Remove Shortcut button.

To reset your shortcut key combinations to their original commands, just click the Reset button.

If you're selecting a keystroke combination that is already assigned as the keyboard shortcut for another command, a message box appears telling you the name of the command that the key combination is already assigned to. If you still want to assign the shortcut key combination to a new command, click Yes.

Customizing ACT!'s Windows and Tabs

As you use ACT!, you may find that you want to customize its look. In each window and tab, you can change the color, size, and style of the font, as well as the color of the window's or tab's background. You make these changes in the Colors and Fonts tab of the Preferences dialog box. Open the Preferences dialog box by choosing the Preferences command from the Edit menu.

From the Colors and Fonts tab, you can do the following to an ACT! window or tab:

- ✔ Change the font, style, size, and color.
- ✔ Change the background color.
- ✔ Display or hide the grid lines for the Contact List and Task List windows, the Notes/History tab, the Activities tab, the Group tab in the Contacts window, and the Contacts tab in the Groups window.

Chapter 28

Managing and Protecting Your ACT! Database

. . . .

In This Chapter

▶ Discovering data synchronization

▶ Exporting and importing contact and group records

▶ Opening, closing, deleting, and copying your Act! database

▶ Backing up your ACT! database

. . . .

*T*his chapter covers the different ways that you can share ACT! data, and it also dealss with the basic day-to-day stuff that you do with an ACT! database.

Sharing Information through Data Synchronization

If you are frequently away from your office, you can easily share contact information with your coworkers. ACT! 2000 includes a data synchronization feature that enables you to exchange information with other ACT! 2000 users so that the contacts in your database match the contacts in the other user's database. This is what database synchronization does:

✔ Database synchronization consolidates the changes you make to your database and creates a file containing these changes. The update file is then attached to an e-mail message and is either sent to a shared folder or directly synchronized with another database.

✔ Synchronization enables you to receive updates that have been sent to you from another user.

✔ Synchronization works on a field-by-field basis, with the latest change taking effect. It merges contact data and compares the fields to determine which data is the most recent.

✔ Synchronization merges a contact's notes/history items and activities.

Synchronization ensures that you and your colleagues have the most up-to-date information about all your contacts and groups of contacts, including their notes, histories, and activities. And even if you don't need to share data with other ACT! users, you may need to synchronize data between a laptop and a desktop computer.

Data synchronization is a very powerful feature. And though it is beyond the scope of this book, I'm going to point you to some places where you can get all the synchronization information that you need.

ACT!'s online help

The first thing you should do is consult ACT!'s online help features. This is what you do:

1. **Select Help⇨Help Topics.**

   The Help Topics: ACT! dialog box opens.

2. **Click on the How To section.**

3. **Scroll through the list until you find the Synchronize Contact Data With Other ACT! Users section and click Open.**

   The list of synchronization topics appears.

4. **Go through the list and read each of the synchronization help topics.**

Print out each topic and read it so that you thoroughly understand how to utilize ACT!'s synchronization feature.

Using ACT!'s Knowledge Base

This is how you access ACT!'s Knowledge Base over the Internet:

1. **Go to the Symantec ACT! Web site.**

   The address is `www.symantec.com/act`.

2. **Click on Service & Support.**

   The Service & Support page opens.

3. **Select the Knowledge Base & FAQ link.**

   The Knowledge Base page opens.

4. **Select the ACT! link.**

   The ACT! Knowledge Base page opens.

5. **Select the ACT! 2000 for Windows 95/98/NT link**.

   The ACT! 2000 Genie page opens.

6. **Type** SYNCHRONIZATION **in the Search field**.

   The complete list of synchronization articles appears.

From these articles you've complete access to Symantec's synchronization library.

At the end of each article, there's a Printer Friendly Version button. Click on it and you can view the article in a format that makes it easy to print.

If you find you need additional help or assistance in setting up and designing your ACT! synchronization program, I suggest that you contact an ACT! Certified Consultant (ACC). See Chapter 30 for information on finding an ACT! Certified Consultant. You can also get information about ACT! Certified Consultants on Symantec's ACT! Web site at www.symantec.com/act.

Exporting and Importing Contact and Group Records to Another Database

When you want to copy ACT! contact or group records from one database to another database, you use the Export or Import commands.

Exporting contacts

This is how you export contact and group records:

1. **Select File⇨Data Exchange, Export.**

   The Export Wizard appears.

2. **From the Export Wizard, select ACT! 2000 (*.DBF) as the file type.**

3. **Click the Filename and Location Browse button, which opens the Save As dialog box.**

4. Select the database that you want to export these records into, if you want to create a new database give the new database a name and click Save.

You return to the Export Wizard.

5. Click the Next button.

The Wizard asks, "What kind of records do you want to export?" You have the following choices:

- Contact Records Only

- Group Records Only

- Contact and Group Record

You can also select your merge options by clicking the Merge button. I explain how to use the features of the Merge Options dialog box later in this chapter.

6. Make your choice and click the Next button.

The Wizard asks you which contact or group records do you want to export.

- If you selected the Contact Records Only option, you can choose from the Current Contact, the Current Lookup, or All Records.

- If you selected Group Records Only or Contact and Group Records, your only choice is All Records.

7. Click the Next button.

The Import Wizard's Contact Map appears (see Figure 28-1). The Contact Map is only available if you selected Contact Records Only or Contact and Group Records in Step 5.

Map the contact fields of the database that is being imported with the database that is open. Mapping ACT! fields is discussed later in this chapter.

Figure 28-1:
The Import
Wizard's
Contact
Map.

8. **Click the Next button.**

   The Import Wizard's Group Map appears. (The Group Map is only available if you selected Group Records Only or Contact and Group Records in Step 5.)

9. **Map the group fields of the database that is being imported with the database that is open.**

10. **Click the Finish button to export your records into the selected database.**

Saving a database as a delimited (.TXT) file

If you want to copy your ACT! database for use in another program, you can save it as a delimited file. A delimited file is a word processing file that has special codes, called delimiters, that separate the individual fields. There are two types of delimited files: tab and comma.

✔ Tab delimited: A tab stop indicates the beginning of a new field; that is, the fields are laid out in spreadsheet form.

✔ Comma delimited: All the fields are enclosed in quotation marks and separated by a comma.

You create a delimited file by following the same steps that were described in the previous section with a few changes.

✔ In the first Export Wizard you select Text - Delimited as the file type, and give it a name with the *.TXT extension.

✔ In the next Wizard you are asked: What kind of records do you want to export? You have two choices: Contact Records Only and Group Records Only.

✔ Click the Options button to open the Export Options dialog box. From the Export Options dialog box, you select your field separators. You can export your database in either a comma delimited or tab delimited format. If you want to export your field names, click the Yes, Export Field Names option.

✔ In the final Export Wizard, you can select which fields you want to export.

Importing contacts

When you want to import the contact or group records of an ACT! database into the currently open database select the File, Data Exchange, Import command. The Import Wizard opens, and you follow the same steps that were described in the "Exporting contacts" section.

Setting your merge options

From ACT!'s Merge Options dialog box — which was referred to in Step 5 of the "Exporting contacts" section of this chapter — you tell ACT! what to do when it finds contact records that match or do not match during the export or import process. The Merge Options dialog box is shown in Figure 28-2.

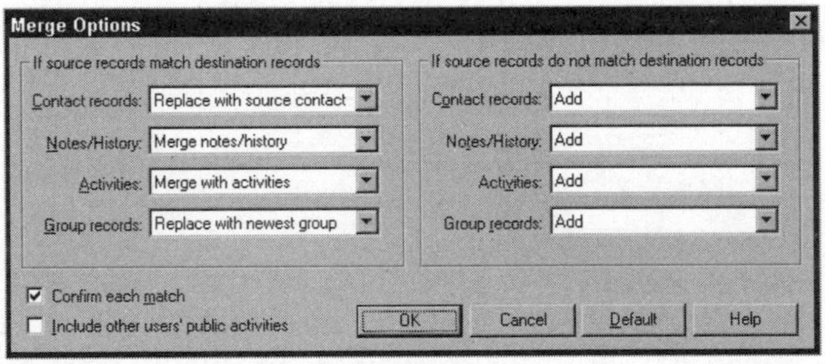

Figure 28-2:
The Merge
Options
dialog box.

- ✔ **Dealing with unique IDs.** In the Merge Options dialog box, you select the data you want to merge from the source database (the database that is currently open) with the destination database (the database that will be receiving the contact records).

  Contacts are always merged on the basis of their unique IDs. The unique ID is an invisible ID number that ACT! stamps on each contact record. ACT! assigns this number when you create or import a contact from one database to another database.

- ✔ **Using the default settings.** The default merge settings should work just fine for the majority of your database merges. When the source records match the destination records, the default settings instruct ACT! to select the newest contact record, and it merges the information in the Notes/History and Activities files together. If the groups match, ACT! selects the newest group.

  If the two sets of contact criteria do not match, ACT! adds the contact as a new contact record to the destination database, along with the contact's notes/history items and activities. If ACT! finds new groups, ACT! adds them to the destination database.

If you don't want to use the default settings, you can tell ACT! what you want it to do if it does or does not find a match. Here are your choices:

✔ **Matching contact records.** When the contact records in the source database match those of the destination database, you have the following choices regarding what ACT! will do with the information in the contact's record:

> • **Replace with newest contact:** ACT! compares the Edit Dates of each contact record in the source and destination database to determine the newest contact record. If the contact record in the source database is newer, ACT! uses that contact information.

> • **Replace with source contact:** ACT! replaces the contact information in the destination database with the contact information from the source database, regardless of which contact record is the newest.

> • **Do not change:** ACT! makes no changes to the information contact fields of the destination database.

✔ **Matching Notes/History files.** If the contact records in the source database match those in the destination database, you have the following choices for notes/history items:

> • **Merge Notes/History:** ACT! adds new notes/history items to the contact's Notes/History file in the destination database and updates matching entries with the latest information.

> • **Replace with source notes/history:** ACT! replaces the contact's notes/history items that are in the destination database with those that are in the source database.

> • **Do not change:** ACT! makes no changes to the notes/history items that are in the destination database.

✔ **Matching schedules.** When the contact records in the source database match those of the destination database, you have the following choices regarding the contact's scheduled activities:

> • **Merge activities:** ACT! adds new activities to the destination database's contact record. (You can also reconcile cleared activities, provided that you select the Merge History option.)

> • **Replace with source activities:** ACT! replaces the contact's scheduled activities in the destination database with the contact's scheduled activities that are in the source database.

> • **Do not change:** ACT! makes no changes to the contact's scheduled activities in the destination database.

✔ **Matching Group Records.** If the Group Records in the source database match those of the destination database, you have the following choices:

- **Replace with newest group:** ACT! compares the Edit Date of the Group Records in the source and destination databases. If the Group Record in the source database is newer, ACT! uses that group information.

- **Replace with source group:** ACT! replaces the Group Record in the destination database with the Group Record from the source database, regardless of which group record is the newest.

- **Do not change:** ACT! makes no changes to the Group Records of the destination database.

✔ **Dealing with non-matching contact records.** When you perform a custom merge, the merge options that you select in the fields of the Merge Options dialog box determines what ACT! will do when it finds contact records from the source database that do not match those in the destination database.

If a contact record in the source database does not match any of the contact records in the destination database — this means that it's a new record — you have to decide what ACT! will do with the contact records, notes/history, activities, and group records. You can have ACT! add them to the destination database, or you can have ACT! not add them to the destination database.

✔ **Confirming each match.** If you want ACT! to confirm each match, select the Confirm Each Match box. When ACT! finds a match, the Confirm Merge dialog box appears, and you can look at the contact's basic information. If you want to accept the merge, click the Merge button. If you don't, click the Skip button, and ACT! moves on to the next current record; otherwise, ACT! makes the changes automatically.

✔ **Including public activities.** If you want to include all public activities, select the Include Other User's Public Activities option.

Here are some additional things to keep in mind:

✔ Because merging has the potential to overwrite contact data, you should back up your destination database before choosing the Merge command. During the merge process, you can only alter the destination database. Backing up the source database is not necessary.

✔ Before you merge an ACT! database, compress and reindex both databases so that all the deleted contacts have been swapped out. This way, you have the newest and freshest indexes available, and you'll complete your merge in half the time.

✔ If you want to clean up an ACT! database that has a number of duplicate records in it, create a new database and merge the old database into the new one. The first time ACT! encounters a contact record, ACT! enters the contact record into the new database. The second time ACT! encounters a contact record with the same secondary-match criteria, it merges the two contact records together.

ACT! uses primary and secondary merge criteria to determine when contact records match. The default merge criteria for Contact records are Company, Contact, and Phone. The default merge criteria for Group records are Group Name and Record Creator. You can change your merge criteria by selecting the Advanced tab in the Define Fields dialog box and changing the duplicate matching fields. (You open the Define Fields dialog box by selecting Edit⇨Define Fields.) Checking your ACT! database for duplicate records is covered in Chapter 9.

✔ The date that you merge a contact record into an ACT! database is recorded in the Merge Date field on the Status tab.

Mapping your Contact and Group fields

When you import one ACT! database into another, you want to make sure that everything ends up in the right place, so you use the Import Wizard's Contact Map and Group Map. The process that I'm describing is identical for both the Contact Map and the Group Map. (The Contact Map is shown in Figure 28-1.)

Mapping, in this instance, is the process of matching the fields of the source database with those of the destination database, which ensures that everything ends up in the right place.

You can map any field in the source database to any field in the destination database. You can also exclude any field you want from the merge process.

The Contact Map dialog box displays the contents of each field of the source database, and it enables you to map, or match, each of those fields to the appropriate field in the destination database.

To map the imported fields with the appropriate ACT! fields, choose a field in the Map This Field column and then select the field that you want to map it to from the drop-down list in the To This Field column.

You then work your way through the list of fields that you're importing into ACT!, one field at a time, and determine which field you want to map the imported field to. If you don't want to import a particular field into ACT!, you can exclude that field by choosing the Do Not Map selection from the drop-down menu, which leaves the field blank.

Here are some more mapping features:

✔ **Viewing the contacts information.** After mapping the fields of your first contact, click the View Next Record button to view the contact information of the next contact in the source database. Viewing the records of several contacts helps you determine how the imported fields should be mapped to the destination database's corresponding fields. To view the previous contact's information, click the View Previous Record button.

Continue this process until all the fields from the source database have been mapped to the correct fields in the destination database (or have been excluded from the importing process).

If the data in a source database's field is larger or longer than the field in the destination database you are mapping it to, ACT! truncates the data.

✔ **Saving your map settings.** After you've mapped your data, you can save your map settings by clicking the Contact Map's Save Map button. Saving your map settings enables you to use the settings again if you need to merge information from the same source into one of your ACT! databases.

✔ **Using your map settings.** When you want to apply one of your previously saved map settings, click the Contact Map's Load Map button and select the setting that you want to use from the list that appears in the Open dialog box. Then click OK.

Opening, Closing, Deleting, and Copying your ACT! Database

This section deals with the basic day-to-day stuff that you do with an ACT! database.

✔ **Opening a database:** To open an ACT! database, select File➪Open or press Ctrl+O, and the Open File dialog box appears. Highlight the database file you want to open, click OK, and ACT! opens the new database.

✔ **Closing a database:** To close an ACT! database, select File➪Close, press Ctrl+W, or Alt+F4, and ACT! closes your database.

If you have an automatic backup system, closing your ACT! database before the backup begins is a good idea. The backup program may not be able to open and copy your ACT! database files if the database is open.

✔ **Deleting a database:** To delete a database from your computer, select File➪Administration➪Delete Database, highlight the database you want to delete, and an ACT! message box asks you if you're sure you want to delete this database. Click Yes, and ACT! deletes the database. Click No, and ACT! cancels the deletion. (If the database has a password, you must enter the password before ACT! deletes the database.)

Deleting a database deletes all the contacts within your ACT! database. After a database is deleted, all of its contact information is gone.

✔ **Copying your database with the File➪Save Copy As command:** When you want to make a copy of your ACT! database, use the Save Copy As command in the File menu. With this command, you can make a copy of your entire database or create an empty database.

After you choose the Save Copy As command, a message box appears that asks whether you want to copy the entire database or create an empty copy.

The Save Copy As command can be useful when you want to back up your database to another directory or onto a different disk, hard drive, or Zip drive.

✔ **Creating a new database with the File➪New command:** When you want to create a brand-new ACT! database, this is how you do it:

1. Select File➪New or press Ctrl+N. The New dialog box appears.

2. Select ACT! Database as your File Type and click OK. The New Database dialog box appears.

3. Give your new database a name and click Save. ACT! begins to create the new database, and the Enter My Record Information dialog box opens.

4. Make any changes to the My Record information and click OK. ACT! creates the new database.

ACT! takes the My Record information (name, address, phone, and so on) from the database that is open at the time the new database is created. The My Record contact record contains information about the user of the database. (In a shared database, the My Record contact record belongs to the currently logged on user.) The name and address information in My Record appears in letters, memos, faxes, and reports, identifying the creator of these documents.

If you want to assign a password to a database, open the Set Password dialog box by selecting File➪Administration➪Set Password.

If you want to create a new database that has all of the ACT! fields, drop-down menus, and field attributes, select the Create Empty Copy option.

You're also given the choice of saving this database in the ACT! 3 or ACT! 4 format.

Backing Up Your ACT! Database

One of the most important things you can do is backup your database. Bad things do happen to computers, and you never want to discover that your hard drive crashed and you just lost years worth of contact information.

Fortunately, you've a number of backup options.

ACT! comes with a backup utility that makes it easy to back up your database to a floppy disk or another directory on your hard drive or your network. This is how you do it:

1. **Select File⇨Backup from the menu bar.**

   The Backup dialog box opens.

2. **Select the directory in which you want to save the database and give the file a name.**

3. **Click the Options tab to select which additional files you want to include with this backup.**

   You can backup Attached Mail, Documents, Envelopes, Labels, Layouts, Reports, SideACT! Data, and Templates.

   Click the Remind Me To Back Up Every ____ Days option to have ACT! remind you to back up your database at regular intervals.

4. **Click Start to start the backup process.**

Once you've backed up your database you restore it by using the File⇨Restore command.

This is how you restore a database that you've backed up:

1. **Select File⇨Restore from the menu bar.**

   The Restore dialog box opens.

2. **Select the file you want to restore.**

3. **Select the folder in which you want to restore it.**

4. **Click the Start button.**

   ACT! restores your files and places the database, Attached Mail, Documents, Envelopes, Labels and other things in the appropriate file.

Part VIII
The Part of Tens

The 5th Wave   By Rich Tennant

"MY GIRLFRIEND RAN A SPREADSHEET OF MY LIFE, AND GENERATED THIS CHART. MY BEST HOPE IS THAT SHE'LL CHANGE HER MAJOR FROM 'COMPUTER SCIENCES' TO 'REHABILITATIVE SERVICES.'"

In this part . . .

Every ...*For Dummies* book ends with lists of ten items. It's tradition. (According to my publisher, it's the law.) Well, I still want to present you with meaty information that you can use rather than a bunch of lists. True, the next few chapters each have at least ten tidbits of information in them, but some of the chapters aren't arranged as easy-to-read lists. I prefer to use my own hard-to-follow prose.

Chapter 29

At Least Ten Database Maintenance Tips

Keeping Your Databases in Tip-Top Shape

You must maintain — compress and reindex — your ACT! databases if you want them to work properly. I can give you two reasons:

✓ **Reindexing:** You want to make sure that ACT!'s indexes are working properly; otherwise, ACT! may begin to have some difficulty locating contact records. The process of fixing ACT!'s indexes is called reindexing.

✓ **Compressing:** Whenever you delete a contact from your database, the disk space holding that deleted contact is not usable; it becomes fragmented. When you compress your database, you remove the wasted space that's inside your database. If you've deleted a substantial number of contacts, you have a great deal of wasted space inside your database, which causes ACT! to slow down.

To perform maintenance on your database, choose File➪Administration➪ Database Maintenance, and the Database Maintenance dialog box appears. The Database Maintenance dialog box has two tabs, the Periodic Maintenance tab and the Data Clean-up tab.

On the Database Maintenance dialog box's Periodic Maintenance tab you've three options:

- ✔ **Reindex database:** Click the the Reindex button, and ACT! reindexes the database. When you reindex a database, the Reindexing Databases progress gauge appears to keep you apprised of the status.

- ✔ **Compress and reindex database:** Select the Compress option and click the Reindex button, and ACT! both compresses and reindexes your database. Depending on the size of the database, compressing can take several minutes. You should compress and reindex your database at least two or three times each week.

- ✔ **Remind me to reindex:** If you want ACT! to remind you to reindex your database every few days, select the Remind Me Again In __ Days option.

On the Database Maintenance dialog box's Data Clean-up tab you can have ACT! automatically remove notes, histories, attachments and a number of other things from your ACT! database.

Select the item(s) you want to remove from your database and then select the number of days you want to go back. You've these choices:

- ✔ Notes older than __ days.

- ✔ Histories older than __ days.

- ✔ Attachments older than __ days.

- ✔ Transaction logs older than __ days.

- ✔ Cleared activities older than __ days.

- ✔ Lost sales older than __ days.

- ✔ Closed/won sales older than __ days.

- ✔ Sales opportunities older than __ days.

Click the Remove Selected Items button and a warning message appears asking you: `Are you sure you want to remove the selected items?` Click Yes and ACT! reindexes your database and removes the selected items.

Here are some reindexing tips:

- ✔ Only the database administrator can compress or reindex a shared ACT! database. The Database Maintenance command is active only when the database administrator is the only user of the database. All other users must be logged off.

✔ Never interrupt ACT! while it is compressing or reindexing your database because you can cause considerable damage to your database.

✔ Protect your computer with a surge protector and a backup power supply. An unexpected interruption of power is often the cause of database corruption. If you're not protecting your computer with a quality surge protector, you need to go out and purchase one this very moment!

✔ Back up your ACT! database! The more you use ACT!, the more important backing up your database on a regular basis becomes. Losing data or other files can be disastrous. And the easiest way to back up your hard drives and your ACT! databases is to use an automatic backup system. (Check out Chapter 25 for more information on backing up your databases.)

A word about indexes

A database index is sort of like the index in the back of a book. You open a book, look for an item in the index, and it points you to a certain page within the book.

Each time you enter contact or activity information into ACT!, ACT! records the location of that information within indexes (tables). When you perform a lookup, ACT! searches through the index to find the lookup criteria, and displays the results.

An ACT! database is composed of many separate database files — an activity database, a contacts, database, an e-mail database, a groups database, and so on — each of which has its own index.

Each time you add, modify, or delete contact information, ACT! saves the information in the appropriate database and updates the indexes.

Every once in a while, you may find that the index within one of your databases has become so damaged (corrupted) that you're unable to open the database. Should this happen, a message appears telling you that you need to reindex your database.

This is how you reindex an ACT! database from the Startup window:

1. **Select File▷Database Maintenance.**

   The Open dialog box appears.

2. **Select the database that you want to reindex and click Open.**

   The Database Maintenance dialog box appears.

3. **Click the Reindex button.**

If you're still having index problems, use ACTDIAG.

Using ACTDIAG

ACTDIAG is a diagnostic utility program that's included with ACT!. It's purpose is to help diagnose ACT! database problems. ACTDIAG is located within your ACT! directory. Double-click on the executable file (ACTDIAG.EXE) and you open ACTDIAG.

ACTDIAG and is not documented nor is it supported by Symantec. Unless you are an experienced ACT! user, you should only use ACTDIAG when on the phone with an ACT! technical support technician. ACT! tech support's phone number is 541-465-8645. An ACT! Certified Consultant can also help solve your database problems. To learn more about the services provided by an ACT! Certified Consultant, turn to Chapter 30.

From within ACTDIAG you can do the following:

- Diagnose the database structure.
- Get system configuration information.
- Undelete deleted records.
- Backup the ACT! Registry keys.
- Remove Index files.
- Remove Unapplied Sync Packets.
- Remove TEMP files.

If you are still having database problems, Symantec has a data recovery program. You can log onto it from within ACT! by selecting Help⇨ Symantec Online Support. Select the Online Support option and then select the Learn About Symantec Data Recovery Services option.

Symantec Data Recovery has created a document that helps you determine if you need to use the ACT! Database Repair Services. Call Symantec's Fax-On-Demand service at 541-984-2490, choose option 2, and request document 918875.

You can also get information about Symantec's Data Recovery program from the ACT! Web site. Go to www.symantec.com/act. Select the Service & Support link. On the Service & Support page there is information about repairing a damaged ACT! database.

Accessing System Information

From within ACT!, you have access to information about your computer. Select Help⇨About ACT!, and click the System Information tab. You have access to the following information:

- **System Properties:** Select System properties, and ACT! displays information about your operating system, processor, and more. You can also open the Windows Network Support dialog box, the System Properties dialog box, the Control Panel, and the Windows System folder.

- **Memory Status:** Select Memory Status, and you can see your system's total physical memory, available physical memory, memory utilization, and available disk space. You can also open the Windows Memory Troubleshooter.

- **Display Settings:** Select Display Settings, and you can see your resolution, color depth, and vertical refresh rates. You can also open the Display Properties dialog box.

- **Library Versions:** Select Library Versions, and you can see a list of each dll file that ACT! is using.

- **Technical Support:** Select Technical Support, and you can log onto Symantec's Web site and check for updates with LiveUpdate.

Updating ACT! with LiveUpdate

ACT!'s LiveUpdate feature, (select Help⇨LiveUpdate), enables you to automatically download patches, bug fixes, enhancements, support tips, and other useful information directly from Symantec's Web site into your computer.

Once you initiate a LiveUpdate session, ACT! downloads the files into your computer and then automatically installs them for you.

You can log onto Symantec's server with either a modem or Internet connection.

The Bare Minimum on Administering a Multi-User Database

You can share your ACT! database with other users, even if you're using ACT! on a stand-alone computer. You, as the administrator, can add new users to your ACT! database. You can also remove a user from your shared ACT! database. To do these tasks, select File⇨Administration⇨Define Users, and the Define Users dialog box appears. From the Users dialog box, you can add a new user or remove an existing user.

That's really all I ought to say about this topic, as anything more would be beyond the scope of this ...*For Dummies* book. I'm assuming that the typical ACT! user isn't the administrator of a shared database.

However, here are some additional sources for database administration information:

✔ **ACT! Online Help:** ACT!'s online help has extensive information about using ACT! in a multi-user environment. Select Help⇨Help Topics and then click the Index tab and enter Multiuser Databases. ACT! then displays the help information on multi-user databases.

✔ **ACT! Users Guide**: The ACT! Users Guide, which is also on the ACT! 2000 CD-ROM, has a whole chapter on Database Administration. Its name is UserGuide.PDF, and it's located in the ACTDOCS folder.

✔ **The Knowledge Base on ACT!'s Web site**: ACT!'s Knowledge Base contains a great deal of information about database administration. You can log onto the Knowledge Base from within ACT! by selecting Help⇨Symantec Online Support and the Technical Support window opens. Click on the Online Support button, and the Online Support window opens. Click on the Search Knowledge Base option. (ACT!'s home page is www.symantec.com/act.)

Chapter 30

More Than Ten Technical Resources

• •

• •

*1*f you have a technical problem, contact ACT! technical support.

If you want to have someone help you set up your ACT! database, show you how to administer it, or just help you discover how to get the most out of ACT!, then you should call an ACT! Certified Consultant. They're trained to solve ACT! problems.

And if you want to share ideas with other ACT! users, attend an ACT! user group meeting.

ACT! Telephone Support

Symantec offers a number of different telephone support packages. For more information about these different support packages, and their costs, you can call Symantec customer service at 541-465-8645 or visit the ACT! Web page at www.symantec.com/act and select the Technical Support link. On the ACT! Technical Support page, select the Telephone Support link, which takes you to the ACT! Telephone Support page.

The following is a brief description of the different types of ACT! technical support that is available.

Standard Care

Standard Care support, available by calling 541-465-8645, is free for all registered users for 90 days from the date of their first call.

Priority Care

Priority Care offers two access options that guarantee faster service:

- **Per Incident Fee:** If you have an in-depth problem, this is a good option for receiving technical support. The phone number for this service is 800-927-3989.
- **Per Minute Fee:** If you have a quick question, use this technical support service. The phone number for this service is 900-646-0001.

Gold Care Support

Gold Care is a membership program offering ongoing priority support for you or your small company.

Gold Care provides cost-effective support programs for customers who need ongoing technical support. You can select the level of Gold Care that meets your needs and receive priority support on a toll-free 800 number with a minimal hold time.

Call Customer Service at 800-441-7234 to become a member and receive these benefits:

- Priority support on a toll-free 800 number
- Average hold times of three minutes or less
- Support hours from 6:00 a.m. to 5:00 p.m. Pacific Time; 9:00 a.m. to 8:00 p.m. Eastern Time

Platinum Support

Platinum Care is the corporate solution. Platinum Care customers receive unlimited use of a toll-free number and access to the Platinum Web site.

Platinum Support gives corporate customers all the features they need to be successful: unlimited toll-free calls, extended hours of operation, and access to the most senior technical analysts. In addition, you receive quarterly updates of your software, detailed "inside information," and much more.

ACT! Certified Consultants

ACT! Certified Consultants (ACCs) are trained individuals who set up and design ACT! databases to meet the specific needs of ACT! users. They offer a variety of services:

- ✔ **Training:** Many ACCs offer individual and group training. Classes range from introductory to advanced. Some ACCs can customize their courseware to meet your needs.

- ✔ **Network installation and configuration:** Setting up ACT! on a network can be an involved task. You need to explore different user options and to take into account your organization's objectives. An ACC can provide a needs analysis before proceeding with this implementation.

- ✔ **Data conversion:** Often times, data needs to be converted and manipulated before being brought into ACT!. ACCs have a great deal of experience in a variety of data conversion situations.

- ✔ **Consulting:** An ACC consulting service can offer you a great deal of information, depending upon your needs and requirements.

In addition, Symantec provides ACT! Certified Consultants with the latest information regarding Symantec's products and keeps them informed about other software products that integrate with ACT!.

For an up-to-date list of all the ACT! Certified Consultants worldwide, visit Symantec's Web site at www.symantec.com/act.

You can also call Symantec Customer Service at 800-441-7234 (United States and Canada). Finally, you can obtain the current list of ACCs from Symantec's Fax on Demand service, whose 24-hour number is 541-984-2475.

If you would like to become an ACT! Certified Consultant, send e-mail to acc@symantec.com or call the Education Hot Line 800-786-8620.

ACT! User Groups

Table 30-1 lists ACT! user groups that ACT! enthusiasts or ACT! Certified Consultants support.

These ACT! user groups exist for the benefit of ACT! users of all types who attend the meetings: small business owners, ACT! users who work in large organizations, and resellers of computer- or software-related products.

Most user groups meet monthly and attract anywhere from 25 to 75 ACT! users who come to exchange tips and tricks, see new products, and find out how to use ACT! better. Some groups sponsor special event meetings once or twice per year in which they can attract 200 to 250 ACT! users who come to see new versions of ACT! or hear ACT! insiders talk about where ACT! is going in the future.

The best way to get more out of using ACT! is to share your experiences with other users. If you can't find an ACT! user group in your community. Why not think about starting one yourself?

For an up-to-date list of ACT! users groups visit the ACT! Web site at www.symantec.com/act and click the User Groups link.

Table 30-1	ACT! User Groups	
City	*Contact*	*Phone No.*
Charlotte, NC	Andy Kaplan	704-593-1998
Chicago, IL	Alan Lee	847-619-2000
Denver, CO	Philip McBride	303-321-3341 X-11
Eugene, OR	Michael Syman-Degler	541-345-9681
Houston, TX	Robert Malone	713-461-3096
Independence, MO	Cathy Long	800-409-2567
Indianapolis, IN	Art Russ	317-843-0186
Minneapolis, MN	David Sunnarborg	612-789-7053
Pittsburgh	Don Reed	412-682-5435
San Diego	Doug Wolf	800-449-9653
San Francisco, CA	Linda Keating	650-323-9141
Sacramento, CA	Bari D. McMillan	916-772-2144
Stamford, CT	Andy Kaplan	203-328-3720

Index

• D •

• *E* •

• H •

Notes

Notes

Notes

Notes

Notes

Notes

Notes

Notes

Notes

Notes

Notes

Notes